Fresh Tastes

FROM

A well-seasoned kitchen®

Fresh Tastes

FROM

A well-seasoned kitchen®

....

by LEE CLAYTON ROPER

To Jennifer and Don —
[signature] Lee Clayton Roper

OVER 170 FLAVORFUL RECIPES,
ESSENTIAL COOKING TIPS &
DELIGHTFUL STORIES
TO SPARK INSPIRATION
IN YOUR KITCHEN

PHOTOGRAPHY
Rick Souders

FOOD STYLING
Stephen Shern

MLC PUBLISHING, LLC

DENVER, COLORADO

Published in the United States by
MLC Publishing, LLC
P.O. Box 6374
Denver, Colorado 80206

"A Well-Seasoned Kitchen" and "Fresh Tastes" are trademarks of MLC Publishing, LLC. All rights in and to these trademarks are claimed exclusively by the publisher. No claims with respect to any other brand name or mark used in this book are made; such names and marks are used for reference purposes only, they are and remain the property of their respective owners and no endorsement or affiliation is expressed or implied.

Roper, Lee Clayton.
Fresh tastes from a well-seasoned kitchen : over 170 flavorful recipes, essential cooking tips & delightful stories to spark inspiration in your kitchen / by Lee Clayton Roper ; photography, Rick Souders ; food styling, Stephen Shern. -- First edition. -- Denver, Colo. : MLC Publishing, LLC, [2015]
pages ; cm.
ISBN: 978-0-9841163-6-2
Includes index.
Summary: Inspiration can come from just about anywhere. For the author, most of her inspiration comes from the kitchen-- her own, her friend's and her family's. In her new cookbook she has compiled a unique collection of recipes designed to nurture confidence and creativity in the kitchen. From appetizers to surprisingly simple main courses to desserts and handcrafted menus, she serves up dishes to inspire readers; including cooking tips, serving suggestions, and personal reflections.--Publisher.
1. Cooking, American. 2. Cooking. 3. Menus. 4. Dinners and dining. 5. Entertaining. 6. Make-ahead cooking. 7. Cookbooks.
I. Souders, Rick. II. Shern, Stephen. III. Title.

TX715 .R66 2015   2015946648
641.5/973--dc23   1511

Library of Congress Control Number: 2015946648

Printed in China
Printed on acid-free paper

10 9 8 7 6 5 4 3 2 1
First edition

Lee's Kitchen designed by Angela Otten, Wm Ohs
Construction by Encore Homes 2005, Inc.

Photographer: Rick Souders, Souders Studios, Inc.
    Producer & Set Stylist: Brenda Christy
    Studio Manager: Austin Beadles, Souders Studios, Inc.
    Imaging Specialist: John Wood, Square Pixels
Food Stylist: Stephen Shern
    Food Styling Assistant: Jen Fletcher

Design and Art Direction: Agency Off Record

Manufacturing and Distribution: Favorite Recipes Press, an imprint of Southwest Publishing Group

WWW.SEASONEDKITCHEN.COM

Dedication

To all the friends and family who have inspired me —
you'll see your recipes, names and faces throughout
the pages of this book. Your love of food, cooking and
entertaining always help keep my kitchen creativity
alive. Thank you all for encouraging and supporting
me through a major career change, my first book and,
now, *Fresh Tastes*.

White Chocolate and Lime Tart with Strawberries | 238

Contents

9 | Thanks

11 | Recipe Testers

13 | Introduction

14 | Appetizers

36 | Breakfast & Brunch

54 | Soups

70 | Salads

98 | Poultry

120 | Meats

146 | Fish & Seafood

166 | Pasta

180 | Vegetarian Main Dishes

198 | Side Dishes

228 | Desserts

262 | Menus

268 | Index

Thanks

Fans of *A Well-Seasoned Kitchen* know that my mother, Sally Clayton, was the inspiration behind the original project. Much like my first book, *Fresh Tastes* is too a labor of love. With mom no longer here to guide me, for this collection I looked to the authentic people, places, and flavors that inspire me in my kitchen. Without them, *Fresh Tastes* would not have been possible.

First and foremost, I give thanks to my incredibly supportive and loving husband, Robert, who immediately insisted I write another book after the first came out — even before its success was evident. He supports me at every turn, providing sound advice and encouragement (and recipes!) just when I need it.

I am grateful for my fabulous production team, comprised of Agency Off Record (my ad/design agency) and The Nagler Agency (my communications/PR firm). Supporting design, production, branding, messaging, and copy editing, they understood my vision and successfully turned my ideas into reality — including coordinating production with Free Recipes Press, the printer for *Fresh Tastes*. I am indebted to Matt Keeney, Elena Mlotkowski, Alyssa Peters, Tom Comber and Jessie Woodhead at Agency Off Record and Diane Nagler and Talia Haykin at The Nagler Agency for all that they have done — and continue to do — for me and all things *Fresh Tastes*.

I am especially grateful to the talented photographer Rick Souders, who translated our recipes into works of art, with the support of his Studio Manager Austin Beadles, Producer and Prop Stylist Brenda Christy, and Imaging Specialist John Wood; our food stylist Stephen Shern and his capable Assistant Jen Fletcher, who made every single dish look perfect and inviting (without altering the recipe)!

Special thanks goes to Bailey Jeann Ruskus, a professional chef whose help was invaluable during the final round of testing and assisting me in retesting and modifying recipes in our quest for the best recipes for *Fresh Tastes*.

Additionally, *Fresh Tastes* would not have a name — or a tagline — without the independent feedback and guidance provided by Tamara O'Brien, Evie Haskell, Paul Maxwell and Cody Maxwell. A special thanks to Dave Eck and Lisa Ekus for their guidance on ensuring *Fresh Tastes* would resonate with readers. I must also thank Amy Hall of Amethyst Harbor — her detailed work ensured that the index in *Fresh Tastes* is thorough and easy to use.

Many thanks to all my friends and family who shared recipes, inspiration and constant support — there are too many to name, but you know who you are! Most of all, thank you to my mom and dad, whose love and encouragement were the original inspiration behind this collection. They made me believe I could do anything, and continue to inspire me on my journey today.

Recipe Testers

In addition to Chef Bailey Jeann Ruskus, I want to thank the many volunteer recipe testers and their friends and families who gave their time to help. Our testers spent many hours preparing, serving and analyzing several different recipes, often making the dishes two or three times. Their independent observations and unbiased feedback on directions, flavors, presentation and overall appeal have ensured that the recipes in *Fresh Tastes* are reliable, clear and concise, resulting in delicious, beautiful dishes for you to share with your friends and family.

Stephanie Akhter
Cynthia Ballantyne
Char Beales
Maggie Bellville
Annie Bement
Marilyn Berryman
Bob Block
Lisa Block
Susan Burgstiner
Bobbi Carney
Deborah Cassel
Peggy Chandler
Jim Chiddix
Lauren Dorsey
Mollie Uhl Eaton
Jane Ellis

Amanda Faison
Sue Parker Gerson
Heather Halas
Mary Hale
Crawford Hamilton
Anne Knutson Hargrave
Diane Heidel
Jessie Hickam
Denise Hitchcock
Jake Johannesen
Dona Johnson
Mark Kieffer
Gerri Kier
Lisen Kintzele
Chris Losier
Mary Jane Lovelie

Lori Mark
Abbe McKenna
Laura Parker
Diane Reeder
Rebecca Richardson
Cheri Ruskus
Sheila Schroeder
Gail Springsteen
Andrea Spronk
Wendy Stahl
Kimberly Lord Stewart
Mary Talbot
Allison Wendler
Tina Wilson
Angie Wolf

Rolled Turkey Breast with Roasted Red Pepper Stuffing | 118

Introduction

Inspiration can come from just about anywhere. Like many other people who love to cook and entertain, I'm often impressed by recipes that spark the imagination. While my first cookbook, *A Well-Seasoned Kitchen*, was inspired by my mother Sally Clayton's love of cooking and entertaining, this second volume, *Fresh Tastes*, was born from looking at and creating dishes with a new and "fresh" perspective.

Friends, family, places, and even my very own, newly remodeled kitchen all contributed to producing the collection you see here. These 173 recipes are a combination of my own spin on dishes shared with me by my friends and family, as well as flavorful creations I crafted based on my experiences during the many decades I've been cooking and entertaining.

My approach in *Fresh Tastes* starts with the confidence that, with the right preparation and a pinch of creativity, every dish can be extraordinary. I've taken the "complicated" out of preparing a dish — simplifying the process while ramping up the flavor, using fresh ingredients when and where possible. Sometimes, seasonality requires that packaged organic ingredients be used instead of fresh — to ensure the most flavor in a dish. This approach allows you to make our Sautéed Chicken Breasts with Tomato-Olive-Caper Sauce in the winter, but have it taste like summer! Geography also plays a role in the availability of ingredients. I intentionally keep recipes and ingredients easily and widely accessible, often providing alternative substitutions.

Inside you will discover how selecting the proper ingredients or adding a new twist on an old favorite can accentuate the flavor and make even the simplest meal memorable. I share my personal reflections on how great meals and conversation can bring friends and family together, along with 65 beautiful color photographs of the finished dishes and 18 process shots of key preparation steps (such as peeling a butternut squash or putting a foil collar on a soufflé dish). Indispensable cooking tips are included throughout the recipes, as well as serving suggestions and a helpful menu section with recommendations for some of my favorite seasonal combinations.

From delectable appetizers and creative salads to flavorful main courses and luscious desserts, recipes included in *Fresh Tastes* were evaluated by a team of volunteer testers across the country. Only the best, most flavorful, eye catching dishes made the cut.

I'm confident each recipe in this book, both updated classics and contemporary fare, will inspire you to create fresh, delicious and sophisticated dishes — and empower you to explore your own creativity in the kitchen.

Appetizers

"A great appetizer sets the stage for a warm, family dinner. Everyone together sharing and enjoying appetizers is a great way to start the meal." — *Executive Chef Robert Williams*

Just like my mom Sally, I love appetizers — small, colorful bites bursting with flavor, in all sizes and shapes. In *Fresh Tastes*, you'll find an assortment of appetizers for every occasion designed to keep your guests happy — with a delicacy in one hand and a cocktail in the other!

16 | Chorizo, Cheese and Jalapeño Turnovers

17 | Goat Cheese, Pesto and Tomato Crostini

18 | Green Chile Canapés

20 | Mushroom Paté

21 | Hot Onion Soufflé

22 | Prosciutto, Fig and Goat Cheese Tarts

24 | Spicy Chicken Wings

25 | Zesty Pimiento Cheese Spread

26 | Tomato Shortbread with Olive Tapenade

28 | Smoked Salmon Mousse

29 | Poppy Seed Puffs

30 | Hearts of Palm Dip

31 | Taco Salad Dip

32 | Champagne Cocktail

34 | Robert's Perfect Martini

35 | Robert's Perfect Manhattan

CHORIZO, CHEESE AND JALAPEÑO TURNOVERS

Always a crowd pleaser, these turnovers have just the right amount of spice — not too strong, but enough kick for friends and family who like it hot. For this recipe, it's crucial you use Mexican chorizo, an uncooked, ground meat sausage, *not* Spanish (cured, ready-to-eat in link form, similar to salami). They're quite different in both flavor and composition, which makes all the difference in the taste and texture of this dish.

MAKES: about 9 dozen

1 pound ground Mexican chorizo sausage

1/2 cup chopped fresh jalapeño peppers, seeded and ribs removed

1 (8-ounce) package cream cheese, softened

1 cup (4 ounces) freshly grated Parmesan cheese

Salt, to taste

1 (16-ounce) package frozen phyllo dough, thawed

1/2 to 1 cup (1 to 2 sticks) butter, melted

Preheat the oven to 400 degrees. Lightly butter two large rimmed baking sheets.

In a medium skillet, brown sausage over medium heat, breaking up meat with a spatula as it cooks; drain. Let cool 1 to 2 minutes. Transfer to a food processor; pulse until chopped into small pieces. Transfer to a medium mixing bowl and stir in chopped peppers and cheeses. Season to taste with salt. Set aside.

Place one sheet of phyllo dough on work surface and brush lightly with melted butter *(see Tip below)*. Place a second sheet of phyllo on top and lightly brush with butter. Cut crosswise into 7 to 8 equal strips about 12 inches long by 2 inches wide.

Place about 1 teaspoon of filling on bottom of each strip. Fold one corner of phyllo diagonally over filling to form a triangle. Continue folding back and forth (like folding a flag) to the end of the strip. Place, seam side down, on a prepared baking sheet. Repeat with remaining phyllo and filling. Lightly brush the tops of the triangles with butter. Bake 10 minutes or until tops are golden brown. Serve immediately or cool to freeze. Cut triangles in half to serve, if desired.

MAKE AHEAD Turnovers can be made up to 1 month ahead and frozen. To freeze, place cooled baking sheets in the freezer. Once frozen, carefully transfer turnovers to a zip top plastic bag and freeze. To serve, place turnovers on a parchment paper lined baking sheet; thaw. Reheat at 325 degrees for 10 minutes or until thoroughly hot.

TIP

When working with phyllo dough, it is important to keep it from drying out. Place phyllo sheets on a flat surface, cover with plastic wrap and then a moist dishcloth. Take out sheets one at a time, keeping remaining sheets covered.

GOAT CHEESE, PESTO AND TOMATO CROSTINI

These little crostini bites are colorful, beautiful and super easy to prepare. Festive red tomatoes top the pesto, making this the perfect dish to serve during the holidays. Choosing the right bread for the crostini is key. I usually look for a nice Ciabatta bread in the bakery section at Whole Foods and ask them to machine slice it for me to save time. Note the faster variation below; it uses the same ingredients in a dip.

SERVES: 6 to 8

1 loaf Ciabatta or other Italian bread, sliced about 1/2-inch thick

8 ounces goat cheese, softened

2 tablespoons cream cheese, softened

1/2 cup prepared basil pesto

6 to 8 large Roma or plum tomatoes, seeded and chopped

1/4 cup toasted pine nuts

Kosher salt, to taste

Freshly ground black pepper, to taste

Preheat oven to 350 degrees.

Cut bread slices into 1- to 2-inch pieces and place on a baking sheet. Bake 5 to 7 minutes or until toasted and light golden brown.

In a medium bowl, combine goat cheese and cream cheese, stirring just until smooth (don't over-mix or it will become runny). Spread mixture on toast pieces. Top with pesto. Sprinkle tomatoes evenly over the pesto. Sprinkle top with pine nuts. Season with kosher salt and fresh ground pepper and serve immediately.

VARIATION Serve as a dip. Spread goat cheese in bottom of shallow baking dish. Spread pesto evenly over the top. Scatter tomatoes over top of pesto. Scatter pine nuts over tomatoes. Season with salt and pepper, to taste. Serve with crackers.

TIP

Our favorite pesto recipe is Spinach Basil Pesto, which can be found on our website, at www.seasonedkitchen.com. You can use your own favorite recipe, or store bought works okay, too. Just make sure to purchase the fresh, refrigerated pesto, not the jarred stuff.

GREEN CHILE CANAPÉS

My childhood best friend's mother, Dorothy Hartwell, grew up in Michigan and moved to Colorado in the early '60's. Here, she quickly grew to love Mexican food, especially dishes with green chiles. I've always referred to Dorothy as my "second" mother because I spent almost as much time at the Hartwells as I did in my own home! Like my mom, Dorothy was an excellent cook and I have many fond memories of dinners in their home. When Mrs. Hartwell passed away a few years ago, Katey, her sister Anne and brother David kindly shared their mom's recipes with me. This appetizer is one of my favorites. While the recipe makes around six dozen canapés, it can easily be cut in half. But as delicious as they are, you may not want to — since they always all seem to disappear!

MAKES: about 6 dozen

3 to 4 (1 pound) loaves pumpernickel or whole wheat cocktail bread*

1 cup (2 sticks) butter, softened (see Tip)

8 ounces mild green chiles, seeded, roasted and chopped (see Tip on page 38)**

Chopped garlic or shallots, to taste

2 cups (8 ounces) finely shredded Monterey Jack cheese

1 cup mayonnaise

*usually found in the deli or bakery section of major grocery stores

** Can substitute 2 (4-ounce) cans chopped green chiles, drained

Preheat broiler.

Cut 1 1/2- to 2-inch rounds out of each slice of bread (not using crusts). Set aside.

In a medium mixing bowl, stir together the butter, chiles and garlic or shallots. Spread a small amount evenly on one side of bread slices. In another medium mixing bowl, stir together the cheese and mayonnaise. Spread a thick layer on top of the chile mixture. Place canapés on baking sheets. Broil until puffy and lightly browned. Cool slightly, then serve immediately.

MAKE AHEAD Butter mixture and cheese mixture can be prepared, covered and refrigerated separately up to 3 days in advance. Bring to room temperature before assembling the canapés.

TIP

Forgot to bring your butter to room temperature? No problem. Just put it in the microwave on 30 percent power for 30 seconds. If it still isn't soft, continue heating at 30 percent power in 15 second increments just until it is soft to the touch.

MUSHROOM PATÉ

One night, I had guests coming in from out of town and needed a quick appetizer. I wanted something hearty yet vegetarian, so I immediately thought of mushrooms. This appetizer was born and it was a hit. It's now made its way into my regular rotation...and hopefully yours too!

SERVES: 8 to 10
MAKES: about 2 cups

16 ounces baby portabella (cremini) mushrooms

3 tablespoons butter

1 1/2 teaspoons chopped garlic

1/3 cup chopped green onion (white, light green and some of the dark green portion)

1/4 cup sherry

2 teaspoons fresh thyme leaves

6 ounces cream cheese

Juice from 1/2 to 1 lemon

Cayenne pepper, to taste

Salt, to taste

Freshly ground black pepper, to taste

1/4 cup chopped toasted pecans
  (see Tip on page 216)

Crackers or toast points

Remove the stems from the mushrooms, cut the caps in half and thinly slice.

In a large sauté pan or skillet, melt butter over medium heat. Add the garlic and mushrooms; cook, stirring occasionally, until mushrooms are soft and liquid evaporates. Stir in the green onion and sherry; cook until liquid evaporates.

Reduce heat to low; stir in thyme and cream cheese. Cook, stirring constantly, just until the cheese melts and mixture is blended. Remove from heat and season to taste with the lemon juice, cayenne pepper, salt and pepper. Stir in pecans.

Press mixture into a serving bowl. Cover and refrigerate several hours. Bring to room temperature before serving. Serve with crackers or toast points.

MAKE AHEAD Paté can be made up to 2 days ahead, covered and refrigerated.

HOT ONION SOUFFLÉ

Who doesn't love the flavor combination of onion and cheese mixed with a bit of mayonnaise? This soufflé is such a fan favorite, I've been told I should serve it with spoons instead of tortilla chips. Be prepared for friends and family to request this recipe...it happens to me every time I make it!

MAKES: about 6 cups

1 tablespoon butter, plus additional for buttering dish

1 tablespoon olive oil

3 1/2 cups finely chopped onion

3 (8-ounce) packages cream cheese, cut into 1-inch squares

2 cups (8 ounces) freshly grated Parmesan cheese

1/2 cup mayonnaise

Kosher salt, to taste

Tortilla chips

Preheat oven to 425 degrees. Butter a shallow 1 1/2 to 2 quart soufflé or baking dish.

In a large skillet or sauté pan, combine butter and oil over medium-low heat; stir occasionally until butter melts. Add onions and cook, stirring occasionally, until soft and starting to turn a light brown color.

Remove from heat; add the cream cheese and stir until melted. Add the Parmesan cheese and mayonnaise; stir until well combined. Season with salt to taste. Transfer mixture to the prepared baking dish and bake 15 minutes or until golden brown and puffy. Serve immediately with tortilla chips.

MAKE AHEAD Dip can be assembled up to 24 hours in advance, covered and refrigerated. Bring to room temperature before baking, or if baked immediately from the refrigerator, increase cook time by 5 to 10 minutes.

PROSCIUTTO, FIG AND GOAT CHEESE TARTS

For one of Robert's birthdays, I created this easy, make-ahead recipe and it was a winner. The salty prosciutto and sweet fig spread pair beautifully — especially when topped off with tangy goat cheese.

Note that you need to start preparation several hours in advance, as they must be frozen before baking.

MAKES: 6 dozen

1 (17.3 ounce) package (2 sheets) frozen puff pastry, thawed in refrigerator *(see Tip below)*

1 (8 to 8.5-ounce) jar fig spread*

1 cup (6 ounces) chopped prosciutto

1 cup (4 ounces) crumbled goat cheese

*Available in the cheese section at Whole Foods and at specialty food stores

Remove 1 sheet of puff pastry from refrigerator. On a lightly floured surface, roll puff pastry into a 12-inch square. Cut into 2-inch squares. Press pastry into small mini-muffin pans and prick with a fork. Spoon a scant 1/2 teaspoon of fig spread into center of each square. Top with chopped prosciutto and goat cheese. Remove remaining puff pastry sheet from refrigerator; repeat procedure with second pastry sheet. Freeze in muffin pans.

Preheat the oven to 400 degrees.

Bake frozen tarts (in mini-muffin pans) 10 to 15 minutes or until hot and pastry is golden. Serve immediately.

MAKE AHEAD Tarts can be kept frozen for up to 3 months (any longer and they won't bake properly). Remove frozen tarts from the muffin pans and place in heavy-duty freezer bags. To bake, place tarts back into mini-muffin pans.

TIP

Tip on using puff pastry: It is important when working with puff pastry to keep it cold. If it gets warm, it will be difficult to roll and cut, and won't puff as much when baked.

SPICY CHICKEN WINGS

I love this recipe for chicken wings as it has just the right amount of spice — not overly spicy but far from bland. I also like serving these wings with guacamole instead of blue cheese dressing, a trick I picked up at a neighborhood cocktail party. You could also serve them with Ranch salad dressing. As a main dish, serve with homemade French fries and a tossed salad — oh, and beer!

SERVES: 8 to 10 as an appetizer, or 4 to 6 as a main dish

Vegetable cooking spray

3 pounds chicken wings or drumettes

2 tablespoons olive oil

1 tablespoon ground cumin

1 1/2 teaspoons garlic salt

1 1/2 teaspoons onion powder

1 1/2 teaspoons paprika

1 1/2 teaspoons lemon-pepper seasoning

1/2 teaspoon dried oregano

1/4 to 1/2 teaspoon cayenne pepper

2 cups prepared guacamole
(see Note 1, page 126)

Preheat the oven to 425 degrees. Spray rack of a broiler pan or wire cooling rack inserted in rimmed baking sheet with cooking spray. Set aside.

Pat chicken wings dry with paper towels and place in a large bowl.

In a small bowl, whisk together olive oil, cumin, garlic salt, onion powder, paprika, lemon-pepper, oregano and cayenne pepper. Pour over the chicken, tossing to coat with your hands. Arrange wings in a single layer on prepared broiler pan.

Bake for 30 minutes or until wings are tender, browned and cooked through. Serve hot or at room temperature with the guacamole on the side.

MAKE AHEAD The wings can be made earlier in the day, covered and refrigerated. Bring to room temperature or warm in a 350 degree oven before serving.

ZESTY PIMIENTO CHEESE SPREAD

Mom loved pimiento cheese and made it often, sometimes just for our family to enjoy. She never measured the ingredients, just mixed them to taste. This is my version of her "recipe". I add cayenne pepper to give it a little kick. It's delicious as a filling in grilled cheese sandwiches, too *(photo, page 16)*.

SERVES: 6 to 8

1 cup (4 ounces) grated yellow sharp Cheddar cheese

1 cup (4 ounces) grated white sharp Cheddar cheese (We like Cracker Barrel brand)

6 tablespoons mayonnaise

1 (2-ounce) jar chopped pimientos, drained

Cayenne pepper, to taste

Salt, to taste

Freshly ground black pepper, to taste

Crackers and/or celery stalks

In a medium mixing bowl, combine cheeses, mayonnaise and pimientos. Mash together with a fork until well mixed. Season to taste with cayenne pepper, salt and black pepper. Serve with crackers and/or celery stalks.

MAKE AHEAD The cheese spread can be made up to 3 days before serving, covered and stored in the refrigerator.

A WELL-SEASONED INSPIRATION

SALLY CLAYTON *Known far and wide for her effortless style and sensibility when it came to home cooking and entertaining, my mother was a truly amazing woman from whom I learned so much, both in and out of the kitchen. She never lost her cool if things went awry. She taught me to always remain calm and wear a smile; there's a solution for everything and it's best to leave those mistakes in the kitchen. Her philosophy, "fabulous dinners don't have to be complicated or time consuming," was ingrained in me from a young age. Mom's sage advice — to use the best quality ingredients available, always have a menu (and a plan) identified, make ahead as many dishes as possible, and make sure to infuse the food (and the party) with lots of love and laughter — has been my ultimate recipe for success!*

TOMATO SHORTBREAD WITH OLIVE TAPENADE

Robert and I were lucky enough to attend a fun potluck dinner party at the beautiful home of our good friends Trudy and Jim Chiddix in Evergreen — a community just west of Denver in the foothills of the Rocky Mountains. We sat on their patio for cocktails, a magical setting beside a pond fed by a stream coming down the side of the mountain. Another guest, Joel Benson, brought the most amazing appetizer, and fortunately for us, shared his recipe for these shortbreads. The tomato and olive combination can't be beat and the dish makes for a great presentation. Joel tells me they're easy to make gluten free — simply substitute gluten-free flour and you're good to go.

MAKES: about 5 1/2 dozen
(recipe may be
halved)

2 cups all-purpose flour

2 tablespoons sugar

2 tablespoons freshly grated
Parmesan cheese

2 tablespoons fresh thyme leaves

1 teaspoon kosher salt

1/2 teaspoon cayenne pepper

Pinch freshly ground black pepper

1/2 cup tomato paste

1 cup (2 sticks) cold butter, cubed

3/4 cup purchased Kalamata olive
tapenade (*see Note*)

In a food processor, combine flour, sugar, cheese, thyme, salt, cayenne and black pepper; process until well blended. Add the tomato paste and pulse until well blended. Add the butter and pulse until the dough starts to come together.

Scrape the dough onto a large sheet of plastic wrap and roll it into 2 (1 1/2- to 2-inch wide) logs. Wrap the dough in plastic wrap and refrigerate at least one hour or until well chilled.

Preheat the oven to 350 degrees. Line 3 to 4 baking sheets with parchment paper.

Slice the shortbread logs into 1/4-inch-thick rounds and arrange on the prepared baking sheets. Bake 18 minutes, or until the edges are lightly browned. Transfer the shortbreads to a wire rack to cool. To serve, place around 1/2 teaspoon olive tapenade on each shortbread.

MAKE AHEAD Shortbread logs can be prepared but not sliced, well wrapped and frozen for up to 2 months. Thaw in refrigerator. They can also be baked earlier in the day, covered and stored at room temperature.

NOTE One day, Whole Foods was out of their Kalamata olive tapenade, so I went to the olive bar and filled a small plastic container with pitted Kalamata olives, a few roasted red peppers, roasted garlic and capers. I went home, whirled them around in a food processor and then stirred in some toasted pine nuts. The resulting tapenade was perfect with these shortbreads!

SMOKED SALMON MOUSSE

This recipe originally came from my Aunt Bobbie, who got it from friends in Alaska, where they know quite a bit about cooking with salmon! I provide two ways to serve this mousse — one as a dip, the other piped into poppy seed puffs (*see recipe on next page*) for a passable, two-bite appetizer. It's delicious both ways.

> MAKES: around 2 cups or 32
> (2 tablespoon
> servings)

4 ounces smoked salmon, preferably lox

12 ounces cream cheese (regular or low fat)

1 teaspoon liquid smoke

1 teaspoon caper liquid (from a jar of capers)

2 teaspoons fish sauce

2 tablespoons chopped fresh dill

Juice from 1/2 small lemon, or more to taste

Salt, to taste

White pepper, to taste

In a food processor, combine salmon, cream cheese, liquid smoke, caper liquid, fish sauce, dill and lemon juice. Process until well blended. Season with salt and white pepper to taste (it won't need much salt). Add more lemon, if needed. Serve with crackers or toast points, or pipe into Poppy Seed Puffs (*see recipe on next page*).

MAKE AHEAD Mousse can be made up to 24 hours ahead, covered and refrigerated.

NOTE The mousse is best if made an hour or two ahead, covered and refrigerated to allow the flavors to blend.

POPPY SEED PUFFS

These little puffs are incredibly versatile and surprisingly easy to make. The dough ("*pâte à choux*") is a classic French pastry, traditionally used for everything from gougères to cream puffs and éclairs. Once baked and cooled, I like to fill them with our Smoked Salmon Mousse — amongst many other delicacies. Simply slit the side and pipe (or split in half and fill) with your favorite sweet or savory filling.

MAKES: about 5 dozen
small puffs

1 cup water

1 stick unsalted butter, cut into
tablespoons

1 teaspoon kosher salt

1 cup all-purpose flour

4 large eggs

2 to 3 tablespoons poppy seeds

2 cups filling of your choice (I like
Smoked Salmon Mousse)

TIP

On piping: Fit a plain tip into a pastry bag. Fold top half of bag over the outside (like a cuff). Spoon filling into bag, no more than half full. Pull up cuff and twist bag closed (above filling); keep twisting until filling is visible in the tip. Point tip around 1/2 inch above where you want to pipe, guiding it with your non-dominant hand. Use your other hand to push filling from the top of the bag (where it's twisted) out of the tip, to the desired size. Stop and move tip in a circle to disengage it from the dough. Pull straight up. Flatten any points on top of dough mound with moistened fingertip.

Preheat oven to 400 degrees. Lightly grease or line with parchment paper 2 large rimmed baking sheets.

In a medium saucepan, bring the water, butter and salt to a boil over medium-high heat. Cook, stirring, until the butter melts. Add the flour all at once and, using a wooden spoon, stir vigorously until combined and it forms a ball (takes just a few minutes). Transfer the mixture to a mixing bowl and beat at medium speed with an electric mixer for about 30 seconds to 1 minute. Add the eggs, one at a time, beating well after each addition, until the mixture becomes a smooth, shiny dough.

Transfer dough to a pastry bag fitted with a 1/2-inch plain tip. Pipe 3/4-inch mounds, about 1-inch apart, onto the prepared baking sheets (*see Tip at left*). Using moistened fingertips, flatten the tops. Sprinkle generously with poppy seeds (some will fall off during baking and also during filling) and bake 15 to 20 minutes or until the puffs are risen and just beginning to brown.

Using a sharp knife, poke a hole into the side of each puff and continue baking another 5 to 10 minutes or until golden brown (puffs will sound hollow when tapped on the top). Transfer to a rack and cool. Can freeze at this point (*see directions below*).

Just before serving, pipe filling into puffs through the cut hole in the side and serve immediately. You can also cut off the tops and pipe or spoon filling in that way, replacing top once filled.

MAKE AHEAD Puffs can be frozen for up to 1 month. Place in a single layer on a baking sheet and freeze. When frozen, place in a zip top bag. To use, thaw and re-crisp in a 325 degree oven for just a few minutes.

HEARTS OF PALM DIP

Since no one can ever guess the main ingredient (and they always ask), I should really call this "Mystery Dip." Another one of my favorite dishes from my mom, I often serve this when unexpected guests drop by, since I usually have all the ingredients on hand. Plus, it takes only 10 minutes (or less) to prepare!

SERVES: 6 to 8

1 (14-ounce) can hearts of palm, drained and finely chopped

3/4 cup (3 ounces) freshly grated Parmesan cheese (or more to taste)

3 tablespoons chopped green onion (white, light green and some of the dark green portion)

2/3 cup mayonnaise

1/4 cup sour cream

2 tablespoons chopped pimientos, drained

1/8 teaspoon cayenne pepper

Kosher salt, to taste

Crackers

Preheat oven to 350 degrees. In a medium bowl, combine hearts of palm, Parmesan cheese, green onion, mayonnaise, sour cream, pimiento and cayenne. Season to taste with salt. Spread mixture in a small, shallow baking dish. Bake 20 minutes or until hot and bubbly. Serve with crackers.

MAKE AHEAD Dip can be assembled up to 24 hours in advance, covered and refrigerated. Bring to room temperature before heating.

TACO SALAD DIP

A variation of the well-known Seven Layer Dip, this recipe has no refried beans and is a snap to put together. It was given to me several years ago and continues to be a crowd pleaser today.

Note that this dip tastes best if you let the cream cheese mixture sit about an hour or two before serving to allow the flavors to blend. Don't worry if you don't have time though — it also tastes great when served immediately!

SERVES: 8 to 10

1 (8-ounce) package cream cheese, softened

1 1/2 cups sour cream

2 tablespoons Mexican seasoning blend*

3/4 cup salsa (We like Pace brand)

6 green onions, chopped

3/4 cup (3 ounces) shredded sharp Cheddar cheese, or more to taste

1 (2.25-ounce) can sliced black olives, drained

1 ripe avocado, chopped

1 small tomato, seeded and chopped

1/2 cup chopped lettuce

Tortilla chips

*Recipe at www.seasonedkitchen.com. Prepared Mexican (or taco) seasoning is also available in the spice aisle at most major grocery stores

In a medium mixing bowl, stir together cream cheese, sour cream, and taco seasoning. Spread evenly in the bottom of an 8- or 9-inch pie plate or other shallow 4-cup dish. Spread salsa evenly over the top of cream cheese mixture. Top with ingredients in this order: onions, cheese, olives, avocado, tomato and lettuce. Serve with tortilla chips.

CHAMPAGNE COCKTAIL

Who needs an excuse to enjoy bubbles? A great alternative to the traditional Mimosa, this recipe perfectly complements brunch, special occasions and, of course, New Year's Eve celebrations.

SERVES: 12

1 1/4 cups pomegranate juice or cranberry juice cocktail

1 cup Cointreau or other orange-flavored liqueur

1/2 cup fresh lime juice, or more to taste

2 (750 ml) bottles champagne or other sparking wine

Garnish: fresh or frozen raspberries or cranberries

In a medium pitcher, stir together the pomegranate juice, Cointreau, and lime juice. Cover and chill.

To serve, fill champagne glasses with half juice mixture and half champagne. Place a raspberry or cranberry or two in each glass for garnish.

MAKE AHEAD The juice mixture can be prepared, covered and refrigerated one day in advance.

Champagne Cocktail, Robert's Perfect Martini, Robert's Perfect Manhattan

ROBERT'S PERFECT MARTINI

From the time we first started dating, Robert and I have always enjoyed sharing a martini together. Before they closed, we'd frequent this great restaurant in Denver called Mel's, sit at the bar with martinis and truffle french fries, listening to live jazz from their piano player. These days, we tend to enjoy our martinis at home and Robert's become known far and wide for his fabulous martinis. He doesn't really measure, just pours the ingredients into a shaker. But don't worry — as long as you use good quality vodka and don't go crazy adding a ton of liqueur, yours too will be a surefire success! *(photo, page 33)*

PER SERVING

5 ounces (about 2/3 cup) good
    quality vodka

Splash to 1 ounce (2 tablespoons
    Cointreau or other orange flavored
    liqueur or ginger liqueur)

Lemon twist *(see Tip)*

Fill martini or coupe glasses with ice water to quickly chill; let stand 1 to 2 minutes. Drain and dry.

Fill a cocktail shaker with ice cubes (large cubes won't melt as quickly as small cubes in the spirits and/or liqueur). Add vodka and Cointreau. Shake well. Pour through a cocktail strainer into a chilled martini glass. Rub a lemon twist around the rim of the glass; then drop it into the martini. Serve!

TIP

Making a lemon twist: Using a vegetable peeler, start near one of the poles of the lemon and cut downward to get a wide strip of lemon peel. Try to get as little of the white part as possible as it is bitter.

ROBERT'S PERFECT MANHATTAN

To celebrate our anniversary one year, Robert and I visited the Palace Arms restaurant at the Brown Palace Hotel in downtown Denver. Opting to enjoy a pre-dinner cocktail in their beautiful lobby, Robert noticed a "Traditional Rye Manhattan" while perusing the drinks menu. While he wasn't partial to Manhattans in the past (he felt they were too sweet), on this night he thought their use of rye instead of the traditional bourbon might lend better flavor. He was right and this recipe is now his drink of choice for special occasions! *(photo, page 33)*

PER SERVING

4 ounces (1/2 cup) good quality rye whiskey

2 ounces (1/4 cup) sweet vermouth

1 ounce (2 tablespoons) dry vermouth

Several shakes of bitters

Garnish: maraschino cherries

Fill a martini or coupe glass with ice water to quickly chill; let stand 1 to 2 minutes. Drain and dry.

Fill a cocktail shaker with ice cubes (large cubes won't melt as quickly as small cubes in the spirits and/or liqueur). Add rye, vermouths and bitters. Shake well. Pour through a cocktail strainer into a chilled martini glass. Garnish with cherries, if desired, and serve.

Mini Raspberry Nut Muffins and Apple Butterscotch Muffins | 53 & 52

Breakfast & Brunch

"All happiness depends on a leisurely breakfast." — *John Gunther, author*

Breakfast and brunch can be a home gourmet's best ally — and most of these dishes can be made ahead or prepared quite quickly. Designed for lazy Sundays or holiday celebrations, these recipes were chosen for effortless and beautiful morning gatherings!

38 | Southwestern Chile-Cheese "Soufflé"

39 | Pesto, Sausage and Parmesan Cheese Strata

40 | Cheese Blintz Soufflés with Blueberry Balsamic Sauce

42 | Banana Caramel Baked French Toast

43 | Spiced Bacon Twists

44 | Smoked Salmon Eggs Benedict with Mustard-Dill Sauce

46 | Huevos Rancheros

47 | Mushroom, Spinach and Onion Frittata with Goat Cheese

48 | Toasted Bagels with Egg Salad and Smoked Salmon

49 | Mini Sticky Pecan Rolls

50 | Cinnamon Loaf

52 | Apple Butterscotch Muffins

53 | Mini Raspberry Nut Muffins

SOUTHWESTERN CHILE-CHEESE "SOUFFLÉ"

While this dish can't be prepared ahead of time, it takes just minutes to execute, since you don't need to separate the eggs or whip egg whites. The southwestern flavors are mild; feel free to increase the amount of green chiles and/or cumin to ramp it up a bit if you like.

SERVES: 10

10 large eggs

1/2 cup butter, softened *(see Tip on page 18)*

2 cups small-curd cottage cheese

1/2 cup all-purpose flour

1 teaspoon baking powder

1/2 teaspoon dried oregano

1/2 teaspoon ground cumin

1/2 teaspoon salt

1/4 teaspoon garlic powder

1/8 teaspoon freshly ground black pepper

4 cups (16 ounces) Monterey Jack cheese, grated (can also use Cheddar or a blend)

4 ounces mild green chiles, seeded, roasted and chopped *(see Tip)**

1/4 cup or 1 (2-ounce) jar chopped red pimiento, drained

*Can substitute 1 (4-ounce) can diced green chiles

Preheat oven to 350 degrees. Butter a 13- by 9-inch baking dish.

In a large mixing bowl, beat eggs with an electric mixer (or process in a blender) until light. Add butter and cottage cheese; beat until well mixed.

In a small mixing bowl, whisk together the flour, baking powder, oregano, cumin, salt, garlic powder and pepper. Add to the egg mixture and beat just until mixed. Stir in cheese, chiles and pimiento. Pour into prepared pan and bake 30 to 35 minutes or until golden brown, set (not jiggly) and puffy. Serve immediately.

> **TIP**
>
> *To roast chiles or other peppers: Line a large rimmed baking sheet with foil. Lay peppers on prepared pan and broil (5 to 6 inches from heat) for 7 to 8 minutes or until top side is blackened. Using tongs, turn over and continue roasting another 5 to 7 minutes, or until both sides are blackened. Transfer to a plate or bowl and cover with plastic wrap (seal the edges). Let sit until cool. Remove charred skins from cooled peppers and discard. Cut in half lengthwise and remove seeds and veins (leave some for spicier flavor).*

PESTO, SAUSAGE AND PARMESAN CHEESE STRATA

Craving a breakfast strata one Sunday morning, I came up with this recipe that, unlike most stratas, can be prepared, cooked and served without being refrigerated overnight. This recipe can be proportionately increased as needed, depending on how may individual gratin dishes (and guests) you have. It can also easily be made in one large baking dish to feed a crowd.

SERVES: 2

2 slices whole wheat bread (or 1 multigrain or plain English muffin)

2 cooked turkey or chicken sausage links (Jimmy Dean brand works well)

2 tablespoons (about 4) chopped green onions

4 large egg whites

1/4 cup milk (skim or whole)

1 1/2 tablespoons whipped cream cheese

1 tablespoon mayonnaise

1 tablespoon prepared pesto*

2 teaspoons Dijon mustard

4 teaspoons freshly grated Parmesan cheese, divided

Salt, to taste

Freshly ground black pepper, to taste

For this dish I like to use Spinach Basil Pesto; the recipe can be found on our website www.seasonedkitchen.com. You can also use your own favorite recipe, or purchase fresh, refrigerated pesto (not the shelf stable jarred stuff)

Preheat oven to 375 degrees. Generously oil 2 small individual gratin dishes or 2 large ramekins.

Cut bread into (1/2-inch) small squares, place on a baking sheet and toast until just lightly brown. Heat sausages for 45 seconds in the microwave and then slice into small rounds.

Arrange bread cubes on bottom of prepared dishes; top with sausage slices and green onions. In a medium bowl, whisk egg whites, milk, cream cheese, mayonnaise, pesto, mustard and 2 teaspoons Parmesan cheese until well blended. Season to taste with salt and pepper.

Pour evenly over bread mixture, pushing down bread cubes to make sure they are soaked. Sprinkle 1 teaspoon of remaining Parmesan cheese over the top of each dish. Bake 15 minutes or until cooked through, puffy and slightly brown on top.

MAKE AHEAD Strata can be prepared, covered and refrigerated for up to 24 hours. Bring to room temperature before baking.

VARIATIONS 1. Strata can be made in one dish. Increase cooking time 5 to 10 minutes. 2. If you don't have whipped cream cheese, cube block cream cheese and scatter among the bread cubes and sausage before pouring over the egg mixture.

CHEESE BLINTZ SOUFFLÉS
WITH BLUEBERRY BALSAMIC SAUCE

An unusual, delicious and impressive brunch dish, this soufflé comes direct from mom's recipe box, while the sauce is my creation. The soufflé can easily be doubled for a crowd, using a 9- by 13-inch baking dish. Serve with our Spiced Bacon Twists *(page 43)* and a fresh fruit medley on the side. Double the balsamic sauce and put half in the freezer to use later on pancakes or waffles.

SERVES: 6

BLUEBERRY BALSAMIC SAUCE

1 cup sugar

2 tablespoons cornstarch

1/2 cup water

1 1/2 cups fresh blueberries

1 tablespoon unsalted butter

2 tablespoons Blueberry Balsamic Vinegar *(see Note)*

CHEESE BLINTZ SOUFFLÉS

3 large eggs

3/4 cup sour cream

1/4 cup (1 large navel orange) freshly squeezed orange juice

1/2 cup butter, softened

3 tablespoons sugar, divided

1 teaspoon baking powder

1/2 cup all-purpose flour, sifted

4 ounces cream cheese

1 cup small-curd cottage cheese

1 egg yolk

1/2 teaspoon vanilla extract

Garnish: additional fresh blueberries (optional)

To make the sauce: In a medium saucepan, stir together sugar, cornstarch and water. Bring to a boil, reduce heat to medium and cook, stirring occasionally, for 5 minutes or until sugar dissolves. Stir in blueberries and cook, stirring occasionally for 10 minutes. Reduce heat to low, add butter and stir until melted. Stir in balsamic vinegar. Remove from heat and set aside.

To make the soufflés: Preheat oven to 350 degrees. Butter 6 individual (6- to 8-ounce) soufflé dishes or 6 large ramekins.

Using an electric mixer or food processor, blend together the eggs, sour cream, orange juice, butter, 2 1/2 tablespoons sugar and baking powder. Add flour and blend until smooth. Pour half the batter (about 1/4 cup each) into the prepared baking dishes.

Beat together the cream cheese, cottage cheese, egg yolks, vanilla and remaining 1/2 tablespoon sugar. Drop by spoonfuls over the top of the batter in the baking dishes. Gently drizzle remaining batter over the top (about 1/4 cup per dish). Put ramekins on a large baking sheet and bake uncovered, for 30 to 35 minutes or until puffed, set in the center and golden brown. Serve with warm sauce spooned over the top. Garnish with additional fresh blueberries.

MAKE AHEAD Blueberry Balsamic Sauce can be made up to two days ahead, covered and refrigerated. Can also be frozen for up to 6 months. Soufflés can be assembled but not baked up to 12 hours ahead, covered and refrigerated. Bring to room temperature before baking.

NOTE Blueberry Balsamic Vinegar can be purchased at specialty food stores or online. If you can't find it, substitute white balsamic vinegar and add a few more blueberries (to taste).

ONE-DISH VARIATION Make the soufflé in one dish. Butter an 8- by 8-inch baking dish. Pour half the batter (about 1 1/2 cups). Top with cheese mixture as described, then drizzle remaining batter over the top. Bake, uncovered, 40 to 45 minutes or until puffed and set in the center and golden brown. Serve with Blueberry Balsamic Sauce on the side.

BANANA CARAMEL BAKED FRENCH TOAST

This French toast dish is a good excuse to have the traditional New Orleans dessert Bananas Foster for breakfast. Similar in flavor, bananas cooked in a yummy caramel sauce are the star of this dish. I add depth and texture by using an egg bread, like Challah. I've served this dish to friends who aren't typically French toast fans and they love it! Serve with fresh berries on the side.

Note that you need to start this dish at least 8 hours before serving.

SERVES: 6 to 8

1/2 cup butter

1 cup firmly packed light brown sugar

2 tablespoons light corn syrup

1 tablespoon plus 1 teaspoon Kahlua or other coffee flavored liqueur, or dark rum

2 large bananas, cut into 1/4-inch slices

8 (3/4-inch) slices Challah or other egg bread

5 large eggs

1 1/2 cups half and half

1 teaspoon vanilla extract

1/4 teaspoon salt

1/2 cup sliced almonds

Powdered sugar (optional)

Butter a 13-by 9-inch baking dish.

In a medium saucepan, combine the butter, brown sugar and corn syrup over medium heat. Cook, stirring constantly, until the butter melts and blends with the sugar. Stir in 1 tablespoon liqueur. Pour into prepared baking dish.

Arrange banana slices over the top of sauce. Arrange the bread slices in one layer over the bananas, trimming the bread to fit as needed (depending on the size of your bread, you will likely need 6 full slices and then cut up the remaining 2 slices to fill in the gaps). Set aside.

In a medium mixing bowl, whisk together the remaining 1 teaspoon liqueur, eggs, half and half, vanilla and salt. Pour evenly over the bread slices, soaking bread thoroughly with the milk mixture. Cover, and refrigerate at least 8 hours, up to 24 hours.

To serve, remove dish from refrigerator and bring to room temperature (about 1 hour). Preheat oven to 350 degrees.

Sprinkle the top of the dish with almonds. Bake for 35 to 40 minutes or until golden brown and the top is set; let stand 5 minutes. Dust with powdered sugar, if desired, and serve.

SPICED BACON TWISTS

My good friend Missy Eliot hosts a wonderful ladies brunch and ornament exchange every Christmas. One year, she served the most divine bacon — a wonderful combination of sweet, savory and spicy. It turns out the recipe comes from another good friend, Judy Grant. Fortunately for us, Judy and Missy were both willing to share the recipe!

SERVES: 6 to 8

1/2 cup firmly packed light brown sugar

2 tablespoons dry mustard

1/2 teaspoon ground cinnamon

1/2 teaspoon ground nutmeg

1/2 teaspoon cayenne pepper

1 pound sliced bacon (peppered bacon is even better)

Arrange oven racks in the middle and bottom positions of the oven. Preheat oven to 350 degrees.

Line the bottom of a broiler pan or large rimmed baking sheet with aluminum foil. Place broiler rack or metal cooling rack over foil-lined pan. Set aside.

In a small bowl, combine the brown sugar, mustard, cinnamon, nutmeg and cayenne, blending with a fork until evenly blended. Transfer mixture to a large sheet of wax paper. Dip bacon strips into sugar mixture to coat evenly. Twist each strip several times to make a spiral. Place bacon on prepared rack.

Bake 25 to 30 minutes or until bacon is almost crisp and sugar is bubbly — it may take 45 minutes depending on the oven. Watch carefully so they don't burn. Transfer strips to clean aluminum foil or parchment paper to cool (don't use a paper towel — they will stick!).

MAKE AHEAD May be prepared a day or two ahead of baking and refrigerated. Or bake, refrigerate and reheat in microwave or low (250 degree) oven.

SMOKED SALMON EGGS BENEDICT
WITH MUSTARD-DILL SAUCE

I recently started poaching eggs instead of frying them, as I prefer the more delicate texture of a poached egg. One morning as I was debating how to serve Robert his poached egg, I decided to create a version of Eggs Benedict with the smoked salmon we had on hand. I love how the flavors of mustard and dill complement salmon, so I created this sauce in place of the more traditional Hollandaise sauce. It's now one of our favorite breakfasts!

Note that you need to make the sauce the night before serving. You are likely to have some sauce leftover; it keeps in the refrigerator for a week or so and is also great on grilled fish or chicken.

SERVES: 6

2/3 cup half and half, plus more if needed to thin sauce

6 tablespoons olive oil

6 tablespoons Dijon mustard

5 tablespoons coarsely chopped fresh dill

4 teaspoons white wine vinegar

2 shallots, finely chopped

6 English muffins, split in half

4 tablespoons butter

12 ounces smoked salmon

12 large eggs

In a small mixing bowl, whisk together the half and half, olive oil, mustard, dill, vinegar and shallot. Transfer to a glass jar, cover and refrigerate overnight to allow the flavors to blend.

Place jar in a bain marie (bowl or pan of simmering water) to warm the sauce. Add 1 to 3 teaspoons half and half if sauce is too thick. Set aside and keep warm.

Toast the English muffin halves; spread with butter. Top each piece of toast with smoked salmon. Place two halves on 6 individual plates and set aside.

Poach the eggs to desired doneness (see Tip); place eggs on top of smoked salmon. Drizzle mustard-dill sauce over the top. Serve immediately.

MAKE AHEAD Mustard sauce can be made up to 3 days ahead, covered and refrigerated. Bring to room temperature before serving. Eggs can be poached the night before, placed in water, covered and refrigerated. Drop in hot but not boiling water for just a minute or so to reheat just before serving.

TIP

How to poach an egg: Put 2 inches of water in a sauté or saucepan; add 2 teaspoons of cider or white wine vinegar. Heat to the point where bubbles form on the bottom of the pan, with just a few bubbles (or none) rising to the top. Crack a cold, very fresh egg into a fine mesh strainer over a bowl (or sink) and gently swirl around to drain off excess water in the whites. Stir the almost boiling water to form a whirlpool. While the water is swirling, gently pour the egg into the middle. Cook to desired doneness, around 3 to 4 minutes for a runny egg. If egg sticks to the bottom of the pan while cooking, use a spatula to gently unstick. Remove egg from water with a slotted spoon and place egg (in spoon) on paper towel to drain. Serve immediately or place in cold water to hold (see make ahead instructions).

HUEVOS RANCHEROS

I first fell in love with the traditional Mexican egg dish Huevos Rancheros on vacation with a group of girlfriends in Cabo San Lucas. We were staying in a condo on the beach and the tiny restaurant in the complex made the most amazing huevos for us every morning. This recipe is my quick and easy version of this delicious breakfast entrée.

SERVES: 2; may be expanded

1/4 cup sour cream

1/2 teaspoon Mexican seasoning or taco seasoning blend*

2 tablespoons olive oil, divided

2 corn tortillas

1 cup prepared refried beans

2 large eggs

2 tablespoons grated cheddar cheese, or more to taste

2 to 3 tablespoons prepared guacamole, at room temperature (see Note 1, page 126)

2 to 3 tablespoons prepared pico de gallo, at room temperature (see Note 2, page 126)

1 tablespoon sliced black olives, or more to taste

1 tablespoon chopped green onion, or more to taste

*Recipe at www.seasonedkitchen.com. Prepared Mexican (or taco) seasoning is also available in the spice aisle at most major grocery stores

In a small mixing bowl, whisk together the sour cream and Mexican seasoning. Set aside to allow the flavors to blend.

In a large skillet, heat 1 tablespoon of the oil over medium-high heat. Cook each tortilla about 1 minute per side or until crisp and lightly browned. Drain on paper towels.

In a small saucepan, cook the refried beans over low heat, stirring occasionally, until hot.

Meanwhile, in a large skillet, heat the remaining 1 tablespoon oil over medium heat. Fry the eggs to desired degree of doneness.

Spread the heated beans over the tortillas. Top with ingredients in this order: sour cream mixture, eggs, cheese, guacamole, pico de gallo, olives and onions. Serve immediately.

MUSHROOM, SPINACH AND ONION FRITTATA WITH GOAT CHEESE

Frittatas are much easier to make than omelets, yet equally impressive to serve. This version combines fresh vegetables and herbs with tangy goat cheese for a wonderful breakfast treat. Serve with turkey sausage and Nama's Buttermilk Biscuits (*page 223*).

SERVES: 4

Olive oil or olive oil cooking spray

1/2 cup thinly sliced onion

6 ounces fresh mushrooms (button, baby bella, or cremini), stems removed and sliced

Chopped fresh herbs (chives, thyme, rosemary), to taste

2 cups packed baby spinach

1 cup egg whites

2 to 3 tablespoons crumbled goat cheese

Kosher salt, to taste

Freshly ground black pepper, to taste

Preheat the broiler with oven rack 5 to 6 inches away from heat.

Coat an oven-safe large skillet with olive oil and heat over medium-low heat. Add the onion and cook until starting to wilt. Stir in the mushrooms and cook, stirring occasionally until the mushrooms are cooked through and soft. Stir in the chopped herbs and spinach. Cook, stirring constantly, until the spinach wilts.

Stir in the egg whites and cook until the egg is set on the bottom and starting to cook on the top. Sprinkle with goat cheese.

Broil until the egg is set and the frittata is just starting to brown on top. Season with kosher salt and ground pepper and serve immediately.

A WELL-SEASONED INSPIRATION

NAMA *Born and raised in Kentucky, Nama, my maternal grandmother, was a true southern woman. She loved cooking and entertaining, and her relaxed approach in the kitchen fascinated me. While Nama was a taster, not a measurer, using only the palm of her hand to "measure" ingredients, her meals were always perfectly delicious. Nama taught me that tasting while cooking lets you adjust ingredients as needed and that proper seasoning brings out the natural flavor in food.*

TOASTED BAGELS WITH EGG SALAD AND SMOKED SALMON

Robert loves egg salad and smoked salmon, so combining the two in an open-faced sandwich for his breakfast one morning was a no-brainer. Making egg salad is not an exact science; it depends on the size and freshness of your ingredients. My proportions are a good place to start; add more mustard for more zing and/or more mayonnaise for more moisture. Be careful with the onions — if you're using large green onions and they're very fresh, you may need only one. These sandwiches are on the rich side; Robert and I find one half, combined with a serving of fresh fruit, is plenty for each of us.

SERVES: 2 to 4

4 large eggs

2 heaping tablespoons mayonnaise

2 teaspoons Dijon mustard

2 green onions, chopped (white part and some of the green)

1 tablespoon chopped fresh chives

Paprika, to taste

Kosher salt, to taste

Freshly ground black pepper, to taste

2 bagels, sliced in half (I like to use whole wheat or poppy seed)

3 to 4 ounces smoked salmon

In a large saucepan, place eggs in one layer and cover with water. Bring to a boil over high heat. Reduce heat to simmer and cook for 6 to 8 minutes (cook for longer time if at higher altitude). Remove from heat and leave eggs in hot water for another 3 to 5 minutes. Drain and run eggs under cold water until cooled.

Remove shells. Chop eggs and place in a medium mixing bowl; stir in mayonnaise, mustard, onion and chives. Season to taste with paprika, salt and pepper. Adjust the mayonnaise and mustard, if necessary.

Lightly toast the bagel halves, then spread egg salad mixture on each half. Top with slices of salmon and serve.

MAKE AHEAD Egg salad can be made up to 24 hours in advance, covered and refrigerated.

VARIATION Use toasted mini bagels or pumpernickel cocktail bread instead of the regular-size bagels and serve as hors d'oeuvres or a side dish for a brunch.

MINI STICKY PECAN ROLLS

Another great recipe from mom — gooey, caramel deliciousness (*photo, page 51*). We like them with our Southwestern Chile-Cheese Soufflé (*page 38*). The beauty in these scrumptious little bites is that they can be prepared the night before (*see Make Ahead instructions*).

MAKES: 3 dozen

2 1/2 cups all-purpose flour (may need more), divided

1/4 cup granulated sugar

1 (1/4-ounce) package active dry yeast

1/4 teaspoon baking soda

1 teaspoon salt

1 cup buttermilk

3 tablespoons vegetable oil

2 tablespoons water

1/4 cup water

6 tablespoons butter, melted, divided

3/4 cup firmly packed light brown sugar, divided

1 cup pecan halves, finely chopped

1 teaspoon ground cinnamon

Generously butter 36 mini-muffin cups.

In a large mixing bowl, whisk together 1 cup of the flour, sugar, yeast, baking soda and salt. Set aside.

In a small saucepan, heat the buttermilk and oil over medium heat just until it reaches 100 to 110 degrees. Add to the flour mixture and using the dough hook of an electric mixer, beat at medium speed for 2 minutes. Add remaining 1 1/2 cups flour and continue mixing until dough clings to hook and cleans sides of bowl. Knead on low or speed 2 for another 2 minutes until dough is smooth and elastic. Place dough on a floured surface and knead a few times, adding additional flour if dough is too sticky. Place in a greased bowl, turning to coat. Set aside in a non-drafty area while topping is prepared.

In a small mixing bowl, stir together water, 1/4 cup melted butter and 1/2 cup brown sugar. Spoon into prepared mini muffin cups. Sprinkle chopped pecans on top.

On a lightly floured surface, roll half of dough into an 8- by 14 to 16-inch rectangle. Brush with 1 tablespoon butter. Sprinkle 2 tablespoons brown sugar and cinnamon evenly over dough. Tightly roll into a cylinder starting with the long side (so you will have a 14 to 16-inch long cylinder when it's rolled up). Cut off rough or uneven ends, then cut cylinder into 1/2 to 3/4-inch slices (depending on depth of muffin cups) and place in muffin cups. Repeat with second half of dough. Let rise in a warm (85 degrees) place about 1 to 1 1/2 hours or until close to doubled in size.

Preheat oven to 350 degrees. Bake rolls 10 minutes or until golden brown. Remove from oven and let cool 1 to 2 minutes, then invert the rolls onto parchment paper or foil (scoop any remaining pecans or sauce onto the rolls using a small spoon). Let cool, then serve.

MAKE AHEAD Rolls can be prepared through slicing and placing in the mini-muffin tins, covered and refrigerated overnight. Let rise for around 1 1/2 hours before baking.

CINNAMON LOAF

The sour cream in this recipe keeps the loaf super moist, while the cinnamon and brown sugar flavor bring back fond childhood memories of eating cinnamon toast in my grandmother Nama's kitchen. Another recipe from mom's files — this one I found written on a bank deposit slip!

MAKES: 1 large or
4 small loaves

2 cups all-purpose flour

1 1/2 teaspoons baking powder

1 teaspoon baking soda

1/2 teaspoon salt

1/2 cup butter, softened (see Tip on page 18)

1 1/4 cups sugar, divided

2 large eggs

1 teaspoon vanilla extract

1 cup sour cream

1/4 cup whole milk

2 teaspoons ground cinnamon

1 1/2 teaspoons orange zest (from about 1 large navel orange)

Preheat oven to 350 degrees. Grease 1 large (9- by 5-inch) loaf pan, or 4 small (5 1/2- by 3-inch) loaf pans.

In a medium mixing bowl, whisk together the flour, baking powder, baking soda and salt; set aside.

In a large mixing bowl, using the paddle attachment of an electric mixer, cream the butter and 1 cup of the sugar on medium speed until light and fluffy. Add the eggs, one at a time, beating well after each addition. Beat in the vanilla, sour cream and milk until well blended. At low speed, slowly add the flour mixture, beating just until blended (do not overmix). Dough will be very thick. Spread half of batter into prepared loaf pan(s).

In a small bowl, stir together the remaining 1/4 cup sugar and cinnamon. Using your hands, blend in the orange zest; set aside 1 tablespoon. Sprinkle remaining cinnamon-sugar mixture over the batter in the pan. Carefully spoon the remaining batter over the top and smooth so top is level. Using a sharp knife, make a cut along the top of the batter lengthwise to within 1 inch of each end. Sprinkle remaining 1 tablespoon cinnamon-sugar mixture over the top of the cut.

Bake for 40 to 45 minutes or until a toothpick inserted in the center (but not through the cinnamon sugar) comes out clean. Cool in pan on a wire rack 10 minutes. Run a knife around the outside of the bread to loosen. Transfer loaf to a wire rack; cool completely.

HIGH ALTITUDE No adjustments necessary.

MAKE AHEAD Bread can be made up to 24 hours in advance, loosely covered with foil and stored at room temperature.

Cinnamon Loaf and Mini Sticky Pecan Rolls

APPLE BUTTERSCOTCH MUFFINS

With a flavor reminiscent of candy apples, I especially enjoy making these muffins (*photo, page 36*) in the fall. They're actually terrific any time of the year and I think they taste best the day after baking.

MAKES: 22 muffins

Nonstick cooking spray or paper muffin liners

2 1/2 cups all-purpose flour

1 1/2 teaspoons ground cinnamon

1 1/4 teaspoons baking powder

1 teaspoon baking soda

1 teaspoon salt

1/2 cup unsweetened applesauce

1/3 cup vegetable or olive oil

1 large egg, beaten

1 egg white

1 1/4 cups sugar

1/2 cup chopped pecans, or more to taste

3 cups (about 2 to 3 large) peeled and chopped Granny Smith apples

4 ounces (about 2/3 cup) butterscotch chips

Preheat oven to 350 degrees. Spray 22 muffin cups with nonstick cooking spray or line with muffin paper cups.

In a small mixing bowl, sift together the flour, cinnamon, baking powder, baking soda and salt. Set aside. In a large mixing bowl, stir together the applesauce, oil, eggs and sugar. Stir in flour mixture just until combined; do not over mix. Stir in pecans and apples (batter will be very thick).

Spoon batter into prepared muffin cups. Sprinkle butterscotch chips over the top of the batter, pushing down slightly. Fill any empty muffin cups in the pan halfway with water to prevent burning. Bake for 20 to 25 minutes until slightly golden brown and a toothpick inserted into the middle of a muffin comes out clean. Cool 5 minutes in pan on a wire rack; remove from pan and cool completely.

HIGH ALTITUDE Reduce the baking powder and baking soda each by 1/8 teaspoon, increase applesauce by 1 tablespoon, increase oil by 2 teaspoons and use extra large eggs. Bake 5 additional minutes, if necessary.

MAKE AHEAD Muffins can be prepared up to 24 hours in advance; they can also be frozen.

TIP

Muffin baking tips: Don't over mix the batter (it makes the muffins tough). Use a spring-loaded scoop to fill muffin cups with batter — it's faster and the muffins come out the same size. Fill empty muffin cups with water to prevent burning. Don't let the batter sit in the cups for any length of time; it keeps them from rising when baked. Let baked muffins sit in the cups for around 5 minutes before removing, then put on a wire rack to cool.

MINI RASPBERRY NUT MUFFINS

These muffins are best made when raspberries are in season. Frozen berries simply won't do the recipe justice, but with fresh raspberries, they're refreshing and fun to serve — and gone in just two bites! *(photo, page 36)*

MAKES: one dozen regular or
3 dozen mini muffins

3 tablespoons chopped pecans

1/3 cup plus 2 tablespoons light
brown sugar, divided

2 teaspoons ground cinnamon,
divided

1 1/2 cups all-purpose flour

2 teaspoons baking powder

1/4 teaspoon salt

1 large egg, beaten

1/4 cup vegetable oil

1/2 cup milk (2% or whole)

36 fresh raspberries (1 1/4 cups or
about 5 to 6 ounces)

1 cup powdered (confectioners)
sugar

4 to 6 teaspoons freshly squeezed
lemon juice

Preheat oven to 350 degrees. Spray 36 mini muffin cups with cooking spray.

In a small bowl, stir together the chopped pecans, 2 tablespoons brown sugar and 1 teaspoon cinnamon; set aside.

In a medium mixing bowl, whisk together the remaining 1/3 cup brown sugar, remaining 1 teaspoon cinnamon, flour, baking powder and salt. In a large mixing bowl, whisk together the egg, oil and milk; add dry ingredients and gently stir just until combined. Do not over mix or muffins will be tough (batter will be thick).

Spoon batter 3/4 full into prepared mini cups. Press 1 raspberry into batter (they will stick partially out the top of the batter). Sprinkle pecan topping mixture over the top, pushing down lightly with your fingers to adhere.

Bake for 8 to 12 minutes or until golden brown and a toothpick inserted into a muffin (into the batter, not the raspberry) comes out clean. Remove from pan to a wire rack to cool at least 30 minutes.

In a small bowl, stir together powdered sugar and 4 teaspoons lemon juice until well blended. Mixture should be fairly thick, yet thin enough to drizzle. If too thick, add more lemon juice. Drizzle over the top of the muffins (I like to put it in a squeeze bottle and drizzle it in lines).

HIGH ALTITUDE Decrease baking powder by 1/4 teaspoon, increase vegetable oil by 1 1/2 teaspoons and increase milk by 1 tablespoon.

MAKE AHEAD Muffins can be made a day ahead, placed on a wire rack at room temperature and covered with a dry, clean towel. Store any leftovers in an airtight container that has been lined with paper towels to keep the muffins from getting soggy.

Soups

"A first-rate soup is more creative than a second-rate painting."
— *Abraham Maslow, Psychologist*

There's nothing quite like a great soup, both hot and cold. From hearty to light, casual to sophisticated, this fresh collection of recipes takes you from summer picnics (just add a thermos) to cold winter nights by the fire!

CHILLED SOUPS

56 | Cucumber Leek Vichyssoise

58 | Chilled Minted Pea Soup

HOT SOUPS

59 | Butternut Squash Soup

60 | Carrot-Ginger Soup

62 | Puréed Black Bean Soup

63 | Roasted Eggplant and Tomato Soup

64 | Split Pea Soup with Country Ham

66 | Italian Sausage, Spinach and Orzo Soup

68 | Soy-Ginger Shrimp and Rice Soup

69 | Chinese Chicken Noodle Soup

CUCUMBER LEEK VICHYSSOISE

Robert doesn't like cucumbers on their own but will eat them mixed in with other foods. I love cucumbers, so to accommodate him I often experiment, finding new ways to incorporate them into a dish. Growing up, I loved the vichyssoise at the country club where my family belonged (and Robert and I still belong today). Traditionally served very cold (often over ice), adding cold cucumber seemed a natural fit.

SERVES: 6

1 tablespoon butter

1/2 teaspoon chopped garlic or shallots

1/4 cup (1/4 large) chopped onion

1 1/2 cups (2 large) chopped leeks, white and light green parts

2 cups chicken stock

1/2 teaspoon salt

2 cups (2 large) peeled, seeded and chopped cucumber

1/2 cup packed chopped fresh baby spinach

1 large russet potato, peeled and thinly sliced

3/4 cup half and half

Juice from 1/2 lemon

Kosher salt

Ground white pepper

Garnish: thinly sliced radish, chopped fresh chives

In a large skillet or sauté pan, melt butter over medium-low heat. Add garlic (or shallots), onion and leeks. Cook, stirring frequently, about 5 to 7 minutes or until soft and the leeks are just beginning to turn brown. Remove from heat. Set aside.

In a large saucepan, bring chicken stock and salt to a boil over medium-high heat. Add cucumber, spinach and potato. Cover, reduce heat to low, and simmer about 10 to 15 minutes or until potatoes are tender. Remove from heat, uncover and cool for 15 minutes.

Stir in leek mixture and half and half. Purée with an immersion blender or transfer to a blender in 2 batches and purée until smooth. Season to taste with lemon juice, salt and ground white pepper. Cover and chill for several hours. Adjust seasonings, as needed. Serve cold; garnish servings with thinly sliced radishes and chopped chives.

MAKE AHEAD Soup can be made up to 2 days ahead, covered and refrigerated.

CHILLED MINTED PEA SOUP

From the age of two up until my early 40's, my family and I spent one to two weeks each summer on the Gordon Ranch in Wyoming. Here, I learned many things about good food, cooking and entertaining. Dinner was formal — at 7pm, after cocktails at 6. A first course was always on the menu, often a soup. When Valerie and Mark Gordon inherited the ranch after their parents' passing, they graciously shared the Ranch's recipe box with me. This delicious soup recipe came from that fabulous box of memories.

SERVES: 6 to 8 as a
first course

3 cups shelled fresh (about 2 1/2 pounds in the pod) peas*

1 tablespoon butter

1/3 cup (about 2 medium) thinly sliced leeks, white part only

3 1/2 cups chicken broth

2 tablespoons chopped green onion

1 1/2 cups loosely packed fresh mint leaves, plus more for garnish

1 tablespoon fresh lemon or lime juice

3/4 cup heavy whipping cream

Salt, to taste

Freshly ground black pepper, to taste

Garnishes: fresh grated Parmesan, fresh mint leaves

*If fresh peas aren't in season, substitute 15 ounces frozen and thawed peas

Cook fresh peas in boiling water until tender, about 5 to 7 minutes. Drain, plunge in ice water, and drain again. (If using frozen peas, no need to cook them; simply thaw under running hot water and drain.) Set aside.

In a large stockpot, melt butter over medium heat. Add leeks and cook about 4 to 5 minutes until soft. Add chicken broth and bring to a boil. Reduce heat to simmer and stir in peas, green onion and mint. Cook for 2 minutes. Remove from heat and cool 15 to 20 minutes or until mixture is room temperature.

Stir in lemon or lime juice and whipping cream. Purée with an immersion blender or transfer to a blender in batches; purée until smooth. Cover and chill.

Before serving, season to taste with salt and fresh ground pepper. Garnish servings with Parmesan cheese and a mint leaf.

MAKE AHEAD Soup can be made up to 24 hours in advance, covered and refrigerated.

BUTTERNUT SQUASH SOUP

Sometimes the best recipes arise from kitchen-related disasters. My cousin Dave Berry is one of those natural cooks who can create delicious recipes from scratch. When following his original recipe for Butternut Squash Soup, I accidentally added too much chicken stock, resulting in a very watery, flavorless soup. I needed to amp it up to give it more flavor. Instead of adding more steamed squash, I opted to layer in more flavor — seasoning the squash with curry and onion powder and roasting it. I decided a bit of apple would add a nice bit of sweetness. According to our dinner guests (and recipe testers), my "fixes" were a success!

SERVES: 10 to 12

3 pounds (12 cups) peeled, seeded and cubed butternut squash (about 4 to 4 1/2 pounds whole squash), divided

2 tablespoons olive oil

1 1/2 teaspoons curry powder, divided

1/2 teaspoon onion powder

Salt, to taste

Freshly ground black pepper, to taste

2 tablespoons butter

2 medium yellow onions, chopped

1 tablespoon chopped fresh rosemary, or more to taste

6 cups chicken stock

1/2 apple, peeled, cored and chopped

1 cup half and half

Garnish: 1/4 cup chopped roasted pecans

Preheat oven to 425 degrees.

Arrange half of the squash in a single layer in a large roasting pan; toss with olive oil, 1/2 teaspoon curry powder and onion powder. Season to taste with salt and pepper. Roast squash about 25 to 35 minutes or until very soft. Cool slightly, then mash with a potato masher until smooth.

In a large soup pot or Dutch oven, melt butter over medium heat. Add the chopped onion and rosemary; cook until the onion is soft. Add the remaining uncooked cubed squash, chicken stock, chopped apple and remaining curry powder. Bring to boil, reduce heat to medium-low and simmer about 30 to 40 minutes or until the squash is tender when tested with a fork. Add half and half, stirring until well blended.

Remove from heat. Purée with an immersion blend or cool slightly and transfer to a blender in batches; purée until smooth. Return mixture to pan and reheat, if necessary. Stir in the mashed squash. Season to taste with salt and pepper. Serve warm; garnish with about 1 teaspoon chopped pecans per serving.

MAKE AHEAD: Soup can be made up to 2 days in advance, covered and refrigerated (I actually think it tastes better if it sits for awhile). Reheat over medium heat until hot.

CARROT-GINGER SOUP

I think carrot and ginger are a match made in heaven. Enhanced with a hint of chipotle, garlic and onion, this soup got rave reviews from my book club when I shared it with them. If you can't find chipotle-flavored olive oil, simply add a small amount of puréed chipotle peppers.

SERVES: 6 to 8

1 tablespoon butter

1 tablespoon chipotle flavored or plain olive oil*

1 1/2 to 2 teaspoons grated fresh ginger

1/2 teaspoon chopped garlic

1 1/2 cups chopped onion

1 cup chopped celery, reserving any leaves for garnish

2 pounds carrots, peeled and sliced

2 cups chicken stock

1 1/2 cups water

1/2 cup regular or skim evaporated milk or half and half

2 tablespoons dry sherry (or more to taste)

Salt, to taste

Freshly ground black pepper, to taste

Garnish: celery leaves

*If using plain olive oil, add 1/4 to 1/2 teaspoon puréed chipotle peppers in adobo sauce

In a large stockpot, melt butter with the olive oil over medium heat. Stir in ginger, garlic, onion, celery and carrots. Cook, stirring frequently for 3 to 5 minutes or until starting to soften. Stir in chicken stock and water; bring to a boil. Cover, reduce heat and simmer until carrots are tender, about 15 to 20 minutes.

Remove from heat. Purée with an immersion blender or cool and transfer to a blender in batches; purée until smooth. Return soup to pan, if necessary, and stir in milk and sherry. Season to taste with salt and pepper. Reheat over medium-low heat. Serve hot or warm. Garnish each serving with celery leaves, if desired.

MAKE AHEAD Soup can be made up to 2 days ahead, covered and refrigerated.

PURÉED BLACK BEAN SOUP

Robert and I belong to a ski club in Colorado and once a year a group of members plan, cook and serve a four to five-course gourmet dinner for everyone. The year we chaired the committee, our friend and committee member Diane Reeder contributed this soup recipe to the menu. Since then, it has become a favorite in our household. The black beans in this meat-free soup are flavored with a wonderful mix of onion, jalapeño pepper, cumin, tomato and cilantro.

SERVES: 6

3 tablespoons olive oil

12 green onions, chopped

3 (15-ounce) cans black beans, rinsed and drained *(see Note)*

3 to 4 teaspoons chopped garlic

3 jalapeños, seeded and finely sliced (include a few seeds to make it spicier)

2 teaspoons ground cumin

1 1/2 teaspoons ground coriander

2 tablespoons tomato paste

4 1/2 cups chicken stock or broth

1 1/2 small bunches fresh cilantro, chopped

1 1/2 tablespoons light brown sugar

Salt, to taste

Freshly ground black pepper, to taste

Garnishes: fried corn tortilla strips, sour cream and fresh lime wedges or slices

In a large stockpot, heat olive oil over medium heat. Add green onions and sauté just until soft. Stir in the beans, garlic, jalapeños, cumin, coriander and tomato paste. Continue cooking, stirring frequently, about 5 minutes. Stir in chicken stock, cilantro and sugar; bring to a boil, reduce heat and simmer, partially covered, about 20 minutes.

Purée with an immersion blender or cool slightly and transfer to a blender in batches; purée until smooth. Return soup to pan, if necessary and season to taste with salt and pepper. Reheat at a low simmer when ready to serve. Garnish with fried tortilla strips, sour cream and either a squeeze or slice of fresh lime.

MAKE AHEAD Soup can be prepared up to 2 days ahead of time, covered and refrigerated.

NOTE You can make this soup with 3/4 pound (2 to 2 1/4 cups) dried black beans. Rinse beans and add to soup at the same time as canned. Increase cook time to 1 1/2 to 2 hours.

ROASTED EGGPLANT AND TOMATO SOUP

My good friend Cynthia Ballantyne shared with me a delicious recipe for an eggplant soup she got from the chef at a fabulous hotel in Big Sur, California. Amazingly similar to an eggplant soup recipe I'd been making for years, I decided to combine the two recipes, and this is the result. It's delicious with our Italian Popovers *(page 227)*.

SERVES: 6 to 8

1 1/2 pounds eggplant, peeled and cut into 1-inch pieces

3 tablespoons extra virgin olive oil, divided

1/2 teaspoon salt

1/4 teaspoon freshly ground black pepper

1 cup chopped yellow onion

1 teaspoon chopped garlic

2 large tomatoes, chopped and seeded*

1 tablespoon fresh thyme

2 tablespoons chopped fresh chives, divided

3 to 4 cups vegetable broth, divided

1 tablespoon red wine vinegar

When fresh tomatoes aren't in season, for more flavor substitute 2 1/2 cups canned diced tomatoes, drained

Preheat the oven to 450 degrees.

In a small roasting pan, toss the eggplant with 1 1/2 tablespoons of the olive oil, salt, and pepper. Roast 20 minutes, stirring occasionally, until well browned. Set aside.

In a medium stockpot, heat the remaining 1 1/2 tablespoons of olive oil over medium heat. Add the onion, garlic and tomatoes and cook 8 to 10 minutes or until the onion is soft. Stir in the roasted eggplant and cook for 5 minutes. Add the thyme, 1 tablespoon chives and 3 cups vegetable broth. Bring to a boil, reduce heat and simmer about 10 to 12 minutes, until eggplant is very soft. Stir in vinegar.

Remove from heat. Purée with an immersion blender or cool slightly and transfer to a blender in batches; purée until smooth. Return soup to pot and season to taste with salt and pepper. Stir in more vegetable broth (up to 1 cup) if soup is too thick. Reheat over medium-low heat, stirring frequently. Spoon into individual bowls, garnishing with remaining 1 tablespoon chopped chives.

MAKE AHEAD Soup can be made up to 2 days ahead, covered and refrigerated.

SPLIT PEA SOUP WITH COUNTRY HAM

A big fan of split pea soup, I decided to try making a batch using the bone and leftover scraps from our Christmas country ham — it was yummy! Warning: country ham tastes smokier and saltier than regular ham, so if you're not accustomed to its flavor, you might want to avoid using the ham bone. I still recommend stirring in the chopped ham at the end and make sure to use fresh split peas. If they're old, they'll never soften — no matter how long you cook them.

SERVES: 4 to 6

2 cups dried split peas, rinsed and picked over

2 tablespoons olive oil

1 cup (1 very large) chopped carrots

1 cup (1/2 large) chopped yellow onion

1 cup (3 medium) chopped leeks

1/4 cup (2 large stalks) chopped celery

2 to 3 quarts chicken broth

1 country ham bone

1 cup chopped cooked country ham

In a medium mixing bowl, cover dried peas with water with 1-inch on top. Soak overnight. Drain, rinse and set aside.

In a large stockpot, heat the olive oil over medium heat. Add the carrots, onion, leeks and celery. Sauté, stirring occasionally, 15 minutes or until soft and just beginning to brown.

Add 2 quarts of the chicken broth and ham bone. Bring to a boil, partially cover, reduce heat and simmer for 30 minutes. Stir in the peas; reduce heat to low, uncover and simmer, stirring occasionally, for 1 1/2 hours or until the peas are tender. The longer you cook it, the creamier the consistency of the soup.

Remove the ham bone and stir in the chopped country ham. Thin with additional chicken broth, as needed. Serve hot.

MAKE AHEAD Soup can be prepared up to 2 days ahead of time, covered and refrigerated.

TIP

I think this soup tastes best if you stir in the ham and then let it set for a bit off the heat – at least 30 minutes, or even overnight in the refrigerator. It thickens as it sits, so you will want to thin it with more broth.

ITALIAN SAUSAGE, SPINACH AND ORZO SOUP

Our good friend Carol Nollsch gave me this recipe and recommends making it the day before serving to allow the flavors to blend. It's my favorite kind of recipe — quick and easy to prepare from items usually on hand (with limited chopping!) and full of flavor. Carol recommends serving it with cornbread; our testers also liked it with sourdough bread.

SERVES: 8

1 tablespoon extra virgin olive oil

1 pound uncooked Italian sausage, casings removed if necessary

2 cups chopped onion

1/2 to 1 teaspoon chopped garlic

2 teaspoons Italian seasoning

1/2 teaspoon red pepper flakes

2/3 cup dry white wine

7 cups chicken broth or stock

2 cups seeded and diced fresh tomatoes, or 1 (16-ounce) can diced tomatoes undrained (see Tip) .

1 cup orzo pasta

5 cups packed shredded fresh baby spinach

3/4 to 1 cup (3 to 4 ounces) freshly grated Parmesan cheese

In a large stockpot, heat oil over medium-high heat. Add the sausage and sauté until browned, breaking up meat with a spatula. Drain and discard oil.

Stir in onion, garlic, Italian seasoning and red pepper flakes and cook 3 to 4 minutes. Stir in the wine; reduce heat to low and simmer, scraping up any browned bits from bottom of pan, until wine is almost evaporated. Stir in the chicken broth, tomatoes and orzo. Bring to boil, reduce heat and simmer about 10 to 12 minutes or until pasta is cooked.

Stir in spinach; cook about 3 to 5 minutes or until wilted. Ladle in to soup bowls and sprinkle with freshly grated Parmesan cheese.

TIP

If using canned tomatoes, don't drain and reduce chicken broth about 1/2 cup.

SOY-GINGER SHRIMP AND RICE SOUP

Really good soup doesn't need to take hours to make. This Asian-inspired recipe can be on the table in less than 30 minutes, is spicy, aromatic (lots of ginger, soy and lime) — and healthy too. While Robert likes it with 3/4 teaspoon cayenne pepper, I prefer it a bit less spicy. To compromise, I make it with 1/2 teaspoon cayenne pepper and then put out some sriracha sauce for him to add more heat if he wants it. *(photo, page 54)*

SERVES: 4 to 6

1 tablespoon peanut oil

1 tablespoon grated fresh ginger

1/2 to 3/4 teaspoon cayenne pepper
(higher amount is pretty spicy!)

5 cups chicken broth

2 to 3 teaspoons soy sauce, divided

2 tablespoons lime zest (from around
2 large limes)

1/2 cup uncooked long grain rice

1 cup unsweetened coconut milk

2 cups (about 6 large) chopped
white mushrooms

1/2 cup (1/2 large) chopped onion

1 heaping tablespoon chopped
fresh cilantro

16 ounces medium (41 to 50 per
pound) shrimp, peeled and
deveined (tail shells removed)

2 tablespoons fresh lime juice

Garnishes: chopped green onion
and cilantro

In a large saucepan, combine peanut oil, ginger and cayenne pepper over medium heat; sauté for 1 minute. Add chicken broth, 2 teaspoons soy sauce, and lime zest; bring mixture to a boil. Stir in rice, cover, reduce heat and simmer 15 minutes.

Stir in coconut milk, mushrooms, onion and cilantro. Bring to a boil; reduce heat and simmer, covered and stirring occasionally, for 5 minutes.

Add shrimp and simmer, uncovered, for 3 to 5 minutes or until shrimp are cooked through and turn pink. Remove from heat and stir in lime juice. Taste and add remaining 1 teaspoon soy sauce, if needed. Season to taste with salt and pepper. Serve hot, garnished with chopped onion and cilantro.

CHINESE CHICKEN NOODLE SOUP

One evening, Robert had a bad cold and I thought some chicken noodle soup would make him feel better. I jazzed it up a bit, adding veggies and ginger, and then decided to give it an Asian twist. I swapped out pasta noodles for bean threads and added some sesame oil and soy sauce. It turned out delicious — and Robert loved it too!

SERVES: 6 to 8

1 tablespoon butter

1 tablespoon sesame oil (not dark or toasted)

3/4 cup chopped green onion

1/2 cup (1 large stalk) chopped celery

1/2 cup (1 medium) chopped red bell pepper

1/2 cup chopped mushrooms, preferably shiitake

1 teaspoon chopped fresh ginger

7 cups chicken stock or broth

12 ounces (about 2 breast halves) boneless, skinless chicken breasts, chopped into bite-sized pieces

1 (3.75 to 4 ounce) package cellophane, glass or bean thread noodles

3/4 cup bean sprouts, cut into 3/4 inch pieces

1 cup shredded baby spinach

1 cup shredded Napa cabbage

1/4 cup soy sauce

2 tablespoons fresh lemon juice

Kosher salt, to taste

Freshly ground black pepper, to taste

In a large stockpot, melt butter with sesame oil over medium-high heat, stirring until blended. Stir in the onion, celery, bell pepper, mushrooms and ginger. Cook, stirring constantly, about 7 to 8 minutes or just until softened. Add chicken stock and bring to a boil. Stir in chopped chicken; reduce heat to simmer, and cook about 10 minutes or until chicken is done.

Stir in noodles, sprouts, spinach and cabbage and simmer 4 to 5 minutes or until noodles are tender. Stir in soy sauce and lemon juice; season to taste with salt and pepper. Cut noodles into smaller pieces using kitchen shears, if desired. Serve hot.

MAKE AHEAD Soup can be made up to 2 days in advance, covered and refrigerated.

Salads

"...The perfect dinner necessarily includes the perfect salad."
— *George Ellwanger, author of "Pleasures of the Table" (1902)*

A beautiful salad can make a meal. The clever presentation of these inspired, new and classic salads (plated, tossed, jarred and more) is second only to the freshness of the ingredients within!

SIDE SALADS

72 | Mixed Greens with Dried Cranberries

73 | Tomato and Peach Salad with Lime-Balsamic Dressing

74 | Tomato and Cucumber Salad with Yogurt-Herb Dressing

76 | Apple, Walnut and Stilton Cheese Salad

78 | Avocado-Mushroom Salad with Chutney Dressing

79 | Roasted Beet Salad with Arugula Dressing

80 | Roasted Butternut Squash and Mushroom Spinach Salad

82 | Spinach Salad with Curry Dressing

83 | Arugula and Spinach Salad with Lemon-Dijon Dressing

84 | Dorothy's Potato Salad

86 | Indonesian Brown Rice Salad

87 | Caesar Salad Dressing

MAIN DISH

88 | Grilled Steak, Roasted Potatoes and Tomato Salad

90 | Layered Salmon Salad with Avocado-Lime Yogurt Dressing

92 | Crab and Shrimp Salad with Curry-Chutney Dressing

93 | Asian Shrimp and Brown Rice Salad

94 | Tuna Salad Niçoise with Lemon-Tarragon Dressing

96 | Tuna and Roasted Red Pepper Pasta Salad with Pesto Dressing

97 | Chicken, Blueberry and Mango Salad

MIXED GREENS WITH DRIED CRANBERRIES

This is an excellent salad to serve around the holidays — the red cranberries and red onion, together with the green lettuce and avocado, make for a very festive presentation. With a light and fruity dressing, this salad pairs well with our Roasted Halibut with a Caper, Pine Nut and Tomato Sauce (*page 149*) or Roasted Lamb with Lemon (*page 134*).

SERVES: 6

2 tablespoons cranberry juice

1/4 cup white wine vinegar

1 1/2 teaspoons Dijon mustard

1/4 teaspoon fresh ground pepper or lemon pepper seasoning

1/2 cup extra virgin olive oil

8 cups mixed salad greens, torn into bite-sized pieces

1 avocado, peeled and chopped

1/4 cup sliced red onion, cut into quarters (*see Tip on page 78*)

1/2 cup dried cranberries

1/2 cup toasted slivered almonds

In a medium glass jar with a fitted lid, whisk cranberry juice, vinegar, mustard, pepper and olive oil until well combined. Cover and set aside.

In a large salad bowl, combine the salad greens, avocado, onion, cranberries and almonds. Toss with desired amount of dressing and serve (you may have some dressing left over).

MAKE AHEAD Dressing can be made several days ahead, covered and refrigerated. Bring to room temperature before using.

VARIATION Toss the greens with 3/4 of the dressing. Divide between individual salad plates. Cut the avocado into slices and arrange in a spiral pattern on top of the greens. Top with the red onion slices and sprinkle with the cranberries and almonds.

TOMATO AND PEACH SALAD
WITH LIME-BALSAMIC DRESSING

I created a slight adaptation to this salad recipe that came from my good friend Kathy Soter, who likes to make it with white peaches. It's best to make this dish when tomatoes and peaches are in season, and is a beautiful salad to serve as part of a buffet. *(photo, page 70)*

SERVES: 4

2 large tomatoes, sliced into rounds

2 large ripe peaches, peeled, pitted and sliced into rounds *(see Tip below)*

1/4 large red onion, very thinly sliced, preferably with a mandolin *(see Tip, page 78)*

2 tablespoons chopped fresh cilantro, or more to taste

Red pepper flakes, to taste

Salt, to taste

Freshly ground black pepper, to taste

1 tablespoon lime olive oil*

1 tablespoon peach balsamic vinegar*

Fresh lime juice, to taste

Pinch sugar

* If you can't find lime olive oil, substitute lemon olive oil, or extra virgin olive oil and add a bit more lime. If you can't find peach balsamic vinegar, substitute white balsamic vinegar

On a serving platter, arrange the tomato and peach slices in a circular pattern, alternating tomato and peach slices. Scatter red onion over the top. Sprinkle with cilantro and red pepper flakes. Season with salt and fresh ground pepper.

In a small mixing bowl, whisk together the oil, vinegar, lime juice and sugar. Season to taste with salt and pepper. Add more lime juice and/or sugar as needed. Drizzle dressing evenly over top of salad just before serving.

MAKE AHEAD Dressing can be prepared 2 to 3 days in advance, covered refrigerated. Bring to room temperature before serving. Tomatoes, peaches and onion can be sliced and plated up to 4 hours ahead. Cover and store at room temperature. Add cilantro, pepper flakes, salt, pepper and dressing just before serving.

TIP

To slice peaches into rounds: after peeling, cut the peach in half along its natural divide. Gently twist to separate into two halves. Remove pit. Starting in the middle, cut into rounds (there will be a hole in the middle where the pit was).

TOMATO AND CUCUMBER SALAD
WITH YOGURT-HERB DRESSING

One fall, my husband Robert and I had a divine two-week vacation in southern France and northern Spain. A highlight was staying at the fabulous home of good friends, near Biarritz. They both love to cook and they treated us to several scrumptious meals featuring a variety of local fresh foods (you can see photos and read about what we ate on my blog at *www.seasonedkitchen.com*). I was asked to make a salad one evening. After I said yes, I discovered that all the olive oil — all the oil in the house in fact — had been used up making the other parts of the dinner. Suddenly, I felt like someone on one of those reality TV cooking shows; I had to quickly figure out how to make a salad dressing with NO oil! This dish is what I came up with — a yogurt-based dressing with fresh herbs from their garden, served over fresh tomatoes and cucumbers. Ingenuity can be quite delicious!

As with all fresh salad dressings, it tastes best if allowed to sit at least 30 minutes for the flavors to blend.

SERVES: 4 to 6

1/2 cup Greek yogurt

2 tablespoons tarragon vinegar

1 teaspoon lemon zest

1 teaspoon chopped garlic

1 tablespoon chopped fresh dill

1 tablespoon chopped fresh mint

Salt, to taste

Freshly ground black pepper, to taste

3 cups shredded Bibb, Boston or
    Butter lettuce

4 to 5 large ripe tomatoes, sliced

1 large ripe cucumber (peeled if not
    English hothouse cucumber),
    sliced

In a medium mixing bowl, whisk together the yogurt, vinegar, zest, garlic, dill and mint. Season to taste with salt and pepper. Cover and refrigerate for at least 30 minutes.

Arrange the lettuce on a serving platter. Arrange tomatoes and cucumbers on top of the lettuce, alternating each one. Season with salt and pepper. Drizzle dressing over the top.

MAKE AHEAD The dressing can be made up to 24 hours ahead, covered and refrigerated. Bring to room temperature before using.

APPLE, WALNUT AND STILTON CHEESE SALAD

The British have known for years that apples and Stilton cheese are a wonderful combination. In this delicious salad, they're mixed together with spinach, walnuts and a walnut-flavored vinaigrette. I like to serve this salad with any grilled meat or with mom's Coq au Vin (*page 114*).

SERVES: 6

1/4 cup raspberry balsamic vinegar*

1 1/2 teaspoons freshly squeezed lemon juice

1/2 cup walnut oil*

Salt, to taste

Freshly ground black pepper, to taste

10 ounces mixed baby greens (spinach, arugula, lettuce)

2 large Gala or other red apples, unpeeled, cored and chopped

1 cup (6 ounces) chopped walnuts, lightly toasted

1 1/2 to 2 cups (6 to 8 ounces) Stilton cheese, crumbled**

If you can't find raspberry balsamic vinegar, use regular raspberry vinegar and add 1 to 2 tablespoons of honey. If you can't find walnut oil, substitute olive oil and add a few more walnuts

**There are 2 types of Stilton cheese: blue and white. Either will work in this recipe. If you can't find Stilton, you can substitute Gorgonzola or other forms of blue cheese*

In a medium glass jar with fitted lid (an empty Dijon mustard jar works well), whisk together the vinegar, lemon juice and oil until well blended. Season to taste with salt and pepper. Cover and set aside.

In a large bowl, toss together mixed greens, chopped apple, walnuts and cheese. Just before serving, toss with just enough dressing to coat the lettuce (you may have some dressing left over). Season to taste with salt and pepper.

VARIATION IN PRESENTATION If you want to have a more formal, individually plated salad, then instead of chopping the apples, core and slice them. Toss the greens with part of the dressing and divide among six individual salad plates. Arrange the apple slices in a circular pattern over the spinach. Sprinkle the walnuts and cheese crumbles over the top. Drizzle with remaining dressing.

AVOCADO-MUSHROOM SALAD
WITH CHUTNEY DRESSING

My Aunt Bobbie had a knack for finding unusual recipes full of flavor, and this one's no different. The dressing is what makes this salad stand out, with the addition of ground ginger and chutney to a traditional Dijon vinaigrette. Serve with Salmon with Lemon-Lime Crumb Topping (*page 155*) or Feta Chicken (*page 105*).

SERVES: 4

2 tablespoons olive oil

2 tablespoons balsamic vinegar

4 large green onions, chopped (white, light green and some dark green part)

1 1/2 tablespoons Dijon mustard

1/8 teaspoon ground ginger

1 tablespoon mango chutney, large pieces chopped*

1 head Butter, Boston or Bibb lettuce, torn into bite size pieces

1 ripe avocado, chopped

4 ounces thinly sliced mushrooms (white or cremini work well)

1/2 cup thinly sliced red onion, cut into quarters

1/2 cup chopped red bell pepper

Salt, to taste

Freshly ground black pepper, to taste

A widely available mango chutney is the brand "Major Grey's Chutney"

In a glass jar with a fitted lid, whisk together the oil, vinegar, mustard, ginger and chutney. Cover and set aside.

In a large salad bowl, toss together the lettuce, avocado, mushrooms, onion and bell pepper. Toss with the dressing just before serving; season to taste with salt and pepper.

MAKE AHEAD Dressing can be made up to 24 hours ahead, covered and refrigerated. Bring to room temperature before tossing the salad.

TIP

To soften the sharp bite of raw red onion: Peel and slice the red onion as called for in the recipe, then place in a bowl covered with water. Let soak for around hour. Drain and pat dry.

ROASTED BEET SALAD WITH ARUGULA DRESSING

I love this salad, frankly because I love the dressing — baby arugula, green onion, garlic, mayonnaise, sour cream, anchovy and lemon topped off with fresh tarragon. I could eat it with a spoon! And the flavors go really well with almost any roasted vegetable, especially beets. I recommend only using fresh tarragon; the dressing just simply isn't as good using dried.

Note you have to make the dressing at least one day ahead. If you have dressing left over, use it as a dip with fresh veggies.

SERVES: 6

1 1/2 cups (about 1 1/2 to 2 ounces) packed baby arugula

1/3 to 1/2 cup (about 4) sliced green onion (white, light green and some dark green part)

1 teaspoon chopped garlic

1/2 cup mayonnaise

1/2 cup sour cream

1 tablespoon fresh lemon juice

1 1/2 teaspoons anchovy paste (in a tube)*

2 tablespoons chopped fresh tarragon

Salt, to taste

Freshly ground black pepper, to taste

6 large beets (red or mixture of red and yellow)

9 to 10 cups Boston, Bibb or Butter lettuce, torn into bite-size pieces

Crumbled goat cheese

Sliced red onion (*see Tip on page 78*)

If you mash anchovy fillets, the flavor will be stronger than mashed anchovy from a tube, as the latter has vinegar and spices added, which make the fish flavor milder. So, I would reduce the amount to 1 teaspoon if you substitute freshly mashed

In a food processor, combine the arugula, green onion, garlic, mayonnaise, sour cream, lemon juice, anchovy paste and tarragon; process until well blended. Season to taste with salt and pepper. Cover and refrigerate for at least 24 hours.

Preheat the oven to 375 degrees.

Wash the beets and trim off the ends. In a large piece of foil, place 2 beets side by side and fold foil edges together tightly to make a packet; repeat with remaining beets and foil. Place in oven directly on oven rack with seam side up (this keeps any beet juice from going into your oven) and bake 45 minutes to 1 hour, or until soft in the center when pierced with a fork. Cool. When the beets are cool enough to handle, peel and cut into wedges.

Divide lettuce among 6 salad plates. Arrange sliced beets in a circle on top of lettuce; sprinkle with goat cheese and red onion. Drizzle with some of the dressing, passing the rest on the side.

MAKE AHEAD The dressing can be prepared and the beets roasted up to 3 days ahead, covered and stored in the refrigerator.

ROASTED BUTTERNUT SQUASH AND MUSHROOM SPINACH SALAD

This delicious and healthy fall or winter salad is excellent served with soup, roast chicken or pork. If you have friends or family who can't eat mushrooms, you can make this dish without them — it's still scrumptious and beautiful. This recipe will likely make more sugared walnuts than you will need, but just save them for another salad — or enjoy them yourself while you are roasting the vegetables!

SERVES: 4 to 6

2 teaspoons butter

1/4 cup sugar

1/2 cup coarsely chopped walnuts

Kosher salt, to taste

1 1/2 cups peeled, seeded and cubed (1/2-inch) butternut squash (*see Tip, page 197*)

1/4 cup extra virgin olive oil, divided

Freshly ground black pepper, to taste

2 cups quartered mushrooms (cremini, shiitake or small portobellos work best)

1 tablespoon balsamic vinegar

4 cups fresh baby spinach

1/4 cup crumbled goat cheese

1/4 cup shredded ham, optional (preferably country ham; *see note*)

Note: If you can't find country ham, substitute either Virginia ham or prosciutto

In a medium skillet, melt the butter over medium heat. Stir in the sugar, then the walnut pieces. Cook, stirring for 5 minutes. Remove from heat and quickly transfer nuts onto waxed or parchment paper, separating the walnuts as much as possible. Sprinkle lightly with kosher salt. Set aside to cool.

Preheat oven to 425 degrees. In a small roasting pan, toss together the squash and 1 tablespoon of the olive oil. Season with salt and pepper; toss again. In a second roasting pan, toss together the mushrooms and 1 tablespoon of the olive oil. Season with salt and pepper; toss again.

Place the pans in the oven and roast the vegetables for 10 minutes. Rotate the pans, stir the vegetables and continue roasting for another 5 to 10 minutes (at this point the mushrooms should be done). Remove mushrooms from oven and set aside. Continue cooking the squash an additional 5 to 10 minutes or until tender. Let both the squash and mushrooms sit at room temperature for at least 20 minutes before serving.

In a small mixing bowl, whisk together the remaining 2 tablespoons olive oil and balsamic vinegar. Season to taste with salt and pepper. In a large bowl, toss the spinach with half of the dressing (just enough to lightly coat the leaves). Divide the spinach among 6 individual salad plates. Arrange ingredients on top of the spinach: roasted squash and mushrooms, cheese, half of the walnuts (save the rest for another use) and ham, if desired. Drizzle a bit of the remaining dressing over the top of the salad; season to taste with salt and fresh ground pepper.

MAKE AHEAD Sugared walnuts can be made up to 3 days in advance, covered and refrigerated. Dressing can be made up to 24 hours in advance, covered and refrigerated. Bring to room temperature before using. Butternut squash and mushrooms can be roasted up to 8 hours in advance, covered and kept at room temperature.

SPINACH SALAD WITH CURRY DRESSING

My college friend Dede Faulkner Graves gave me this recipe. Every few years, Dede collects recipes from her wide network of friends and family and publishes them in a book that she gives to everyone who gave a recipe. This recipe is one she shared after her latest publication. The curry dressing is fabulous and blends perfectly with the spinach, peanuts, raisins and chopped green onion. Serve with Grilled Rosemary-Dijon Chicken Breasts (*page 102*), Grilled Citrus Salmon (*page 154*) or grilled sirloin steak.

SERVES: 8

2 tablespoons white wine vinegar

1 tablespoon vermouth

2 teaspoons Dijon mustard

1 teaspoon soy sauce

1/2 teaspoon curry powder

1/2 teaspoon sugar

1/2 teaspoon salt

1/4 teaspoon freshly ground pepper

1/3 cup extra virgin olive oil

6 to 8 cups baby spinach

1/2 cup peanuts

1/2 cup raisins

1/2 cup green onions chopped
(white, light green and some dark green part)

In a medium glass jar with a fitted lid, whisk together the vinegar, vermouth, mustard, soy sauce, curry powder, sugar, salt, pepper and olive oil until well blended. Set aside.

Remove any tough stems from the spinach. In a large salad bowl, combine spinach, peanuts, raisins and green onion. Add desired amount of dressing, tossing to coat (you may have some dressing left over).

MAKE AHEAD The dressing can be made up to 2 days ahead, covered and refrigerated. Bring to room temperature before using. Spinach can be prepped earlier in the day, place in the salad bowl, covered and stored at room temperature.

ARUGULA AND SPINACH SALAD
WITH LEMON-DIJON DRESSING

This delicious salad's simplicity adds to its appeal. Using lemon juice in place of vinegar combined with Dijon mustard makes this dressing fresh and citrusy, with a hint of thyme. You can use just arugula or spinach rather than both, if you prefer. Delicious with Sally's Bouillabaisse (*page 157*), Beef Stew with Caramelized Root Vegetables (*page 130*) or other complex entrées.

SERVES: 8

5 tablespoons fresh lemon juice

2 tablespoons chopped shallot

1 tablespoon Dijon mustard

2 teaspoons fresh thyme leaves

1/2 cup extra virgin olive oil

Pinch or 2 of sugar

Salt, to taste

Freshly ground black pepper, to taste

5 ounces baby arugula

5 ounces baby spinach

1/2 cup (2 ounces) Parmesan cheese, shaved into strips

In a small mixing bowl, whisk together the lemon juice, shallot, mustard, thyme and olive oil until well blended. Season to taste with sugar, salt and pepper.

In a large serving bowl, combine the arugula and spinach; toss with the dressing. Top with the shaved Parmesan cheese. Salad can be served either in one large bowl or individual salad plates.

MAKE AHEAD Dressing can be made several days ahead, covered and stored in the refrigerator. Bring to room temperature before serving.

TIP

On shaving Parmesan cheese: Let cheese come to room temperature. Drag a vegetable peeler along the long, flat side of a block or wedge of good quality fresh Parmesan cheese.

DOROTHY'S POTATO SALAD

This recipe comes from Dorothy Hartwell, the mother of my childhood best friend Katey. Katey and I became fast friends in first grade — a friendship that's still going strong. As kids, we ate dinner at least one night a week at each other's house. This lasted for years — even after graduating college! One of my favorite treats at the Hartwell house was Mrs. Hartwell's potato salad. Over the years, she grew famous for it, and an annual summer dinner with hot dogs and her potato salad quickly became a tradition. Mrs. Hartwell (I never called her Dorothy, even after becoming an adult) was a lovely woman who will always have a very special place in my heart. Unfortunately she passed away in 2013 and the next summer when Katey came to visit for a few days (she lives in Mexico), it was on me to make the potato salad. Katey had loaned me her mom's recipe books so I have the original recipe in Mrs. Hartwell's handwriting. I made a copy for myself and will cherish it always. Like many of my own mom's recipes, Mrs. Hartwell didn't include the proportions or the directions (except to let the cooked potatoes sit overnight); these are my additions to the recipe, along with a bit of oil and vinegar. Enjoy! *(photo, page 129)*

Note you need to start this recipe at least 4 hours ahead, preferably the day before.

SERVES: 7 to 8

1 to 2 large eggs (optional)

3 medium Idaho (russet) potatoes

Salt, to taste

Freshly ground black pepper, to taste

1 tablespoon olive oil

1 tablespoon white wine vinegar

3 to 4 green onions, chopped (white, light green and some dark green part)

1 small cucumber, peeled, seeded and chopped

6 medium to large radishes, trimmed, thinly sliced and cut in half if large

3 tablespoons mayonnaise, or more to taste

In a large saucepan, cover eggs with water. Bring to a boil over high heat. Reduce heat to simmer and cook for 6 to 8 minutes (cook for longer time if at higher altitude). Remove from heat and leave eggs in hot water for another 3 to 5 minutes. Drain and run eggs under cold water until cooled. Peel and chop eggs; place in a bowl and refrigerate until ready to use.

In a large saucepan, cover potatoes with salted water. Bring to a boil and cook until just fork-tender (do not overcook or your salad will be mushy!). Drain the water from the pan and return pan to the heat. Shake the potatoes constantly over medium heat about 1 minute or until dry. Let cool enough to handle then peel and cut into bite-size chunks. Transfer to a large bowl and season to taste with salt and pepper.

In a small bowl, whisk together the olive oil and vinegar. Pour over potatoes and toss carefully, making sure not to mash them. Place potatoes in the refrigerator, uncovered, overnight.

1 to 2 teaspoons yellow mustard
  (French's works well)*

Salt, to taste

Freshly ground black pepper, to taste

Mrs Hartwell never used Dijon mustard in this salad, only French's yellow mustard

Take the potatoes out of the refrigerator and add the reserved chopped eggs, cucumbers, radishes and green onion; toss gently. Add enough mayonnaise to moisten the salad and toss well. Add the mustard to taste; toss to coat. Refrigerate until ready to serve. Adjust seasonings before serving, if necessary.

NOTE If you are pressed for time, you can refrigerate the potatoes for about 4 hours but it tastes best if you let the flavors blend overnight.

A WELL-SEASONED INSPIRATION

DOROTHY HARTWELL *Dorothy (or "Mrs. Hartwell," as I called her) was my best friend Katey's mother and I always thought of her as my "second" mom. Mrs. Hartwell was an excellent cook and many of my childhood memories revolve around meals at their home, which often focused on "comfort food," always served with a big side of laughter. Her philosophy was "don't worry about trends — just make what you love, your loved ones will surely love it too!"*

INDONESIAN BROWN RICE SALAD

I was first introduced to the flavors of Indonesian cuisine when I was 8 years old and my family visited Amsterdam on our first European vacation. For more than 300 years, until 1942, Indonesia was a Dutch colony and over the years Dutch colonials fell in love with Indonesian food. There are numerous Indonesian restaurants in Amsterdam and one night my family was treated to a unique Dutch-created Indonesian meal, called a Rijsttafel — or "rice table." It's basically a table full of small bowls filled with numerous Indonesian dishes from various regions, all combined into one meal. We loved it! Years later, when I lived and worked in Amsterdam, I would treat myself to a Rijsttafel dinner at least once a year. Like Rijsttafel, this brown rice salad includes many of the flavors, colors and textures Indonesian food is known for — it's a combination of sweet, sour, salty, spicy and crunchy. It's great as a vegetarian main dish salad, or served as a side salad — and perfect for summer potlucks and barbeques.

SERVES: 6 to 8 as a side dish or 3 to 4 as a main dish

1 teaspoon orange zest

1/2 cup fresh orange juice

1/4 cup olive oil

2 teaspoons chopped fresh ginger

1 tablespoon soy sauce

1/2 teaspoon chopped garlic

4 ounces snow peas

1 green apple, cored and chopped

1 (8-ounce) can water chestnuts, drained and chopped

2 cups cooked brown rice, cooled completely

1 cup chopped celery, with leaves

1 cup chopped red, yellow, or orange bell pepper

1 cup seedless green grapes, halved

1/2 cup chopped fresh cilantro

1/2 cup chopped roasted cashews

1/2 cup raisins

3 green onions, chopped (white, light green and some dark green part)

Kosher salt, to taste

Freshly ground black pepper, to taste

1/4 cup toasted sesame seeds

In a glass jar with a fitted lid, whisk together the orange zest, orange juice, oil, ginger, soy sauce and garlic. Set aside for at least 30 minutes to allow the flavors to blend.

In a steamer basket over boiling water, steam snow peas for 2 to 3 minutes or until crisp-tender. Remove from heat and plunge into ice water. Drain and pat dry. In a large mixing bowl, combine snow peas, apple, water chestnuts, rice, celery, bell pepper, grapes, cilantro, cashews, raisins and green onion. Add dressing, tossing to coat. Season to taste with kosher salt and fresh ground pepper. Sprinkle with sesame seeds and toss again just before serving.

MAKE AHEAD Salad and dressing can be made up to 24 hours ahead, covered and refrigerated separately. Bring to room temperature before tossing and serving.

TIP

On storing cilantro: cut 1/2 inch off the stem end of the cilantro and place in a glass around half to 2/3 full of water; place in the refrigerator. Refill the water as needed, and change the water if it becomes cloudy.

CAESAR SALAD DRESSING

This recipe had a fun roundabout way of getting into this cookbook. One night, Robert and I were treated to a fabulous dinner at the home of our good friend Tammy Smith. She served a salad with truly the best Caesar dressing I had ever tasted, and happily agreed to share the recipe. Tammy sent it via email with the heading, "recipe from Mary Talbot." What struck me as funny was that, while I didn't know Mary at the time, I'd heard wonderful things about her from my college roommate Cynthia Ballantyne, who lives in Boston. A few months later, I finally met Mary — and told her I had her Caesar salad dressing recipe! She then told me it came from her sister Cappy Shopneck, who then told me she got it from a woman on a ranch in Mexico where she and her husband Bob were bird hunting. I haven't yet met the woman in Mexico…but at this rate, it's only a matter of time!

SERVES: Makes around 1 1/4 cups or 12 to 14 servings

2 medium to large garlic cloves

3 to 5 anchovy fillets (around 1/3 to 1/2 of a 2-ounce can)

1 large egg

1 tablespoon Dijon mustard

1 heaping teaspoon granulated chicken broth

A few dashes Worcestershire sauce

Juice from 1/2 to 1 lemon, or to taste

Freshly ground pepper, to taste

1/4 cup extra virgin olive oil

3/4 cup vegetable oil

Kosher salt, to taste

In a blender, combine garlic, anchovies, egg, Dijon mustard, broth granules, Worcestershire sauce, lemon juice and pepper. Blend until smooth.

In a measuring cup, combine oils. With the blender running, slowly add the oil mixture (if the dressing comes out runny, it probably means you added the oil too fast. It should be a drizzle as you pour it in). Season to taste with kosher salt and fresh ground pepper.

MAKE AHEAD Dressing can be made up to 3 days ahead, covered and refrigerated.

GRILLED STEAK, ROASTED POTATOES AND TOMATO SALAD

Inspiration struck one evening when I had some leftover grilled steak and roasted potatoes. This dish is simple to arrange — place chopped cooked steak and potatoes in rows over torn lettuce, alongside chopped hard-boiled eggs and fresh tomatoes, making for a beautiful presentation. I top if off with some quick-pickled red onions and a yogurt-sour cream based dressing spiked with vinegar, horseradish, chives and paprika.

SERVES: 6

2 tablespoons red wine vinegar

1/2 teaspoon kosher salt

1 cup water

1/2 medium red onion, cut in half and thinly sliced

6 small to medium new potatoes (about 3/4 to 1 pound), quartered

1 tablespoon olive oil

1/3 cup sour cream

2 to 3 tablespoons Greek yogurt

1 teaspoon balsamic vinegar

1 tablespoon horseradish, or more to taste

1 tablespoon chopped fresh chives

1/2 teaspoon paprika, preferably smoked

Freshly ground black pepper, to taste

1 pound sirloin steak (bottom round, flat iron or flank steak will also work)

3 hard-boiled eggs, coarsely chopped

2 large tomatoes, coarsely chopped

1 large head red leaf lettuce or spinach, or a mixture of greens, torn into bite-sized pieces

Preheat oven to 425 degrees. Lightly grease or spray an 8- by 8-inch baking dish with cooking spray.

In a medium saucepan, combine red wine vinegar, salt and 1 cup water and bring to a boil. Stir in red onion and remove from heat. Set aside to cool.

In the prepared baking dish, toss potatoes with olive oil and kosher salt to taste. Bake, stirring occasionally, for 35 to 40 minutes or just until potatoes are tender when pierced with a fork (don't overcook). Remove from oven and set aside.

While the potatoes bake, prepare the dressing. In a medium mixing bowl, whisk together the sour cream, yogurt, balsamic vinegar, horseradish, chives and paprika. Season to taste with salt and pepper. Cover and refrigerate until ready to serve.

Preheat grill. Season steak on both sides with salt and pepper. Place on greased grill rack and grill to desired doneness (130-135 for medium rare or 135-145 for medium). Remove from grill and let rest for at least 5 minutes; thinly slice crosswise into 1 to 2-inch pieces. Set aside.

Lightly toss the lettuce with some of the dressing and arrange on a large serving platter. On top of the lettuce, arrange the potatoes, steak, chopped eggs, and tomatoes in rows. Drain red onions, sprinkle over the top. Season to taste with salt, pepper and paprika. Serve, passing remaining dressing on the side.

MAKE AHEAD Pickled red onion, steak, potatoes and dressing can be made up to 24 hours in advance. Bring to room temperature before assembling and serving.

VARIATION The salad can be arranged and served on individual plates.

LAYERED SALMON SALAD
WITH AVOCADO-LIME YOGURT DRESSING

Warm summer evenings are the perfect time to serve a main dish salad for dinner, and since this recipe doesn't require turning on the oven or cooktop, your kitchen stays nice and cool. Layers of lettuce, salmon, capers, onion, tomato, olives, goat cheese and pine nuts are accented by the avocado-lime yogurt dressing. Layering the ingredients in a pretty glass bowl results in a beautiful, impressive presentation; you can also layer the salad in large mason jars for a picnic. The avocado dressing is delicious on most any tossed or chopped lettuce salad.

Note the salad needs to chill for several hours or overnight, mainly to allow the dressing flavors to combine.

SERVES: 6

SALMON SALAD

4 cups shredded lettuce

2 cups flaked cooked salmon

2 tablespoons capers

1/2 cup chopped red onion

2 cups chopped fresh tomato

1/2 cup chopped Kalamata olives (optional)

4 ounces goat cheese, crumbled

1/4 cup toasted pine nuts

Salt, to taste

Freshly ground black pepper, to taste

**AVOCADO-LIME
YOGURT DRESSING**

2 avocados, peeled and pitted

3/4 cup plain yogurt

3 tablespoons fresh lime juice

1 garlic clove, minced

1/2 teaspoon salt

Dash ground cumin

Freshly ground black pepper, to taste

To make the salmon salad: In a deep 3 or 4 quart glass bowl, layer lettuce, salmon, capers, onion, tomato, olives, goat cheese and pine nuts. Sprinkle with salt and pepper. Set aside.

To make the dressing: In a food processor, purée avocados until smooth. Add yogurt, lime juice, garlic, salt and cumin; pulse 2 or 3 times to mix. Add salt and pepper as needed. Spread over top of salad. Cover and chill for several hours or overnight. If desired, toss the salad before serving.

CRAB AND SHRIMP SALAD
WITH CURRY-CHUTNEY DRESSING

My good friend Diane Reeder thought it would be fun for the two of us to cook together, so she invited Robert and me over for dinner one summer evening. I asked Diane if she would mind making a few recipes with me that I wanted to test for this book; she readily agreed. This salad was a winner — Diane, her husband Richard and son Cameron all loved it! The addition of coconut milk in the chutney dressing adds depth to the flavor; and the celery and nuts provide a nice crunch to this pretty, colorful salad. Note that the dressing needs to sit at least 30 minutes for the flavors to blend.

SERVES: 6

CURRY-CHUTNEY DRESSING

1 cup mayonnaise

1/4 cup coconut milk

1/4 cup sour cream

1/4 cup mango chutney, large pieces chopped*

2 teaspoons curry powder, or more to taste

Kosher salt, to taste

Freshly ground black pepper, to taste

CRAB AND SHRIMP SALAD

1 1/2 cups small (61 to 70 count) cooked shrimp, peeled and deveined (including tails)

8 ounces lump crabmeat, rinsed, drained and patted dry

1 cup chopped celery

1/2 cup sliced water chestnuts, chopped

1/2 cup toasted pine nuts

1/4 cup green onions chopped
   (white, light green and some dark green part)

3 tablespoons dried currants
   (or raisins)

Kosher salt, to taste

Freshly ground black pepper, to taste

3 to 4 cups mixed salad greens

2 ripe avocados, sliced

*A widely available mango chutney is the brand "Major Grey's Chutney"

To make the dressing: In a glass jar with a fitted lid, whisk together the mayonnaise, coconut milk, sour cream, mango chutney and curry. Season to taste with kosher salt. Cover and refrigerate for at least 30 minutes.

To make the salad: In a large serving bowl, toss together the shrimp, crab, celery, water chestnuts, pine nuts, onion and currants. Pour half of dressing over seafood mixture and toss until well mixed. Add additional dressing as needed. Season to taste with kosher salt and fresh ground pepper.

Divide mixed greens among 6 dinner plates. Place a scoop of shrimp salad on top of greens. Place avocado slices on the side of the shrimp salad, in a fan pattern. Serve with remaining dressing on the side.

MAKE AHEAD Dressing can be made up to 2 days ahead, covered and refrigerated.

ASIAN SHRIMP AND BROWN RICE SALAD

One night, I decided to get a little creative with our dinner and this dish was born. Toss shrimp with brown rice, almonds, water chestnuts, green onions, cilantro and cabbage, then dress with a soy-ginger-sesame dressing. Our recipe testers say the nuts and cabbage give it a great "crunch." For a more elegant presentation, serve this salad stuffed into hollowed out large tomato halves. Leftover dressing is delicious on sandwiches and turkey burgers.

SERVES: 6

1 3/4 cup mayonnaise

6 tablespoons sour cream

3 tablespoons soy sauce

1 1/2 tablespoons dark or toasted sesame oil

1 1/2 tablespoons rice vinegar

1 1/2 teaspoons chopped fresh ginger

Cayenne pepper, to taste

Kosher salt, to taste

36 (1 pound) medium to large cooked shrimp, peeled, deveined and chopped

1 1/2 cups cooked brown rice, cooled completely

3/4 cup shredded cabbage

3/4 cup (8-ounce can) drained, chopped water chestnuts

3/4 cup chopped fresh cilantro (optional)

6 tablespoons toasted, coarsely chopped or slivered almonds

6 large green onions, chopped (white, light green and some dark green part)

Freshly ground black pepper, to taste

In medium mixing bowl, whisk together the mayonnaise, sour cream, soy sauce, sesame oil, vinegar, ginger and cayenne pepper. Season to taste with kosher salt (may not need any). Set aside.

In a large mixing bowl, stir together shrimp, rice, cabbage, water chestnuts, cilantro, almonds and green onions. Stir in spoonfuls of the dressing until desired consistency is reached (you may not need to use all the dressing). Season with kosher salt and ground pepper to taste.

MAKE AHEAD Dressing and salad can be assembled separately up to 24 hours in advance, covered and refrigerated. Bring to room temperature before tossing and serving.

TUNA SALAD NIÇOISE
WITH LEMON-TARRAGON DRESSING

You can never go wrong with Salad Niçoise, a French composed salad with tuna, hard boiled egg, tomatoes, black olives (preferably Niçoise) and sometimes cooked green beans and potatoes, artfully arranged over a bed of lettuce. For my recipe, I created a lemony dressing accented with tarragon, flavors I associate with French food. I also add capers to the salad for more tangy flavor. I think it's important to layer in the lemon-tarragon flavors by tossing each major ingredient with some of the dressing, then passing the rest on the side. I once served this dish to my book club as a buffet, salad-bar style (*see details below under Variation*).

SERVES: 6

LEMON-TARRAGON DRESSING

7 tablespoons extra virgin olive oil

2 1/2 tablespoons tarragon white wine vinegar

1 heaping teaspoon lemon zest, or more to taste

1 teaspoon chopped fresh tarragon

1/8 teaspoon ground nutmeg

SALAD

3 medium new potatoes, cut into wedges

1 pound green beans, trimmed and cut into 1-inch pieces

3 (5-ounce) cans white tuna, drained

6 cups torn salad greens such as Bibb, Boston or Butter lettuce

Salt, to taste

Freshly ground black pepper, to taste

3 hard boiled eggs, peeled and chopped

2 cups seeded, coarsely chopped fresh tomatoes

1 cup Niçoise or Kalamata black olives, cut in half

1/3 cup capers, drained

To make the dressing: In a small mixing bowl, whisk together the olive oil, vinegar, zest, tarragon and nutmeg. Cover and let sit at room temperature.

To make the salad: Place potatoes in a steamer basket over boiling water. Cover and steam potatoes 10 to 15 minutes until fork tender. Remove from heat and set aside.

Place green beans in a steamer basket over boiling water. Cover and steam 8 minutes or until crisp-tender. Remove and plunge them into ice water to keep their bright green color. Drain again and pat dry with paper towel.

In separate bowls for each ingredient, toss potatoes, green beans, tuna and greens each with 1 to 2 tablespoons dressing. Season each to taste with salt and pepper.

To assemble the salad: On either a large platter or 6 individual plates, spread greens evenly. Top with a mound of the tuna in the middle. Surround with the potatoes, green beans, eggs, tomatoes, and olives. Sprinkle capers over the top. Pass additional dressing on the side.

VARIATION Serve salad bar-style. Put each ingredient in a separate bowl and arrange in the following order: mixed greens (in a large bowl), tuna, potatoes, green beans, eggs, tomatoes, olives, capers and remaining dressing.

TUNA AND ROASTED RED PEPPER PASTA SALAD WITH PESTO DRESSING

I found this salad recipe buried in my mom's files; it was given to her by Marne Kellogg — a friend to us both and the daughter of my parents' good friends Margie and Jack Davis. When I make it, I use my favorite Spinach Basil Pesto recipe (which can be found on my website, *www.seasonedkitchen.com*), and substitute shelled edamame for the green peas called for in the original recipe. It's great for a summer picnic — we often take it to concerts at the Denver Botanic Gardens or Hudson Gardens.

Note that the salad needs to chill for at least one hour.

SERVES: 8

1 pound dry rotelle (wagon wheel) or rotini (corkscrew) pasta

1 (10-ounce) package frozen shelled edamame beans*

2 (5-ounce) cans white tuna in water, drained and broken into chunks

16 ounces marinated roasted red peppers, drained and coarsely chopped**

1 cup Spinach Basil Pesto or regular basil pesto

1/2 cup (2 ounces) fresh grated Parmesan cheese

Salt, to taste

Freshly ground black pepper, to taste

If desired, substitute frozen green peas that have been thawed and drained. Skip directions for cooking the beans

**Can use jarred, or look for roasted red peppers in the olive bar at Whole Foods*

In a large pot, cook the pasta according to package directions. Add the edamame beans to the cooking pasta during the last 6 minutes. Drain cooked pasta-bean mixture in a colander; rinse with cold water, drain again. Set the pasta mixture aside to cool and dry.

In a large mixing bowl, combine pasta mixture, tuna, peppers and pesto, tossing to blend. Add the Parmesan cheese and toss again. Season to taste with salt and pepper. Chill for at least 1 hour. Bring to room temperature before serving.

MAKE AHEAD Salad can be made up to 24 hours in advance, covered and stored in the refrigerator.

CHICKEN, BLUEBERRY AND MANGO SALAD

One summer evening, my good friend Tamara O'Brien brought this delicious salad to a girls gathering. Cool, crisp and beautiful — we all loved it! The mango and blueberry flavor combination tastes like summer, and blends perfectly with the chicken and goat cheese. I added toasted chopped pecans for a bit of crunch, and created the vinaigrette to layer in even more mango flavor *(photo, cover)*.

SERVES: 6

3 cups (3 large) peeled and sliced fresh mangoes, divided

3 tablespoons fresh lime juice

4 1/2 tablespoons extra virgin olive oil

3 tablespoons white balsamic vinegar

1 1/2 teaspoons chopped shallot

10 cups torn Bibb, Boston, or Butter lettuce

3 cups sliced or torn grilled or roasted chicken

1 cup fresh blueberries

Kosher salt, to taste

Fresh ground pepper, to taste

6 tablespoons roasted chopped pecans

3/4 to 1 cup goat cheese crumbles

Place 3/4 cup (around 1/2 large) sliced mango, lime juice, olive oil, vinegar and shallot in a blender or food processor and purée until smooth. Cover and let sit for at least 30 minutes to allow the flavors to blend.

In a large mixing bowl, combine the lettuce, chicken, blueberries and remaining sliced mango. Toss with dressing to taste (you may not need all of it). Season to taste with salt and pepper. Divide salad among 6 dinner plates. Sprinkle chopped pecans and goat cheese over the top. Serve.

MAKE AHEAD Dressing can be made up to 24 hours in advance, covered and refrigerated. Bring to room temperature before serving.

Poultry

"I've always said fashion is like…chicken: You don't have to think about it to know it's delicious." — *Alber Elbaz, Israeli fashion designer*

The anchor for many a meal, well-prepared chicken is both inspired and versatile. Hot or cold; baked, broiled, grilled, roasted, sautéed — in the end, it all comes down to the seasoning. From pot pie to Coq au Vin, these chicken recipes are anything but boring…and always a hit!

100 | Pesto Chicken with Black Beans

101 | Sautéed Chicken Breasts with Tomato-Olive-Caper Sauce

102 | Grilled Rosemary-Dijon Chicken Breasts

104 | Baked Chicken with Artichoke Topping

105 | Feta Chicken

106 | Arroz Con Pollo

108 | Ginger-Orange Chicken with Spicy Couscous

110 | Dijon Curry Chicken

111 | Parmesan-Onion Breaded Chicken Breasts

112 | Mexican Baked Chicken

114 | Coq Au Vin

116 | Chicken Pot Pie

118 | Rolled Turkey Breast with Roasted Red Pepper Stuffing

PESTO CHICKEN WITH BLACK BEANS

Italy meets Mexico in this easy, colorful one dish meal (*photo, page 98*). "Pesto" is an Italian sauce traditionally made with basil, garlic, pine nuts, olive oil and Parmesan cheese. For this recipe, I like to make a Southwestern-inspired pesto sauce, substituting cilantro for the basil and adding in a bit of Serrano pepper and lime juice. The flavor combination of the pesto and black beans works exceptionally well together!

Note that the chicken needs to marinate for 1 to 8 hours.

SERVES: 6

4 large boneless, skinless chicken
   breast halves

1/4 cup white wine

1/2 cup plus 2 tablespoons cilantro
   pesto*, divided

2 (15-ounce) cans black beans,
   rinsed and drained

3/4 cup chicken broth

1/2 teaspoon lime zest

Juice from 1/2 to 1 lime

Tabasco sauce, to taste

2 tablespoons sour cream

Salt, to taste

Freshly ground black pepper, to taste

1/2 to 2/3 cup chopped fresh
   tomatoes or halved grape tomatoes

*Recipe is on our website
www.seasonedkitchen.com.
You can also substitute your own
favorite pesto recipe, or purchase
fresh, refrigerated pesto (not the
shelf stable jarred stuff)*

With a sharp knife, carefully cut each chicken breast in half horizontally, starting on the thicker side to create 2 pieces from each breast half (*see Tip on page 104*).

In a shallow dish large enough to hold the breasts in one layer, whisk together the wine and 1/4 cup of the pesto. Add the chicken, turning to coat well. Cover and refrigerate for 1 to 8 hours.

In a medium saucepan, stir together the black beans, chicken broth and 2 tablespoons pesto. Bring to simmer and cook for 5 to 7 minutes, stirring frequently. Reduce heat to low and stir in lime zest, lime juice, Tabasco sauce and sour cream; continue cooking, stirring, just until heated through. Season to taste with salt and pepper. Keep warm over very low heat, stirring occasionally (beans should become partially mashed by the time you serve them).

Prepare a medium-hot fire in a charcoal grill, or preheat a gas grill on high. Bring chicken to room temperature while the grill is preheating.

Oil the grill grate. Remove chicken from the marinade, place on grill. If using a gas grill, reduce all the burners to medium heat. Grill chicken, covered, for 3 minutes or until seared. Turn over and grill an additional 3 to 4 minutes, or until an instant-read thermometer inserted into thickest portions registers 165 degrees.

Divide black bean sauce among 6 individual dinner plates. Top with 1 or 2 chicken breast pieces; season with salt and pepper. Divide remaining 1/4 cup pesto evenly on top of the chicken. Sprinkle with chopped tomatoes. Serve immediately.

SAUTÉED CHICKEN BREASTS
WITH TOMATO-OLIVE-CAPER SAUCE

These Italian-inspired chicken breasts are quick to prepare for every day meals and elegant enough for entertaining, too. The flavor of the fresh tomatoes, onion, garlic and olives intensifies while cooking, resulting in a delicious, colorful sauce. Serve with Couscous with Dried Cranberries and Pecans (*page 220*).

If your chicken breasts aren't large (or you're serving very hearty eaters!), add one or two more to serve six.

SERVES: 6

4 large boneless, skinless chicken breast halves

1 teaspoon cayenne pepper

1/2 teaspoon ground black pepper

1/2 teaspoon paprika

4 tablespoons olive oil, divided

1/2 cup chopped onion

2 teaspoons chopped garlic

1 1/4 cups seeded and chopped tomatoes*

1/2 cup chicken stock

1 tablespoon chopped fresh oregano

16 Kalamata olives, pitted and chopped

2 teaspoons capers (optional)

2 tablespoons butter

Salt, to taste

When fresh tomatoes aren't in season, for more flavor substitute 1 (15-ounce) can, drained

Butterfly each chicken breast and cut in half to make 8 cutlets (*see Tip on page 104*). In a small bowl, combine the cayenne pepper, black pepper and paprika; rub over both sides of chicken (save any leftover for another use).

In a large nonstick skillet, heat 1 tablespoon olive oil over medium heat. Add 4 chicken cutlets and sauté until beginning to brown and an instant-read thermometer inserted into thickest portion registers 165 degrees. Transfer to a large platter; cover and keep warm. Repeat with 1 tablespoon olive oil and remaining 4 cutlets (don't clean out the skillet).

In the same skillet, heat remaining 2 tablespoons olive oil over medium heat. Add onion and garlic; cook, stirring occasionally, for around 7 to 8 minutes or until the onions are softened. Stir in the tomatoes, chicken stock, oregano, olives and capers (if using); cook, stirring occasionally, 5 minutes or until the tomatoes are softened. Add 2 tablespoons butter and stir until melted. Season to taste with salt and ground pepper. Stir any accumulated juices from the chicken on the platter into the sauce. Spoon sauce over top of chicken breasts to serve.

MAKE AHEAD Chicken and sauce can be cooked earlier in the day, stored separately in the refrigerator. Put sauce in a large skillet with chicken breasts and cook over medium heat just until hot.

VARIATION Sauce is also delicious with sautéed tuna steaks.

GRILLED ROSEMARY-DIJON CHICKEN BREASTS

The fresh flavor of these grilled chicken breasts — with the combination of white wine, rosemary, Dijon and garlic — conjures up memories from trips to the south of France. Whenever I eat this dish, I always I feel like I'm sitting at some wonderful bistro in Provence, no matter where I really am. Serve with Tomatoes Stuffed with Olives and Prosciutto (*page 202*) and Zucchini and Yellow Squash Ribbons (*page 203*).

Note that the chicken needs to marinate for 1 to 8 hours.

SERVES: 4

1/4 cup dry white wine

1/4 cup seasoned or plain rice vinegar

1 tablespoon Dijon mustard

1 1/2 teaspoons Worcestershire sauce

1/2 teaspoon chopped garlic or shallot

1/2 cup extra virgin olive oil

3 tablespoons chopped fresh rosemary

1 tablespoon dried marjoram

Salt, to taste

Freshly ground black pepper, to taste

4 boneless, skinless chicken breasts

In a food processor, combine the white wine, vinegar, mustard, Worcestershire sauce and garlic or shallots; process until well blended. With the machine running, slowly pour the olive oil through the feed tube and process until well mixed. Add the rosemary and marjoram; process until herbs are finely chopped. Season to taste with salt and pepper. Set aside.

Put the chicken breasts between sheets of waxed paper and pound until an even thickness. Place chicken in a glass baking dish that will hold the breasts in one layer. Pour the marinade over the chicken, turning to coat. Cover and refrigerate at least 4 hours, up to 24 hours, turning occasionally.

Prepare a medium-hot fire in a charcoal grill, or preheat a gas grill on high.

Oil the grill racks. Remove chicken from the baking dish, reserving the marinade. Place chicken on grill and if using a gas grill, reduce all the burners to medium heat. Cook chicken, covered, 3 minutes or until seared. Brush with marinade. Turn over, brush with marinade again and grill 3 to 4 minutes until the other side is seared and an instant-read thermometer inserted into thickest portions registers 165 degrees.

MAKE AHEAD Marinade can be made up to 2 days in advance, covered and stored in the refrigerator.

BAKED CHICKEN WITH ARTICHOKE TOPPING

Artichokes were my favorite side dish as a kid — I not only love the flavor, but they're such fun to eat! Today I'm always experimenting with different ways to incorporate them into my recipes. For this one, I simply took mom's artichoke dip recipe and turned it into a topping for chicken — what could be easier? For a quick mid-week meal, serve with quinoa and brown rice mixture and steamed broccoli or tossed salad.

SERVES: 4 to 6

1 (15-ounce) can whole or quartered artichoke hearts in water

2 green onions, chopped

3/4 cup (3 ounces) freshly grated Parmesan cheese

3/4 cup mayonnaise

1/8 teaspoon garlic powder

Salt, to taste

Freshly ground black pepper, to taste

4 boneless, skinless chicken breast halves

Preheat oven to 375 degrees. Grease a baking dish or rimmed baking sheet large enough to hold the chicken in one layer.

Drain the artichoke hearts well, pat dry with paper towels and remove any tough leaves. Chop and place in a medium bowl. Stir in the green onions, Parmesan cheese, mayonnaise and garlic powder. Season to taste with salt and pepper.

Pound the chicken to an even thickness, about 1/2-inch thick. Butterfly larger pieces and cut in half (*see Tip below*). Place chicken in a single layer in the prepared baking dish. Spread artichoke mixture over the top.

Bake, uncovered, for 25 to 30 minutes or until chicken top is lightly browned and an instant-read thermometer inserted into thickest portion registers 165 degrees. If top isn't brown, place under the broiler for a few minutes until golden.

MAKE AHEAD Chicken can be assembled, but not baked, earlier in the day, covered and refrigerated. Bring to room temperature before baking.

TIP

On butterflying and halving boneless chicken breasts: Place one chicken breast half on a cutting board, skin or smooth side up. Place the palm of your non-cutting hand on the top of the breast and using a very sharp knife, slowly cut horizontally through the breast, starting with the thick side and keeping the knife parallel to the cutting board. Cut almost to the other edge. Open up flat, like a book and pound to an even thickness or if desired, cut down the middle to separate into 2 breast cutlets.

FETA CHICKEN

The yogurt marinade in this dish makes the chicken tender and moist, while the feta cheese adds a nice tangy flavor. You can experiment with this recipe, substituting sour cream for the yogurt and goat cheese for the feta cheese. It's also great with flavored feta cheese. Serve with our Saffron Cilantro Rice (*page 216*).

SERVES: 4

2 cups plain Greek yogurt

Juice from 1 lemon

1 teaspoon dried oregano

1 teaspoon chopped garlic or chives

1/2 teaspoon freshly ground black pepper

4 (4- to 5-ounce) boneless, skinless chicken breast halves

Salt, to taste

Freshly ground black pepper, to taste

1/3 cup crumbled feta cheese

In a medium mixing bowl, whisk together the yogurt, lemon juice, oregano, garlic or chives and pepper. Spoon half into a small serving bowl, cover and refrigerate. Spoon remaining half into a shallow, nonreactive baking dish.

Pound the chicken breasts to an even thickness; place on yogurt mixture in the baking dish, turning to coat. Cover and refrigerate for 30 minutes or up to 24 hours.

Preheat broiler. Line the top of a large broiler pan (chicken should fit in one layer) with foil, cutting out vents. Remove the chicken from the marinade and place on the prepared broiler pan, skin or smooth side down, reserving marinade. Sprinkle with salt and pepper.

Broil chicken 4 to 5 inches from the heat about 5 to 6 minutes. Turn over, brush with reserved marinade and sprinkle with feta cheese. Broil 5 to 6 minutes or until chicken is cooked through and an instant-read thermometer inserted into thickest portions registers 165 degrees. Serve reserved chilled sauce on the side.

ARROZ CON POLLO

Shortly after my first cookbook was published, my brother Jim asked, "What ever happened to that delicious chicken and rice dish mom used to make with olives and green chiles?" I knew instantly he was talking about her Latin American dish, Arroz con Pollo. Subsequently, I spent days hunting through mom's various recipe boxes, files, notes and cookbooks looking for the recipe. Thankfully I found it, because it's every bit as delicious today as when we were kids. While Arroz con Pollo starts as a basic chicken and rice dish, there are many different varieties, emanating from Spain to Puerto Rico to Peru. Many include saffron, but mom used turmeric (the "poor man's saffron") in her version and then added garlic, onion, tomatoes, green peas, green chiles and green olives (the ones stuffed with pimientos) to amp up the flavor. Serve with a tossed salad and you have an amazing dinner!

SERVES: 6

5 tablespoons olive oil, divided

2 large garlic cloves, sliced

1 teaspoon salt

3 pounds bone-in, skin-on chicken pieces*

1 large onion, chopped

1 1/2 cups uncooked rice

1 3/4 cups chicken broth

1/2 teaspoon ground turmeric

1 (15-ounce) can tomato sauce

1 3/4 cups chopped fresh tomatoes**

8 ounces poblano peppers, seeded, roasted and chopped (*see Tip on page 38*)**

Salt, to taste

Freshly ground black pepper, to taste

1 cup frozen green peas, thawed

1/2 cup sliced pimiento-stuffed green olives

I like to make this dish with a mixture of split breasts and drumsticks. If the breasts are large, I cut them in half, breaking the bone as needed

**When fresh tomatoes aren't in season, for more flavor substitute 1 (15-ounce) can, undrained. Can substitute 1 (4-ounce) can diced green chiles, undrained, for the fresh poblano peppers*

In a small saucepan, combine 1/4 cup of the olive oil, garlic and salt. Cook over medium heat just until the garlic starts to brown. With a slotted spoon, remove the garlic slices and set aside.

Pat chicken pieces dry with paper towel and brush the garlic-flavored oil over all sides. Place chicken in a glass dish large enough to hold them in one layer, cover and marinate in the refrigerator for at least 1 hour or up to overnight.

Preheat oven to 325 degrees.

In a 4- to 5-quart, cooktop-to-oven baking dish (Le Creuset works well), heat remaining 1 tablespoon olive oil over medium-high heat. Brown chicken pieces on both sides; remove from skillet and place on a plate. Reduce heat to low, stir in onion and rice and cook just until rice begins to brown. Stir in chicken broth and turmeric; cook, scraping any browned bits off the bottom of the pan. Stir in tomato sauce, chopped tomatoes, green chiles and reserved garlic slices. Season to taste with salt and fresh ground pepper.

Place browned chicken pieces on top of rice mixture, skin side up. Cover and bake for 45 minutes. Stir peas and olives into the rice around the chicken pieces, uncover and continue baking 10 to 15 minutes. Season with salt and pepper and serve.

MAKE AHEAD Can be prepared, but not baked, earlier in the day, covered and refrigerated. Bring to room temperature before baking.

GINGER-ORANGE CHICKEN WITH SPICY COUSCOUS

This dish is one of my favorites for entertaining, especially in the summer, as it can be made entirely ahead of time and served at room temperature. It's sort of a backward dish, because the chicken is cooked before it's marinated in the sauce. And the sauce is divine — orange and lemon juices, chutney, ginger, rice vinegar, dark sesame oil and a bit of red pepper flakes for spice. The chicken is served over couscous flavored with dried apricots, cinnamon, pistachios, onions and basil — all the flavors blend together amazingly well.

Note that the chicken needs to marinate overnight, so you'll need to prep a day in advance.

SERVES: 6

GINGER-ORANGE CHICKEN

1/2 cup fresh orange juice

1/4 cup fresh lemon juice

3 tablespoons mango chutney*

2 tablespoons peeled and chopped fresh ginger (*see Tip on page 109*)

1 1/2 tablespoons orange zest

1 1/2 tablespoons seasoned rice vinegar

2 teaspoons dark sesame oil

1/4 teaspoon dried crushed red pepper

6 tablespoons sesame seeds

5 to 6 boneless, skinless chicken breast halves (number depends on size)

4 tablespoons butter, divided

Preheat oven to 400 degrees.

First, prepare the chicken: In a 13-by-9-by-2 inch glass baking dish, whisk together orange juice, lemon juice, chutney, ginger, orange peel, vinegar, sesame oil and crushed red pepper. Set aside.

If chicken breasts are very thick at one end, pound with a meat mallet or rolling pin to an even thickness. If they are very large, butterfly and cut into 2 pieces (*see Tip on page 104*). Sprinkle chicken breasts with salt and pepper.

Place sesame seeds in a shallow bowl. Dredge skin skinned (or smooth) side of chicken in seeds, coating well. In a large skillet, melt 2 tablespoons butter over medium-high heat. Add half of chicken breasts (or as many as will comfortably fit into your skillet), seeds side down, and cook 2 to 3 minutes or until golden brown (watch carefully so sesame seeds don't burn). Turn over and cook 2 minutes longer. Place chicken breasts, seeds side up, in orange juice mixture in baking dish. Thoroughly clean out skillet (otherwise the second batch will burn) and repeat with remaining 2 tablespoons of butter and chicken breasts.

Cover chicken with foil and bake 20 minutes or until cooked through and an instant-read thermometer inserted into thickest portion registers 165 degrees. Remove from oven, remove foil and let chicken cool for around 1 hour in marinade at room temperature. Leave chicken in marinade, cover and chill overnight. Bring to room temperature before serving.

Prepare the couscous: Combine couscous, apricots, cinnamon and allspice in a large bowl. In a large saucepan, bring 2 cups water, olive oil and salt to a boil; remove from heat and stir in couscous mixture.

SPICY COUSCOUS

1 (10-ounce) box couscous

1 cup dried apricots, chopped

1 1/2 teaspoons ground cinnamon

1/4 teaspoon ground allspice

3 tablespoons extra virgin olive oil

1 teaspoon salt

1/2 cup shelled pistachios, toasted and chopped (about 1 cup in the shell)

1/2 cup chopped green onions

1/4 cup chopped fresh basil

Salt, to taste

Freshly ground black pepper, to taste

A widely available mango chutney is the brand "Major Grey's Chutney"

Cover and let stand about 5 minutes or until water is absorbed. When ready to serve, uncover, and fluff couscous with fork. Stir in chopped nuts, green onions and basil. Season to taste with salt and pepper. Serve at room temperature (best if not made too far ahead).

To serve, mound the couscous on a serving platter. Top with chicken breasts. Spoon the sauce from the baking dish over the top of chicken.

TIP

On buying and storing ginger: When purchasing ginger, look for 2- to 4-inch long pieces in the produce section of your grocery store. Make sure you are getting a fresh piece — it should be hard and the skin shouldn't be wrinkled or dry looking. Break off a piece around the size you need if all of the pieces are large. To store ginger, peel it and put it in a jar with a fitted lid. Pour in vodka to cover the ginger, screw on the lid and refrigerate. It will keep for weeks in your frig — and you will have ginger infused vodka to drink in a yummy cocktail. If you don't have vodka, you can use sherry or white wine.

DIJON CURRY CHICKEN

A perfect recipe from mom for busy weeknights when time is tight — it takes less than 15 minutes to prepare, and can be done with ingredients likely to be in your pantry and refrigerator. Serve with Barley Pilaf *(page 219)* or Golden Potatoes *(page 212)* and Shredded Brussels Sprouts with Bacon *(page 201)*.

SERVES: 6

6 boneless, skinless chicken breast halves

Salt, to taste

Freshly ground black pepper, to taste

5 to 6 tablespoons Dijon mustard

6 tablespoons honey

6 tablespoons chopped onion

1 1/2 to 3 teaspoons curry powder, or more to taste

1 teaspoon chopped garlic (optional)

Hot sauce, to taste (Tabasco, Sriracha, or Peri Peri, optional)

Preheat oven to 350 degrees. Grease a shallow baking dish large enough to hold the chicken in one layer.

Rinse chicken breasts and pat dry; if large, butterfly and cut into 2 pieces *(see Tip on page 104)*. Season with salt and pepper.

In small mixing bowl, whisk together the mustard, honey, onion, curry powder, garlic and hot sauce, if desired (mixture will be fairly thick). Brush over top of chicken, cover and bake for 20 to 25 minutes or until chicken is cooked through (no pink inside) and an instant-read thermometer inserted into thickest portions registers 165 degrees.

PARMESAN-ONION BREADED CHICKEN BREASTS

A baked version of fried chicken, this dish features chicken breasts dipped in garlic-infused butter and then rolled in a mixture of breadcrumbs, Parmesan cheese, parsley and French-fried onions. The onions give the crust a nice crunchy texture after baking and the chicken stays very moist and tender. Serve with Broccoli with Curry Mayonnaise Sauce *(page 206)*.

SERVES: 4 to 6

1/3 cup (1 ounce) French-fried onions

1/2 cup panko breadcrumbs

2 to 3 tablespoons freshly grated Parmesan cheese

1 1/2 tablespoons chopped fresh Italian (flat-leaf) parsley

3 large boneless, skinless chicken breast halves

1/4 cup unsalted butter

1 garlic clove, minced

1/2 teaspoon Worcestershire sauce

1/2 teaspoon dry mustard

Preheat oven to 350 degrees. Line a large baking sheet with foil or parchment paper. Set aside.

In a zip top bag, crush the fried onions with a rolling pin or meat mallet until the same consistency as the breadcrumbs. In a shallow dish, combine the onions, breadcrumbs, Parmesan cheese and parsley. Set aside.

Butterfly larger chicken breasts and cut into 2 pieces *(see Tip on page 104)*. Pound smaller breasts to roughly an even thickness.

In a small saucepan, melt the butter over medium heat. Add the garlic and cook for 1 minute. Remove from heat and whisk in the Worcestershire sauce and dry mustard.

Dip each chicken cutlet in the butter mixture, coating both sides, then dredge in the breadcrumbs, coating both sides well (you may have to scoop up some of the crumbs with your hand and press onto the chicken). Place each breaded cutlet on the prepared baking sheet. For a crunchier top, drizzle some of the remaining butter mixture over the top of the cutlets. Bake 20 to 25 minutes, or until chicken is golden brown and an instant-read thermometer inserted into thickest portions registers 165 degrees.

MAKE AHEAD Cutlets can be breaded, covered and refrigerated earlier in the day. Increase cooking time 5 to 10 minutes.

MEXICAN BAKED CHICKEN

A festive and fun one-dish meal — breaded and baked chicken topped with salsa, cheddar cheese and sour cream and served with lettuce, tomatoes and avocado. Instead of just dipping the chicken in beaten egg and then plain breadcrumbs, I layer in more flavor by adding salsa to the eggs and chili powder, cumin, garlic salt and oregano to the breadcrumbs. Another quick and easy midweek meal!

SERVES: 6

4 large eggs

1 1/2 cups Tomatillo-Green Chile Salsa *(page 124)* or purchased salsa verde, divided*

1/4 teaspoon salt

1 1/4 cups panko breadcrumbs

2 teaspoons chili powder

2 teaspoons ground cumin

1 1/2 teaspoons garlic salt

1/2 teaspoon ground oregano

4 large boneless, skinless chicken breast halves

3 tablespoons butter, cut into 3 to 4 pieces

6 cups shredded lettuce

3/4 cup sour cream

6 tablespoons chopped green onion

36 grape or small cherry tomatoes, cut in half

3 ripe avocados, peeled, seeded and sliced

Salt, to taste

Freshly ground black pepper, to taste

6 tablespoons grated sharp Cheddar cheese

6 lime wedges

I like La Victoria brand salsa verde

In a shallow bowl, whisk together the eggs, 3 tablespoons of the salsa and salt. In another shallow bowl, stir together the breadcrumbs, chili powder, cumin, garlic salt and oregano. Butterfly larger breasts and cut into 2 pieces *(see Tip on page 104)*. Pound smaller breasts to roughly an even thickness. Dip each breast in the egg mixture, then dredge in the breadcrumb mixture, coating all sides evenly. Place on a baking sheet and refrigerate for at least 15 minutes and up to 8 hours to allow the coating to set.

Preheat oven to 350 degrees.

Place the butter in a large shallow roasting pan (not glass) large enough to hold the chicken breasts in one layer, and place in preheating oven. As soon as the butter melts, remove pan from the oven (watch closely as the butter burns easily).

Place the chicken pieces in the heated pan, turning to coat with the melted butter. Bake, uncovered, 25 to 30 minutes or until chicken is golden brown and an instant-read thermometer inserted into thickest portions registers 165 degrees.

To serve, place 1 cup of shredded lettuce on each serving plate. Top with a chicken breast. Place a dollop of sour cream and salsa on top of each chicken breast. Sprinkle about 1 tablespoon of green onion over chicken. Arrange 12 tomato halves and slices from 1/2 avocado equally on each plate, placing them decoratively on the lettuce around the chicken breast. Season to taste with salt and freshly ground pepper. Sprinkle Cheddar cheese over each serving. Place a lime wedge on each plate. Pass additional salsa and sour cream on the side.

MAKE AHEAD The chicken breasts can be coated with the breadcrumbs, covered and refrigerated earlier in the day. You may need to increase cooking time by 5 to 10 minutes, depending on how long they are refrigerated.

COQ AU VIN

Mom's take on a classic French dish — chicken is seared, marinated and then baked with a medley of carrots, mushrooms, garlic and green onions — all in a delicious red wine sauce spiked with fresh rosemary, thyme and parsley. The result is fall-off-the-bone tender, juicy chicken with an earthy, rich sauce. Serve with a salad and roasted new potatoes tossed with parsley.

Note that this dish requires starting the prep either the day before or the day it's served, as it needs to sit in the refrigerator for at least four hours or overnight.

SERVES: 8 to 10

32 small white onions, unpeeled

12 ounces center cut bacon

6 tablespoons butter, divided

7 bone-in, skin-on chicken breast halves (*see Note on next page*)

4 bone-in, skin-on chicken drumsticks

Salt, to taste

Freshly ground black pepper, to taste

Paprika, to taste

1 cup plus 2 tablespoons all-purpose flour, divided

10 large carrots, peeled, halved lengthwise and sliced into 1/2-inch pieces

16 medium to large button mushrooms, stemmed and quartered

2 teaspoons chopped garlic

1 cup chopped green onion (white, light green and some dark green part)

1 1/2 teaspoons fresh thyme leaves

1 teaspoon chopped fresh rosemary

1 tablespoon chopped fresh parsley or chopped celery leaves

In a small saucepan, cook the unpeeled onions in boiling water to cover for 2 minutes. Drain, chop off the tip and root ends and peel. Cut in half if larger than a grape. Set aside.

In two large skillets, cook the bacon until crisp. Remove the bacon from the pans, reserving 1 tablespoon bacon grease in each skillet. Drain bacon on paper towels, cool and crumble. Set aside.

Dry the chicken pieces with paper towel and season with salt, pepper and paprika. Place 1 cup flour in a shallow dish and dredge the chicken pieces to lightly coat. In each skillet, add 2 tablespoons butter and melt with the bacon drippings over medium heat. Add chicken pieces and cook 4 to 5 minutes on each side or until lightly brown.

Remove chicken from skillets and set aside on a large plate or pan (don't wipe out the skillets).

To the drippings in each skillet, add the onions, carrots and mushrooms, dividing ingredients equally. Cook over medium heat 10 to 12 minutes or until vegetables start to brown. Stir in the garlic and green onion and cook 5 to 7 minutes. Stir in the thyme, rosemary and parsley and cook for 1 minute. Remove from heat and combine vegetable mixtures into one skillet. Add the brandy; CAREFULLY ignite the brandy, standing back away from the pot. Let the flame subside and place the mixture in the bottom of a 4- to 5-quart, cooktop-to-oven baking dish (I use two Le Creuset pans). Add the chicken (and any juice that has collected) and the crumbled bacon.

In the skillet that held the flambéed vegetables, add the red wine and chicken broth; cook over medium heat, scraping and brown bits from the bottom of the pan. Pour over the chicken and vegetables. Cover and refrigerate chicken mixture for at least 4 hours or overnight.

Preheat oven to 325 degrees.

1/4 cup brandy or Cognac

5 cups dry red wine (Burgundy or
   Pinot Noir)

1 cup chicken broth

Garnish: chopped fresh parsley

Bring the chicken mixture to room temperature. Cover and bake for
2 hours or until chicken is just cooked through and a thermometer
inserted into thickest portions registers 165 degrees. Remove the
chicken pieces from the baking dish and keep warm.

Place the baking dish on top of the stove. In a small mixing bowl,
mash together the remaining 2 tablespoons butter and remaining
2 tablespoons of flour with a fork. Whisk into the sauce mixture
in the pan and bring to a simmer. Cook 5 to 10 minutes, stirring
occasionally, just until thickened. Season to taste with salt and
pepper. Place chicken on a serving platter or individual serving plates
and surround with the vegetables; spoon sauce over the top. Garnish
with chopped fresh parsley.

NOTE Instead of 7 breasts and 4 drumsticks, you can use 3 cut up whole
chickens. If the chicken breasts are very large, cut them in half (breaking the
bone) or trim them down a bit and then poach the extra meat to use in one of
our chicken salad recipes.

VARIATION You can fry the chicken in a combination of the bacon
grease and 4 tablespoons of olive oil (2 tablespoons in each pan) instead of
using butter.

CHICKEN POT PIE

Pot pies can be the best comfort food, and I like to think my version is a modern twist on the traditional dish. In this recipe, I replace the traditional green peas with edamame, and add in white wine and curry powder (I do love anything with curry!). While making this for Robert one night, I accidentally grabbed light coconut milk (instead of evaporated milk) from the pantry. I thought it would make an interesting flavor profile — so I used it, and I was right! Sometimes inspiration comes in the most unusual forms, like grabbing the "wrong" can. I've also created a vegetarian version of this dish *(see Variation below)*.

SERVES: 6 to 7

1 tablespoon butter

6 to 8 ounces chopped fresh mushrooms (any kind)

1/2 large onion, chopped

2 large celery ribs, chopped

2 large carrots, peeled and chopped

3/4 to 1 pound boneless, skinless chicken breasts or thighs, cut into 1/2-inch pieces

2 teaspoons curry powder, divided

1 cup chicken broth

1/2 cup light coconut milk, evaporated milk or half and half

1/2 cup dry white wine

3 tablespoons all-purpose flour

2/3 cup frozen shelled edamame or frozen green peas

2 teaspoons chopped fresh rosemary

3/4 teaspoon fresh thyme leaves

3/4 teaspoon chopped fresh oregano

Salt, to taste

Freshly ground black pepper, to taste

Pinch or 2 of sugar (optional)

4 to 5 large, unbaked Nama's Buttermilk Biscuits *(page 223)*, or prepared biscuits

Preheat oven to 375 degrees. Lightly grease a 9-by-9 inch baking dish or 2-quart oval baking dish.

In a large skillet or sauté pan, melt butter over medium heat. Add the mushrooms, onion, celery and carrots and sauté for 5 minutes. Stir in the chopped chicken and 1 teaspoon curry powder; Cook, stirring frequently, until the chicken is no longer pink.

Slowly stir in the chicken broth, milk and wine. Sift the flour over the top and whisk to blend. Add remaining 1 teaspoon curry powder, edamame and rosemary, whisking until well blended. Bring to a boil, reduce heat and simmer 15 minutes or until thickened. Remove from heat; stir in thyme and oregano and season to taste with salt and pepper. If using evaporated milk, you may need to add a pinch or two of sugar. Spoon into prepared baking dish.

Roll each biscuit flat to make larger. Place over chicken mixture in one layer (biscuits don't have to cover mixture completely). Bake about 15 minutes or until biscuits are browned and chicken mixture is bubbling hot.

ALTERNATIVE PRESENTATION Divide filling between 6 large ramekins, increase number of biscuits to 6 and place 1 biscuit on top of each.

MAKE AHEAD Pot pie filling can be prepared, cooled, covered and refrigerated earlier in the day. Bring to room temperature before covering with biscuits and baking.

VEGETARIAN VARIATION In place of the chicken, use 1/2 bunch fresh asparagus, tough ends removed and sliced into 1/2-inch pieces. Follow same directions as above.

ROLLED TURKEY BREAST
WITH ROASTED RED PEPPER STUFFING

My good friend Ella Spradley hosted a dinner party one evening and served the most wonderful stuffed turkey breast *(photo, page 12)*. Fortunately, she was willing to share the recipe. An alternative to the traditional roast turkey and stuffing, it's a great dish to serve during the holidays, sure to wow your guests *(see our complete Thanksgiving menu on page 266)*. I prefer the additional flavor gained from using prepared roasted peppers (either from a jar or the olive bar at Whole Foods), but you can certainly roast your own.

Ask your butcher to de-bone and butterfly the turkey breast for you (it will be in 2 pieces).

SERVES: 10 to 12

3 tablespoons butter

1 large onion, chopped

1 1/2 teaspoons chopped garlic, divided

2 tablespoons chopped fresh basil

3 tablespoons chopped fresh parsley

1 cup breadcrumbs

Salt, to taste

Freshly ground black pepper, to taste

7-ounces marinated roasted red peppers, drained and patted dry with paper towel

1 (6-pound) skin on turkey breast, boned, halved and butterflied*

Olive oil

2 cups chicken stock or broth, divided

1 cup dry white wine

2 tablespoons cornstarch

1/4 cup water

Equivalent to 4 pounds boneless turkey breast

Preheat oven to 425 degrees.

In a large skillet or sauté pan, heat the butter over medium heat. Add onions and sauté 5 minutes or until soft. Add garlic and basil and sauté 5 minutes. Remove from heat and stir in parsley and breadcrumbs. Season to taste with salt and pepper.

Lay each turkey breast half flat, skin side down and pound with a meat mallet or rolling pin to an even thickness. Spread breadcrumb mixture evenly over each breast, leaving a 1/2- to 1-inch border on the long sides. Arrange red peppers evenly over breadcrumbs. Roll up breast, starting with the long side without skin (skin should be on the outside); tie in several places with kitchen twine.

Place rolled turkey breasts on a rack in a large roasting pan; rub with olive oil and season with salt and pepper. Put turkey in the oven and bake for 35 minutes. Carefully pour 1 cup chicken stock in bottom of pan. Reduce heat to 350 degrees and bake an additional 40 to 50 minutes or until a meat thermometer inserted into the thickest portions registers 165 degrees. Transfer turkey to a platter and let stand 10 minutes.

While the turkey is resting, place the roasting pan on the stove and add white wine. Bring to a boil and cook 7 minutes or until reduced by half. Stir in remaining 1 cup of chicken stock and 1/2 teaspoon chopped garlic. Reduce heat to a simmer and continue cooking, stirring, for 5 minutes. In a small bowl, whisk together cornstarch and water; whisk into wine mixture. Cook until thickened (doesn't take long). Season to taste with salt and pepper. Slice the turkey into thin pieces and serve with the gravy.

MAKE AHEAD Turkey can be stuffed and rolled earlier in the day, covered and refrigerated. Bring to room temperature before baking.

NOTE The turkey can be held in warm oven for a while if needed.

Meats

"The only time to eat diet food is while you're waiting for your steak to cook." — *Julia Child*

Sauces, glazes, marinades and seasonings are the secrets to delicious meat dishes. It's easy to amp up the flavors of fresh beef, pork, lamb and bison with a little inspiration from these recipes!

BEEF, BISON AND LAMB

122 | Cajun Meatloaf

123 | Hill Family Meatloaf

124 | Steak Enchiladas with Roasted Tomatillo-Green Chile Salsa

126 | Kidwell Family Tacos

128 | Oklahoma BBQ Sauce

128 | BBQ Beef Sandwiches

130 | Beef Stew with Caramelized Root Vegetables

132 | Wild Bill's Bison with Shiitake Bourbon Sauce

134 | Roasted Lamb with Lemon

PORK

136 | Slow Cooker Mediterranean Meatball Ratatouille

137 | Eggplant Parmesan with Sausage, Mushroom and Olive Marinara Sauce

138 | Roasted Hoisin Pork Tenderloin

138 | Balsamic-Honey Pork Tenderloin

139 | Asian Pork Tenderloin

140 | Spicy Pork Chops with Argentine Chimichurri Sauce

142 | Grilled Pork Chops with Mushrooms Sauteéd in Bourbon

143 | Sauteéd Pork with a Mustard-Caper Sauce

144 | Lemon Glazed Pork Chops

144 | Pulled Pork Sandwiches

145 | Stir-Fried Pork and Asparagus

CAJUN MEATLOAF

This fabulous meatloaf recipe *(photo, page 120)* comes from chef, author, columnist and lifestyle blogger Sally Schneider. Her focus is on improvising, being resourceful and thinking outside the box (you can find her blog at *improvisedlife.com*). To me, this dish illustrates of all those concepts — and it's delicious too! I like to serve this meatloaf with our Golden Potatoes *(page 212)* and a tossed salad.

SERVES: 8

2 teaspoons salt

1 1/2 teaspoons fresh or 1/2 teaspoon dried thyme leaves

1 1/2 teaspoons freshly ground pepper

1 1/2 teaspoons paprika

1 1/4 teaspoons ground cumin

1 1/4 teaspoons ground nutmeg

3/4 teaspoon cayenne pepper

3/4 teaspoon ground white pepper

1 tablespoon olive oil

1 1/2 cups (1 to 2 onions) chopped yellow onion

1 1/4 cups (3 to 4 ribs) chopped celery

1 cup chopped (1 to 2 peppers) red bell pepper

1 medium jalapeño pepper, seeded and finely chopped

1 tablespoon chopped garlic

1 1/2 tablespoons Worcestershire sauce

1 1/2 teaspoons hot sauce

1/2 cup whole milk

1/2 cup tomato puree

2 teaspoons red wine vinegar

1 1/2 pounds lean ground beef

3/4 pound lean ground pork

1 cup fresh or panko breadcrumbs

3 egg whites

Preheat oven to 350 degrees. Line a 13- by 9-inch baking pan with foil.

In a small bowl, combine the salt, thyme, black pepper, paprika, cumin, nutmeg, cayenne and white pepper.

In a large heavy skillet or sauté pan, heat the oil over medium heat. Add the onion, celery, red pepper, jalapeño, garlic, Worcestershire sauce and hot sauce. Stir in the reserved spice mixture. Cook, stirring occasionally, for 6 minutes or until the mixture starts to stick to the bottom of the pan. Stir in the milk, tomato purée and vinegar. Cook, stirring occasionally, for 12 minutes or until the mixture is thick (reduce the heat if needed to prevent burning). Remove from heat and set aside to cool.

Add the beef, pork, breadcrumbs and egg whites to the cooled vegetable mixture; mix until well combined (I like to use my hands, which is why you need to cool the vegetable mixture). Scoop the mixture into the center of the prepared pan and shape into a loaf about 10- by 5-inches. Bake uncovered for 25 minutes. Increase the oven temperature to 400 degrees and cook an additional 20 to 30 minutes, or until an instant-read thermometer inserted in thickest portion registers 150 degrees. Let rest for at least 5 minutes before serving.

MAKE AHEAD Meatloaf can be prepared but not baked earlier in the day, covered and refrigerated. Bring to room temperature before baking.

HILL FAMILY MEATLOAF

My mom got this recipe from her friend Martha Dietler, who wrote on the recipe card that it was a favorite of the Hill family. I don't actually know the Hill family, but the brown sugar, ketchup, mustard and nutmeg topping is what makes this meatloaf so special — both sweet and savory at the same time. If you are part of the Hill Family, or you know them, please tell them we, too, love their meatloaf!

SERVES: 6 to 8

2/3 cup whole wheat breadcrumbs

1 cup whole milk

1 1/2 pounds ground beef

2 large eggs, beaten

1/4 cup grated onion

1 teaspoon salt

1/2 teaspoon dried sage

1/8 teaspoon fresh ground pepper

1/4 cup ketchup

3 tablespoons light brown sugar

1 teaspoon Dijon mustard

1/4 teaspoon nutmeg

Preheat the oven to 350 degrees.

In a large mixing bowl, stir together breadcrumbs and milk. Stir in ground beef, eggs, onion, salt, sage and pepper. Place mixture in a lightly greased 9- by 5-inch loaf pan or form into a loaf and put on a foil-lined rimmed baking sheet.

In a small mixing bowl, stir together ketchup, brown sugar, mustard and nutmeg. Spread over top of loaf. Bake about 1 hour or until a meat thermometer inserted in thickest portion registers 155 degrees.

MAKE AHEAD Meatloaf can be prepared but not baked earlier in the day, covered and refrigerated. Bring to room temperature before baking.

VARIATION Can put individual servings in muffin tins and bake for 45 minutes.

STEAK ENCHILADAS
WITH ROASTED TOMATILLO-GREEN CHILE SALSA

I created this dish one night when looking for ways to use up some leftover grilled steak. You can substitute leftover pork or chicken in place of the steak as well. The salsa is full of flavor and pretty spicy — if you like less heat, leave out one or two of the Serrano peppers and/or the jalapeño pepper. I like to double the salsa and make it ahead, setting aside the extra portion to use in our Mexican Baked Chicken *(page 112)* and with scrambled eggs. *(See Menu on page 266 for a Mexican Fiesta Dinner!)*

SERVES: 6

TOMATILLO-GREEN CHILE SALSA (MAKES 2 CUPS)

1 pound tomatillos, husked, rinsed and patted dry

1 large poblano chile pepper

3 (2 to 3-inch) Serrano chile peppers

1 (2 to 3-inch) jalapeño pepper

3 tablespoons olive oil, divided

1 cup (around 1/3 large) coarsely chopped onion

1/4 cup chopped fresh cilantro

Juice from 1 lemon

2 tablespoons water

Salt, to taste

STEAK ENCHILADAS

2 teaspoons olive oil

1 pound medium-rare grilled sirloin steak (or leftover cooked beef tenderloin)

1 medium onion, chopped

Chili powder, to taste

Ground cumin, to taste

Salt, to taste

To make Tomatillo-Green Chile Salsa: Preheat broiler. Move upper rack to position around 5 to 6 inches below broiler. Line a large rimmed baking sheet with foil.

Lay the tomatillos and all the peppers on the prepared baking sheet. When the broiler is very hot, broil for 7 to 8 minutes, or until top side of the vegetables are blackened. Using tongs, turn over and continue roasting another 5 to 7 minutes, or until both sides are blackened. Transfer to a large plate and cover with plastic wrap (sealing the edges). Let sit until cool.

In a large skillet, heat 1 tablespoon olive oil over medium heat. Add the chopped onion and cook 5 to 7 minutes or until tender and starting to turn brown.

Remove from heat to cool (leave in pan). Remove the charred skins from cooled peppers and discard *(see Tip on next page)*. Cut in half lengthwise, and using your knife, carefully scrape out and discard the seeds and veins on the inside (if you like super spicy food, leave some of the seeds.)

In a food processor, combine peppers, tomatillos (remove stems but don't peel them) and any accumulated juices on the plate. Add the cooked onion, cilantro, lemon juice, remaining 2 tablespoons olive oil and water. Process until well combined (mixture should be chunky with no large pieces). Season to taste with salt. Transfer to a bowl; set aside.

To prepare Steak Enchiladas: Preheat oven to 350 degrees. Spray 2 (7- by-11-inch) baking pans with nonstick cooking spray.

Cut the steak into 1/4-inch strips then cut the strips into 3 to 4 pieces. In the same skillet used to cook onions, heat the olive oil over medium heat. Add the steak and onions to the pan, and

1/3 cup chopped fresh cilantro, plus more for garnish

1 (15-ounce) can black beans, rinsed and drained

1 3/4 cups chopped fresh tomatoes*

Freshly ground black pepper, to taste

14 to 16 (6-inch) corn tortillas

2 cups (8 ounces) shredded sharp Cheddar cheese (or a mixture of Cheddar and Monterey Jack)

Garnishes: sour cream, fresh cilantro

*When fresh tomatoes aren't in season, for more flavor substitute 1 (15-ounce) can, drained

sprinkle liberally with chili powder, cumin and salt. Cook for 5 minutes, stirring occasionally. Stir in the cilantro, black beans and tomatoes and cook, stirring occasionally, until the onion is soft. Add additional chile powder and cumin, if desired. Season to taste with salt and pepper. Remove from heat and set aside.

To assemble: Spread a thin layer of the salsa over the bottom of the prepared pans, just enough to cover *(see Tip below)*.

Microwave the corn tortillas for around 30 seconds to soften. Dip 1 tortilla in the salsa; spoon about 1/4 to 1/3 cup of steak filling near the edge, sprinkle with grated cheese and roll up. Place, seam side down, in prepared baking dish. Repeat with remaining tortillas, filling and cheese. Spoon remaining salsa evenly over the top of the enchiladas, covering completely. Cover and bake for 20 to 25 minutes or until hot and bubbly. Serve with a dollop of sour cream and a sprinkle of chopped (or whole) cilantro leaves.

MAKE AHEAD Salsa can be made up to 3 days ahead, covered and refrigerated. Enchiladas can be assembled but not baked earlier in the day, covered and refrigerated. Bring to room temperature before baking.

TIP

On roasting peppers: Never rinse peppers (or tomatillos) after roasting — you will wash off all the wonderful smoky flavor! Also, it's best to use gloves when handling hot peppers, as the heat transfers to your hands. If you don't use gloves, take care and never, never touch your eyes before washing your hands thoroughly with soap and water after handling the peppers.

TIP

On assembling enchiladas: It's important to completely cover tortillas (top and bottom) with sauce; it keeps them from turning hard and tough when baked.

KIDWELL FAMILY TACOS

My cousin Jim Kidwell and his daughter Sarah are both fabulous cooks. Their tacos are the best you will ever eat, just ask our other cousins! Jim and Sarah like to use ground elk meat, but I've found this recipe is equally delicious with ground beef, bison or turkey (just omit the butter). They don't really measure the ingredients, so the measurements below are approximate. The best approach to this recipe is to mix together, cook, taste and season again.

SERVES: 4

MAKES: 8 to 10 tacos

1 to 1 1/4 pound ground elk meat (preferably with more than 5% suet), beef, bison or turkey

Chili powder, to taste (preferably a blend of flavors)

Garlic powder to taste

2 teaspoons ground cumin

1 teaspoon kosher salt

1 tablespoon dried Mexican oregano or common oregano

2 to 2 1/2 tablespoons butter, sliced (use only with elk)

8 to 10 taco shells, preferably home made

Prepared guacamole *(see Note 1)*

Pico de gallo *(see Note 2)*

Sour cream

Shredded sharp Cheddar cheese

Chopped green onion

Chopped fresh cilantro

Preheat oven to 325 degrees.

In a large skillet, cook elk meat over medium heat, breaking up meat with a spatula as it browns. Sprinkle a heavy coating of chili powder over the top. Sprinkle with garlic powder to taste, then the cumin, salt and oregano. Cook, stirring and continuing to break up the meat, until the meat is slightly brown. Add butter, stirring until it melts. Sprinkle with another light coating of chili powder and continue cooking until a deep red-brown color (don't overcook otherwise it will dry out).

Divide meat equally between the taco shells. Place in a baking dish that will hold them snugly in one layer; bake 15 to 20 minutes. Serve with guacamole, sour cream, cheese, onions, cilantro and pico de gallo.

NOTE 1 To make your own guacamole, chop and mix together avocado, tomato, shallots or green onions, garlic, cilantro and jalapeño or Serrano pepper. Stir in fresh lime juice and hot pepper sauce. Season with cumin, chile powder, salt and ground pepper.

NOTE 2 If prepared pico de gallo isn't available in your area make your own by chopping and mixing together grape tomatoes, red onion, cilantro and jalapeño pepper. Season with salt and cumin (you can also add some chile powder if you want). Alternatively, substitute purchased salsa.

OKLAHOMA BBQ SAUCE

I found this recipe from mom's friend Ann Reed in mom's recipe box after she passed away. On the back of the card, Ann wrote: "Delicious with ribs, beef, ham or chicken. I have been making this for 20 years and it is special in our house." It's very easy to make, with just the right balance of spice and sweet. Delicious in our BBQ Beef Sandwiches *(below)*, Pulled Pork Sandwiches *(page 144)* and on barbecued chicken.

MAKES: just over 1 quart

2 1/2 cups tomato juice

1 medium onion, minced

3/4 teaspoon garlic powder

1/2 teaspoon celery seed

2 tablespoons butter

1 1/2 cups ketchup

1 cup sugar

1 cup white wine vinegar

1 1/2 tablespoons chili powder

1 1/2 tablespoons
    Worcestershire sauce

2 teaspoons ground cinnamon

1 1/2 teaspoons cayenne pepper

1 1/2 teaspoons ground black pepper

1 teaspoon ground nutmeg

1 teaspoon ground ginger

1 teaspoon ground cloves

In a large saucepan, stir together the tomato juice, onion, garlic powder and celery seed. Bring to a boil, reduce to medium and boil for 15 minutes. Remove from heat and add butter, stirring until melted. Stir in remaining ingredients.

MAKE AHEAD According to Ann, the sauce will keep indefinitely, covered and refrigerated.

BBQ BEEF SANDWICHES

These sandwiches are delicious served with Dorothy's Potato Salad *(page 84)*.

SERVES: 10

4 pounds chuck or arm roast

2 cups water

4 cups Oklahoma BBQ Sauce,
    divided

Hamburger buns, preferably Brioche

In a slow cooker, place the roast in the bottom and add 2 cups water. Cover and cook on high for 4 to 5 hours, or on low for 8 to 10 hours. Take meat out of cooker and drain, reserving about 1/2 cup liquid. Shred the meat with two forks; return to slow cooker. Stir in 2 cups barbeque sauce and reserved liquid. Cover and cook on low for 4 to 6 hours. Taste and stir in more sauce if desired. Serve on hamburger buns, passing remaining sauce on the side.

Oklahoma BBQ Sauce, BBQ Beef Sandwiches, Dorothy's Potato Salad *(page 84)*

BEEF STEW WITH CARAMELIZED ROOT VEGETABLES

Mom had several elegant beef stew recipes for entertaining, this being one of her best. I like to start the dinner with Butternut Squash Soup *(page 59)*, serve Anna Mae's Freezer Rolls *(page 226)* and a light tossed salad alongside this robust stew, and finish off the evening with Pear Kuchen *(page 244)*. I love the slight sweetness the caramelized vegetables add to this dish.

A few notes on this dish: A Le Creuset baking dish works well. All the vegetables should be cut into 1/2 to 3/4-inch size pieces. You can use root vegetables other than those listed here — sweet potatoes, celery root, turnips, etc. This recipe calls for letting the stew rest for at least 30 minutes, up to 24 hours, and then reheating to serve. This step is very important as it allows the flavors to blend and the sauce to thicken.

SERVES: 8

6 to 8 large slices bacon

2 pounds beef stew meat, cut into 1-inch cubes

Freshly ground black pepper, to taste

4 to 6 tablespoons olive oil, divided

1 1/2 cups beef broth

1 1/2 cups good quality Pinot Noir wine

2 tablespoons unsalted butter

2 tablespoons currant jelly

3 teaspoons chopped garlic or shallot

3 carrots, peeled and coarsely chopped

4 medium parsnips, peeled and coarsely chopped

3 medium to large new potatoes

4 large leeks, white and light green part coarsely chopped

4 teaspoons sugar

6 large ripe plum or Italian tomatoes, seeded and coarsely chopped

2 tablespoons fresh thyme leaves

1/2 cup chopped Italian parsley, plus more for garnish

Salt, to taste

Preheat oven to 350 degrees.

In a large (5- to 6-quart) stove-to-oven or cast iron baking dish, cook bacon over medium-low heat until crisp. Remove bacon from pan (don't drain bacon grease out of the dish) and break into 1/2-inch pieces; set aside.

Heat the bacon grease over high heat. Pat beef dry, if necessary, with a paper towel and sprinkle with fresh ground pepper. Sauté 1/4 of meat in the hot bacon grease until browned *(see Tip on page 131)*. With a slotted spoon, transfer beef to small dish and set aside, leaving any accumulated juices in the pan. Repeat with remaining beef (1/4 at a time), adding 1 to 2 tablespoons olive oil if the pan starts to get dry. Don't wipe out the pan when done.

Add beef broth and wine to baking dish and bring to a boil, scraping up any browned bits from the bottom of the pan. Reduce heat to low and stir in the butter, jelly and garlic (or shallot); cook, stirring frequently, until butter and jelly melt (it doesn't take long). Stir in cooked beef. Cover and bake for 45 minutes.

While the beef is cooking, in 2 large skillets or sauté pans, heat 2 tablespoons oil in each pan over medium-low heat. Add carrots, parsnips and potatoes equally to each pan; sauté for 5 minutes. Add leeks and sauté for 3 to 5 minutes. Sprinkle with sugar and cook just until mixture starts to turn brown and caramelize (vegetables may not all be tender, but they will keep cooking in the oven).

After the beef has baked for 45 minutes, remove from the oven and gently stir in leek mixture and chopped tomatoes. Bake, uncovered, for 30 to 40 minutes or until the beef is tender. Remove from oven and stir in thyme, parsley and reserved cooked bacon. Let rest for at least 30 minutes (and up to one day).

Rewarm in a 350 degree oven about 20 minutes. Season to taste with salt and pepper. Garnish with additional chopped parsley.

MAKE AHEAD Stew can be made up to 24 hours ahead, covered and refrigerated. Bring to room temperature before reheating in a 350 degree oven.

TIP

For browning stew meat: To give your stew meat a nice, evenly brown sear on the outside, make sure (1) the meat is dry, (2) the pan and the grease/oil are hot, (3) the beef isn't crowded in the pan (there is space between the pieces) and (4) you don't stir it a lot. Sauté for a few minutes, then turn the pieces over when they don't stick to the pan any more.

WILD BILL'S BISON WITH SHIITAKE BOURBON SAUCE

Bison (or buffalo meat) tastes sweeter and richer than even a high quality cut of beef, is lower in fat and calories and is simply better for you. It adds more iron to your diet, has higher levels of vitamins and minerals and twice as much beta-carotene as other red meats. This bison tenderloin recipe comes from our friend and excellent home gourmet, Bill Hudon. Not only is it delicious, it's a very impressive entrée to serve at a dinner party (*see New Year's Eve Dinner menu on page 267*).

Buffalo really needs to be served rare or medium rare. With the mushroom sauce on the top, your friends and family who prefer their meat more well done won't even notice and will love this dish. Just ask Robert — he likes his meat medium-well to well done and he eats this tenderloin medium rare (as long as he can hide it under the sauce)!

Note the bison needs to marinate for 2 to 3 hours.

SERVES: 12

BISON AND RUB

1 (4- to 5-pound) buffalo tenderloin, strip loin, rib or top sirloin steaks

Olive oil

1/2 cup finely ground coffee

1/2 cup firmly packed light brown sugar

2 tablespoons garlic powder

1 tablespoon dried basil

1 tablespoon Lawry's® seasoned salt

1 tablespoon coarse salt

4 teaspoons smoked paprika

2 teaspoon ground cumin

2 teaspoons ancho chili powder

2 teaspoons ground black pepper

2 teaspoons dried chives

2 teaspoons dried parsley

To make the Bison and Rub: Rub meat all over with olive oil. In a medium mixing bowl, stir together all remaining ingredients. Coat meat evenly with the rub (you will have some rub leftover; save for another use). Let marinate for 2 to 3 hours (this allows the coffee and sugar to dissolve in the oil).

While the meat is marinating, make the shiitake mushroom sauce: Trim the mushrooms and cut into pieces. In a large sauté pan or skillet, melt 3/4 cup (1 1/2 sticks) of the butter over medium heat. Add the mushrooms and sauté until soft. Set aside.

In a large saucepan, melt the remaining 6 tablespoons butter over medium heat. Reduce heat to low, whisk in flour and cook, whisking for 3 minutes. Whisk in the stock, bring to a boil, reduce heat and simmer until thickened. Add mushrooms and simmer 3 to 5 minutes. Add bourbon and cook for 2 minutes. Season to taste with salt and pepper. Remove from heat and set aside.

SHIITAKE MUSHROOM BOURBON SAUCE

1 1/2 pounds shiitake mushrooms

1 1/8 cups butter, divided

6 tablespoons all-purpose flour

6 cups buffalo or beef stock

3/4 cup bourbon

Salt, to taste

Freshly ground black pepper, to taste

Broil or grill bison, turning periodically, until internal temperature reaches 125 degrees for rare, 135 for medium rare (recommended) or 145 for medium. Don't overcook or it will get tough! Let sit for at least 5 minutes before serving. Rewarm the mushroom sauce over medium heat while the meat is resting. Slice bison and serve, spooning sauce over the top.

MAKE AHEAD Rub can be made up to 2 weeks in advance and stored in an airtight container. The mushroom sauce can be made up to 24 hours in advance and stored, covered, in the refrigerator.

ROASTED LAMB WITH LEMON

This recipe was given to me by my late, good friend Thomas Hardy. Having lived and studied in Paris and Italy, Thomas had a large circle of friends all over the world. He was funny, witty and a great entertainer. One friend described him as "Oscar Wilde meets Truman Capote." This lamb was one of his favorite dishes to serve at dinner parties. He said he got it from some famous French countess. I think of him and his big smile and witty sayings every time I make this fabulous and unusual dish.

SERVES: 4

3 tablespoons butter, divided

1 large onion, thinly sliced

1 to 1 1/2 lemons

1 tablespoon olive oil

2 pounds trimmed, cubed lamb*

Salt, to taste

Freshly ground black pepper, to taste

2 tablespoons all-purpose flour

1 cup hot water

1 large pinch saffron

3/4 teaspoon ground cinnamon

1/4 teaspoon ground turmeric

1 large carrot

Cooked basmati or Jasmine rice

*Ask the butcher to trim and cube lamb shoulder for you if cubed lamb meat is not readily available at your grocery store

In a medium skillet, melt 2 tablespoons butter over low heat. Add onions and cook, stirring occasionally, for 35 to 45 minutes or until soft, sweet and dark golden brown. Set aside.

Preheat oven to 325 degrees. Slice the lemon nearly paper-thin. Pick out the seeds. Set aside.

In a heavy cast iron casserole dish (Le Creuset is perfect), melt the remaining 1 tablespoon butter with the olive oil over medium-high heat. Season the lamb with salt and pepper; add to the pan and sear on all sides. Reduce heat to medium-low; sprinkle the flour over the browned lamb and scrape the bottom of the pan to mix the flour with the fat. Stir in 1 cup hot water, saffron, cinnamon and turmeric; season with salt and pepper. Stir in the caramelized onion, bring to a low boil and cook for 2 minutes.

Place a layer of lemon slices over the top of the meat. Put the lid on the pot, place in the oven and bake for 40 minutes.

While the stew cooks, make the carrot flowers: Peel the carrot and cut into 4-inch pieces. Using the channel part of the zester (it's the little loop or groove on the side of the blade which you might never have noticed before), hold one piece of carrot in one hand and using the channel, dig out grooves down the side of the carrot in five places. Slice carrots — they will look like flowers!

To serve, spoon a bed of rice with an indentation in the middle on a large platter or bowl. Stir the stew so the lemons are mixed throughout, and neatly spoon the lamb onto the rice. Smooth out the rice border and decorate with carrot flowers.

MAKE AHEAD Lamb can be prepared earlier in the day, cooled, covered and refrigerated. Rewarm in a 325 degree oven.

SLOW COOKER MEDITERRANEAN MEATBALL RATATOUILLE

My cousin Barb Keller, whom I refer to as the queen of the crockpot, was nice enough to share this delicious dish with me. She makes amazing dishes in her crockpot and this is one of them. Italian sausage meatballs slowly cook for several hours in a rich sauce of mushrooms, eggplant and zucchini. Fresh tomatoes and tomato paste are then added close to the end. People of all ages love this dish! I like to serve it over cooked orzo with a tossed salad on the side.

SERVES: 4 to 6

2 tablespoons olive oil, divided

1 pound mild Italian sausage, casings removed

8 ounces sliced baby portabella mushrooms

1 small eggplant, cut into 1/2-inch pieces

1 zucchini, cut into 1/2-inch pieces

1/2 cup chopped onion

1/2 teaspoon chopped garlic or 1 teaspoon chopped shallot

1 teaspoon dried oregano, divided

1 teaspoon salt, divided

1/2 teaspoon ground black pepper, divided

1 heaping tablespoon tomato paste

2 large tomatoes, seeded and chopped

2 tablespoons chopped fresh basil

1 teaspoon fresh lemon juice

Cooked orzo or rice

In a slow cooker, pour 1 tablespoon oil into the bottom. Shape sausage into 1-inch balls and place on wax paper (makes around 30 meatballs). Place half of the meatballs into the pot. Add half the mushrooms, eggplant and zucchini. Add all of the onion and garlic (or shallot), 1/2 teaspoon oregano, 1/2 teaspoon salt and 1/4 teaspoon pepper. Layer the remaining ingredients on top, in the same order: meatballs, mushrooms, eggplant, zucchini, oregano, salt and pepper. Drizzle remaining 1 tablespoon oil over the top. Cover and cook on low for 6 to 7 hours.

Uncover and stir in tomato paste and diced tomatoes. Cover and cook on low for about 15 minutes. Stir in basil and lemon juice. Serve with cooked orzo or rice.

EGGPLANT PARMESAN WITH SAUSAGE, MUSHROOM AND OLIVE MARINARA SAUCE

My husband Robert has been known for his delicious Eggplant Parmesan for longer than I've known him. One Saturday when he decided to make this delectable dish, I grabbed a pen, paper and camera to capture everything he did. When he was done, he announced it was the best version he had ever made (it was)! Robert serves it with pasta and marinara sauce on the side.

SERVES: 12 to 14

2 medium eggplants, thinly sliced into rounds

6 cups marinara sauce

1 (2.25 ounce) can sliced black olives, drained

1 (14-ounce) can fire roasted tomatoes with garlic, undrained

6 large mushrooms, sliced

1 tablespoon Italian seasoning

1/4 to 1/2 teaspoon red pepper flakes

6 to 8 tablespoons extra virgin olive oil, divided

1 pound mild Italian pork sausage, casings removed (or purchase bulk)

4 large eggs

3/4 cup buttermilk

2 cups Italian-seasoned breadcrumbs

1 cup (4 ounces) freshly grated Parmesan cheese

4 cups (16 ounces) shredded Mozzarella cheese

Slice the eggplant crosswise about 1/4-inch thick; place in a large bowl of cold water to soak.

In a large saucepan or skillet, stir together the marinara sauce, olives, tomatoes, mushrooms, Italian seasoning and pepper flakes. Bring to a boil, reduce heat to low and simmer while cooking the sausage.

In a large skillet, heat 1 tablespoon of the olive oil over medium heat. Add the sausage and cook until no longer pink; drain. Chop briefly in a food processor to break into small pieces. Stir into sauce; continue to simmer while preparing the eggplant.

In a shallow bowl, whisk together the eggs and buttermilk. Place the breadcrumbs in another shallow bowl. Remove eggplant slices from the water one at a time and dip each slice first into the egg mixture, then dredge in the breadcrumbs.

In a large skillet, heat 2 tablespoons olive oil over medium heat. Sauté the eggplant in batches until golden brown on each side. You will be able to cook around 6 slices at a time; add additional oil as needed. Place on paper towels to drain.

Preheat oven to 400 degrees.

In a 13- by 9-inch baking dish, spread marinara sauce to cover the bottom. Layer the eggplant like shingles in two rows, with each row going in an opposite direction (you may be able to fit in three rows, depending on the size of your eggplant). Cover with remaining sauce (Robert likes to save some to serve over pasta on the side).

In a medium mixing bowl, combine the two cheeses. Sprinkle evenly over the top of the sauce. Bake for around 30 to 40 minutes or until the cheese melts and casserole is bubbly hot and golden brown on top. Let rest about 5 minutes before serving.

MAKE AHEAD Eggplant can be prepared and baked up to 24 hours ahead, cooled, covered and refrigerated. Reheat in a 400 degree oven. Can also be frozen after baking.

ROASTED HOISIN PORK TENDERLOIN

While most pork tenderloin recipes require some amount of marinating, this one doesn't. This dish is great for those nights when you haven't planned ahead — no marinating or other up front preparation is required. Just mix together four ingredients, smear on the pork and cook — that's all it takes to prepare this delicious, Asian-inspired entrée.

SERVES: 4 to 6

1/2 cup hoisin sauce, plus more for serving

1/3 cup chopped green onion (white, light green and some dark green part)

1 tablespoon chopped fresh ginger

1 1/2 teaspoons chopped garlic

1 1/2 to 1 3/4 pounds pork tenderloin

Preheat the oven to 500 degrees. Line the bottom and rack of a broiler pan with foil, cutting out the slits through the foil. Set aside.

In a small mixing bowl, stir together the hoisin sauce, green onion, ginger and garlic. Spread over the pork tenderloins. Place on the broiler pan rack and bake for 25 to 30 minutes or until a meat thermometer inserted in thickest portion registers 145 to 150 degrees. Do not turn the meat over.

Transfer to a cutting board and let rest for 10 minutes. Cut into thin slices and serve with additional hoisin sauce on the side. Can be served hot or at room temperature

BALSAMIC-HONEY PORK TENDERLOIN

Try this recipe for an easy-to-prepare and elegant dinner — serve with Cheese Grits Soufflé (*page 213*) and Apple, Walnut and Stilton Cheese Salad (*page 76*). Note the pork must marinate for at least 2 hours.

SERVES: 4 to 6

2 tablespoons honey

2 tablespoons coarse-grain mustard

2 tablespoons balsamic vinegar

1 tablespoon olive oil

1/2 teaspoon chopped garlic or 1 teaspoon chopped shallot

Salt, to taste

Freshly ground black pepper, to taste

1 1/2- to 1 3/4-pounds pork tenderloin

In a small mixing bowl, whisk together the honey, mustard, vinegar, olive oil, garlic (or shallot), salt and pepper. Place in a zip top bag with the pork. Seal bag and place in the refrigerator, turning occasionally, for at least 2 to 24 hours.

Prepare a medium-hot fire in a charcoal grill, or preheat a gas grill on medium-high.

Remove pork from marinade; pour marinade in a small bowl. Place pork on greased grill rack; brush with marinade. Cook, covered with grill lid, for 5 minutes. Turn tenderloins and baste with marinade. Grill 5 minutes; turn and baste. Grill 8 more minutes, or until a meat thermometer inserted in thickest portion registers 145 to 150 degrees. (Do not baste during last 5 minutes.) Transfer pork to cutting board and let rest for 10 minutes. Cut into 1/4- to 1/3-inch thick slices and serve.

ASIAN PORK TENDERLOIN

This flavorful pork recipe comes from the fabulous cook and hostess, Constance Cain. Whenever anyone is invited to the Cain home for dinner, they move heaven and earth to be there. The setting is always lovely, the mix of people interesting and the food delicious. This pork doesn't disappoint; I have served it several times to rave reviews — and our recipe testers loved it too.

I recommend serving this pork with our Saffron Cilantro Rice *(page 216)* and Lemon Dijon Green Beans with Caramelized Shallots *(page 208)*. When entertaining, I follow the directions for finishing the tenderloin in the oven *(see Variation below)* so I don't have to be at the grill during the party for more than 5 minutes.

Note that the pork needs to marinate for at least 1 hour.

SERVES: 4 to 6

1/3 cup low-sodium soy sauce

1/4 cup (2 large limes) fresh
    lime juice

1/4 cup honey

2 tablespoons olive oil

3 to 4 garlic cloves, minced

1 tablespoon chopped fresh ginger

1 tablespoon curry powder

1/2 teaspoon ground black pepper

1 1/2 to 1 3/4 pounds
    pork tenderloin

Sliced green onion (white, light
    green and some dark green parts)

In a medium mixing bowl, whisk together the soy sauce, lime juice, honey, olive oil, garlic, ginger, curry powder and ground pepper. Combine soy sauce mixture and pork in a large zip top bag and marinate in the refrigerator for at least 1 hour and up to 12 hours.

Prepare a medium-hot fire in a charcoal grill or preheat a gas grill on high.

Remove tenderloins from the bag, reserving the marinade and place on a rimmed baking sheet. Pour marinade in a medium saucepan.

If using a gas grill, reduce heat on all burners to medium. Oil grill rack. Grill tenderloins, covered, for 10 minutes. Turn over and continue cooking, covered, for another 5 to 10 minutes or until a meat thermometer inserted into thickest portion registers 145 to 150 degrees. Let rest for 10 minutes before cutting and serving.

While the pork rests, in a small saucepan bring sauce to a boil, reduce heat and simmer for 5 minutes. Slice tenderloins into 1/2-inch thick pieces and place on a large serving platter or individual serving plates. Spoon sauce over the top and sprinkle with green onion.

VARIATION FOR FINISHING IN THE OVEN Sear the outside of the tenderloins on a grill over high heat to mark; it usually takes about 5 minutes. Then place on a parchment paper-lined rimmed baking sheet and roast in a 400 degree oven for around 10 to 15 minutes or until a meat thermometer inserted into thickest portion registers 145 to 150 degrees. Let rest for 10 minutes before cutting and serving.

SPICY PORK CHOPS
WITH ARGENTINE CHIMICHURRI SAUCE

Chimichurri is a sauce from Argentina usually served with meat; typically made with parsley, garlic, olive oil, oregano and wine vinegar. For my Chimichurri I add in red pepper flakes for a bit of spice, and a mixture of lemon juice and white balsamic in place of the wine vinegar. I also like to use a lime-infused olive oil, but you can use regular olive with some lime zest too. The rub on the pork chops is also delicious on pork tenderloin. You can either grill or pan fry the pork *(see Variation below)*.

Note the Chimichurri sauce needs to sit for at least 30 minutes.

SERVES: 4

CHIMICHURRI SAUCE

1 cup packed flat leaf (Italian) parsley

4 large garlic cloves, coarsely chopped

1 1/2 teaspoons dried oregano

1/2 teaspoon kosher salt

1/4 teaspoon red pepper flakes (or more to taste)

1 tablespoon fresh lemon juice

3 tablespoons lemon-flavored balsamic vinegar (can use white balsamic vinegar)

1/2 cup lime olive oil*

If you can't find lime infused olive oil, use extra virgin olive oil and add some lime zest to the sauce

PORK CHOPS

2 tablespoons salt

2 tablespoons paprika

1 1/2 tablespoons light brown sugar

1 tablespoon garlic powder

1 tablespoon onion powder

1 1/2 teaspoons cayenne pepper

1 1/2 teaspoons ground black pepper

3/4 teaspoon freshly ground white pepper

4 boneless pork loin chops, around 3/4-inch thick

2 tablespoons extra virgin olive oil

To make the Chimichurri Sauce: In a food processor, combine parsley, garlic, oregano, salt, red pepper flakes, lemon juice and balsamic vinegar; process until the parsley is evenly chopped. With the machine running, slowly add the olive oil and process just until blended. Taste and add more salt if needed. Let sit at room temperature for at least 30 minutes before serving.

To make the Grilled Pork: In a small bowl, stir together the salt, paprika, brown sugar, garlic powder, onion powder and peppers. Coat both sides of the chops with olive oil, then rub both sides of each chop with spice mixture (around 1/2 to 1 teaspoon per side; save extra for the next time you prepare this recipe or to use on pork tenderloin). Set aside.

Prepare a medium-hot fire in a charcoal grill or preheat a gas grill on high.

Once the grill is heated, bank the coals to one side of the grill, or turn off one burner on a gas grill. Place chops on the hot part of the grill and cook, covered, 3 minutes or until seared. Turn over and grill 2 to 3 minutes or until seared. Move chops to the cooler part of the grill, cover and cook 3 to 4 minutes or until an instant-read thermometer inserted in thickest portion registers 145 degrees. Let rest for around 10 minutes. Serve with some of the sauce spooned over the top, passing the rest on the side.

MAKE AHEAD Chimichurri sauce can be made up to 2 days ahead, covered and refrigerated. Bring to room temperature before serving

VARIATION Chops can be pan-fried in a large skillet in 1 to 2 tablespoons olive oil.

GRILLED PORK CHOPS
WITH MUSHROOMS SAUTÉED IN BOURBON

Rummaging around in mom's files one afternoon, I found one of her fabulous mushroom recipes — mushrooms sautéed with garlic in butter and Jack Daniels (her favorite winter drink), then finished off with Worcestershire, parsley and thyme. I love the rustic flavor of mushrooms and pork together and think mom's mushrooms go well with these grilled pork chops that are seasoned with a garlic-onion-parsley rub.

SERVES: 4

2 slices bacon

1 teaspoon chopped garlic

4 tablespoons butter

1/2 pound shiitake, button or
   cremini mushrooms, sliced

1/2 cup bourbon (preferably
   Jack Daniels)

1/2 cup chicken broth

6 tablespoons Worcestershire sauce

1/4 cup chopped fresh parsley

2 tablespoons fresh thyme leaves

4 (1-inch thick) boneless pork
   loin chops

Wash Park All-Purpose Seasoning
   from Savory Spice*

*Savory Spice is a Colorado-based
company. If you don't have their
seasoning blend, season the chops
with a sprinkle of salt, ground pepper,
garlic powder, onion powder and
dried parsley*

Prepare a medium-hot fire in a charcoal grill or preheat a gas grill on high.

In a large skillet, cook the bacon until crisp. Transfer to paper towels to drain; crumble. Pour off fat from skillet (don't wipe out). Add butter and melt over medium heat. Add mushrooms and cook 5 to 7 minutes or until the mushrooms are soft. Add bourbon; increase heat and bring to a boil. Cook until bourbon is almost evaporated (takes just a few minutes). Stir in chicken broth and Worcestershire sauce; bring to a boil and cook until sauce is slightly thickened. Reduce heat, stir in crumbled bacon, parsley and thyme. Keep warm.

Bank the coals to one side of the grill or turn off one burner on a gas grill. Rub both sides of the pork chops generously with the seasoning mix and place on the hottest part of the grill. Cook, covered, about 3 minutes or until seared. Turn over and cook 2 to 3 minutes or until both sides are seared. Move chops to the cooler part of the grill, cover and cook 3 to 4 minutes or until an instant-read thermometer inserted in the thickest portion registers 145 degrees. Let rest 10 minutes before serving. Transfer to dinner plates and spoon the mushrooms on top.

SAUTÉED PORK WITH A MUSTARD-CAPER SAUCE

Pork and mustard — a perfect combination! Add chopped red onion and capers to broth, mustard and milk, and you have a tangy and bold sauce that perfectly enhances the pork tenderloin. Serve with sautéed spinach and roasted new potatoes for a quick and healthy meal.

SERVES: 4

1 (1- to 1 1/4-pound) pork tenderloin, trimmed

Freshly ground black pepper, to taste

1 tablespoon olive oil

1/2 cup finely chopped red onion

2 cups chicken broth

1/4 cup evaporated milk

2 tablespoons Dijon mustard

2 to 3 tablespoons drained capers

2 teaspoons cornstarch

Cut pork tenderloin into 1/2-inch thick slices and season with fresh ground pepper. In a large skillet, heat olive oil over medium-high heat. Add pork and sauté 2 minutes on each side until browned. Transfer pork to a plate and set aside.

In same skillet, add onions and cook, stirring constantly, 1 minute. Stir in chicken broth and milk. Bring to a boil, scraping up browned bits from the bottom of the pan. Stir in mustard and capers; stir in cornstarch. Place pork in pan, reduce heat to simmer and cook 2 to 3 minutes or until sauce thickens and pork is done.

A WELL-SEASONED INSPIRATION

ROBERT *My smart, handsome and supportive husband Robert loves to cook. His grandparents came from Italy and he grew up enjoying big Sunday dinners at his Aunt Susie and Uncle Billy's house. When he's in the kitchen, Robert never follows a recipe — but always has amazing results. He works backwards, deciding how a dish should taste and look, adjusting ingredients to suit his desired flavor and texture. Robert always says, "If you know where you want to end up, it's a lot easier to get there!"*

LEMON GLAZED PORK CHOPS

Tart lemon is offset with a bit of brown sugar and combined with Dijon mustard to form a coating for the pork chops. Delicious served with Broccoli with Curry-Mayonnaise Sauce *(page 206)*.

SERVES: 4

1/4 cup firmly packed brown sugar

3 teaspoons Dijon mustard

1/2 teaspoon lemon zest

1 tablespoon fresh lemon juice

4 (4- to 5-ounce) boneless pork loin chops (around 1/2-inch thick)

2 tablespoons olive oil 4 lemon slices

2 teaspoons cornstarch

In a small mixing bowl, stir together the brown sugar, mustard, lemon zest and juice. Brush half the mixture evenly on one side of the pork chops.

In a large skillet, heat olive oil over medium heat. Add chops, brushed side down and cook about 4 minutes. Turn over; brush second side with remaining lemon mixture and place 1 lemon slice on each chop. Cook 4 minutes or until an instant-read thermometer inserted into the thickest portion registers 145 to 150 degrees. Let sit for 10 minutes before serving.

PULLED PORK SANDWICHES

Another fabulous slow cooker recipe from my cousin Barb Keller, I especially like to use Ciabatta rolls for these sandwiches. Barb is a great cook and I always seem to leave her house with a new recipe! She recommends cooking this pork over two days. Delicious with our Coleslaw with Lemon-Mayonnaise Dressing (recipe at *www.seasonedkitchen.com*).

SERVES: 8 to 10

2 medium yellow onions, thinly sliced

4 pounds pork loin roast

1 1/2 cups water

1 cup chopped yellow onion (no need to add with our Oklahoma sauce as it has chopped onions in it)

32 ounces (4 cups) of Oklahoma BBQ Sauce *(page 128)* or other barbeque sauce

Hamburger buns or Ciabatta rolls

Place 1/2 of the sliced onions on the bottom of a slow cooker. Add pork, 1 1/2 cups water, then scatter remaining onions (if using) on the top. Cover and cook on low 8 to 10 hours or on high for 4 to 5 hours.

Remove pork and onions; drain slow cooker, reserving about 1/2 cup liquid. Shred the pork with two forks; place back in slow cooker with cooked onions. Stir in 2 cups barbeque sauce and reserved cooking liquid. Cover and cook on low for 4 to 6 hours. Taste and stir in more sauce, if desired. Serve on hamburger buns or Ciabatta rolls, passing remaining sauce on the side.

STIR-FRIED PORK AND ASPARAGUS

This super easy stir-fry is my kind of dish as it doesn't have a ton of chopping — my one complaint about a lot of Asian dishes is that there's a lot of stuff to chop. The oyster sauce, soy, ginger, garlic and onion combine to make a sweet, salty and earthy sauce that pairs well with the pork and asparagus. I like to serve it with brown jasmine rice, topped off with chopped cilantro and toasted cashews.

SERVES: 4

1/4 cup soy sauce (regular or low sodium)

2 tablespoons oyster sauce

2 teaspoons cornstarch

1 pound pork tenderloin, cut into 1/4-inch slices

1 bunch asparagus, tough ends removed

4 teaspoons olive oil, divided

2 tablespoons chopped fresh ginger

1 teaspoon chopped garlic

4 to 5 green onions, chopped

1/4 cup chicken broth (regular or fat-free)

1/4 cup chopped fresh cilantro (optional)

2 cups hot cooked rice (I like brown jasmine)

1/4 cup chopped toasted cashews

In a medium bowl, whisk together the soy sauce, oyster sauce and cornstarch; add pork slices, tossing to coat. Cover and marinate in the refrigerator for around 15 minutes.

Slice the asparagus on the diagonal into 1-inch pieces. In a large nonstick skillet or wok (stir-fry pan), heat 2 teaspoons of the olive oil over medium-high heat. Add asparagus and cook, stirring frequently until crisp-tender. Transfer to a bowl and set aside; don't clean out the skillet.

Reduce the heat to medium and add the ginger, garlic and green onion to drippings in skillet; sauté 1 minute. Add pork and its sauce and stir-fry for 3 to 4 minutes or until the pork is almost done. Add asparagus and chicken broth, reduce heat and simmer for 2 minutes or until thickened. Stir in cilantro. Serve over hot rice and top with chopped cashews.

Fish & Seafood

"In the hands of an able cook, fish can become an inexhaustible source of perpetual delight." — *Jean-Anthelme Brillat-Savarin, author of Physiologie du Goût (1848)*

I love the versatility of fish and seafood — a quick sauce or marinade and it's perfect for a busy weeknight meal. At the same time, its natural elegance allows the same dishes to be served at a dinner party.

FISH

148 | Halibut with Celery Root Pureé and Tomato Garnish

149 | Roasted Halibut with a Caper, Pine Nut and Tomato Sauce

150 | Lemon-Rosemary Swordfish en Papillote

152 | Sea Bass with a Pistachio Crust

154 | Grilled Citrus Salmon

155 | Salmon with Lemon-Lime Crumb Topping

156 | Mahi Mahi with Herb Mayonnaise

SHELLFISH

157 | Sally's Bouillabaisse

158 | Seafood Phyllo Bundles with Creole Mustard Sauce

160 | Scallops with Tomatoes and Pesto

161 | Grilled Shrimp with Tomatillo-Avocado Sauce

162 | Chipotle Lime Shrimp Tacos with Tomato Mango Salsa

164 | Uncle Bill's Shrimp de Jonghe

165 | Ham and Shrimp Jambalaya

HALIBUT WITH CELERY ROOT PURÉE AND TOMATO GARNISH

Adapted from a recipe that ran in Chef John Broening's column in The Denver Post, this dish *(photo, page 146)* is scrumptious, beautiful on the plate and impressive to serve. It's a very flexible recipe — Chef Broening cooks the fish on the stovetop; I cook it in the oven or on the grill. He uses dill, while I use tarragon. I think the secret is the celery root purée. Often people think it's mashed potatoes, and are always surprised at the unique and delicious flavor.

SERVES: 8

4 medium to large celery root bulbs, peeled and cubed

Fresh lemon juice

6 tablespoons unsalted butter, softened and sliced into tablespoons

1 cup crème fraîche

Salt, to taste

Freshly ground black pepper, to taste

Pinch sugar (optional)

2 pints cherry or grape tomatoes, stemmed and halved (or quartered if large)*

3 tablespoons chopped shallots

2 heaping tablespoons chopped fresh tarragon

1/4 cup extra virgin olive oil

4 teaspoons white wine vinegar

2 1/2 pounds fresh halibut, skin removed, cut into 8 pieces

1/4 cup lemon-flavored or extra virgin olive oil

Chef John stresses using vine-ripe tomatoes, preferably black tomatoes if you can find them

In a large saucepan, cover cubed celery root with water. Add squeeze of lemon juice and bring to a boil. Cover, reduce heat and simmer 25 to 30 minutes or until the celery root is very tender; drain. In a food processor, combine celery root and butter; process just until blended. Add the crème fraîche and process until the consistency of mashed potatoes. Season to taste with salt and pepper. Taste, and if it is a bit bitter, add a pinch of sugar. Return to saucepan and keep warm over low heat.

Preheat oven to 450 degrees. Spray a large shallow baking dish with nonstick cooking spray.

In a medium mixing bowl, toss together the tomatoes, tarragon, shallots, olive oil and vinegar. Set aside.

Brush both sides of the fish with the lemon-flavored olive oil. Season with salt and pepper. Spray a nonstick skillet with cooking spray and place over medium heat. When hot (but not smoking), place the halibut top side down in the pan and cook 3 minutes or until golden brown. Turn over and place in prepared baking dish in one layer. Roast in the oven, uncovered, 8 to 10 minutes per 1-inch of thickness (at it's thickest point), until opaque and just cooked through. Let stand 5 minutes. To serve, spoon celery root purée on each plate. Top with fish fillet and spoon the tomato mixture (and juices) over the top. Serve immediately.

MAKE AHEAD Celery root purée can be made up to 24 hours in advance, cooled, covered and refrigerated. Rewarm in a saucepan over low heat. Tomato garnish can be prepared up to 4 hours in advance, covered and kept at room temperature.

VARIATION Grill the fish instead of roasting it. Preheat grill on high. Place a grilling rack or oiled foil on the grill. Place fish on the rack and cook for 10 minutes per 1-inch of thickness, turning it over halfway through cooking time. Let stand for 5 minutes before serving.

ROASTED HALIBUT WITH A CAPER, PINE NUT AND TOMATO SAUCE

The sauce for this dish is both sweet and savory and it combines beautifully with the fish. While this recipe calls for roasting the halibut, you can also grill it, following the directions for Grilled Halibut on the opposite page. Serve with arugula salad and rice.

SERVES: 6

1/3 cup golden raisins

6 tablespoons extra virgin olive oil, divided

1 small onion, chopped

2 tablespoons pine nuts

2 tablespoons capers, drained

1/4 teaspoon dried oregano

1/8 teaspoon red pepper flakes

1 1/2 teaspoons chopped garlic or shallot

2 bay leaves

1 pound ripe tomatoes, seeded and chopped

Salt, to taste

Freshly ground black pepper, to taste

1 tablespoon white wine vinegar

1 teaspoon sugar

6 (4- to 5-ounce) halibut fillets

Preheat oven to 450 degrees. Spray a large shallow baking dish with nonstick cooking spray.

In a small bowl, cover raisins with warm water. Set aside to soak.

In a large skillet or sauté pan, heat 1/4 cup of the olive oil over medium-high heat. When hot, add the onion, pine nuts, capers, oregano and red pepper. Cook, stirring occasionally, for 5 minutes or until the onion is soft. Add the garlic or shallot and sauté for 30 seconds to 1 minute. Add the bay leaves and tomatoes; season to taste with salt and ground pepper and cook 3 to 4 minutes. Drain the raisins and stir into to tomato mixture. Stir in the vinegar and sugar; cook, stirring occasionally, for 5 minutes. Discard the bay leaves. Keep sauce warm on low heat.

Brush both sides of the fish with the remaining 2 tablespoons olive oil. Spray a nonstick skillet with cooking spray and place over medium heat. When hot (but not smoking), place the halibut, skin side up, in the pan and cook 3 minutes or until golden brown. Turn over and place in prepared baking dish in one layer. Roast in the oven, uncovered, 8 to 10 minutes per 1-inch of thickness (at it's thickest point) until moist, opaque and just cooked through. Remove from oven and let stand for around 5 minutes. Season to taste with salt and pepper and spoon sauce over the top.

MAKE AHEAD Sauce can be made earlier in the day, covered and kept at room temperature. Warm over low heat before serving.

LEMON-ROSEMARY SWORDFISH EN PAPILLOTE

En papillote simply means wrapped in parchment or foil. It is a great way to cook very moist fish. I created this light and flavorful dish one evening using specialty flavored olive oil and vinegar that I purchase from a local purveyor here in Denver. For those of you who don't have access to these types of specialty products, I created a modified version using non-flavored oil and vinegar. Directions for both are provided here — and both versions tested very well. You can also substitute halibut for the swordfish.

Note that the fish needs to marinate for 1 to 2 hours.

SERVES: 4

**MARINADE USING
NON-FLAVORED OLIVE OIL
AND VINEGAR**

Zest and juice from 1 lemon

1/2 cup extra virgin olive oil

1/4 cup white balsamic vinegar

2 tablespoons chopped fresh
  rosemary

1 teaspoon chopped garlic or
  1/2 teaspoon garlic powder or
  1 teaspoon chopped shallot

Dash sugar (optional)

**MARINADE USING FLAVORED
OLIVE OIL AND VINEGAR**

Zest from one lemon

1/2 cup rosemary olive oil

1/4 cup lemon balsamic vinegar

1 tablespoon chopped fresh rosemary

1 teaspoon chopped garlic or
  1/2 teaspoon garlic powder or
  1 teaspoon chopped shallot

SWORDFISH

4 (6- to 8-ounce) swordfish fillets

Kosher salt, to taste

Freshly ground black pepper, to taste

8 thin lemon slices

4 (4-inch) rosemary sprigs

In a shallow glass dish large enough to hold the fish in one layer, whisk together marinade ingredients. Add fish, cover and place in refrigerator for 1 up to 2 hours, turning occasionally.

Preheat oven to 425 degrees.

Tear off 4 pieces of foil or parchment paper, each about 16 to 18 inches or long enough to wrap around fish fillets. Brush foil (if using) with olive oil. Place 1 fish fillet in the center of each piece of foil/paper, drizzling with some of the marinade. Season with kosher salt and fresh ground pepper. Place 2 lemon slices on top of each fillet; top with 1 rosemary sprig. Fold up two opposite edges of the foil/paper and fold over to seal.

Place packets in one layer on a large baking sheet. Bake about 15 minutes (10 minutes per 1-inch of thickness, plus an additional 5 minutes). Remove from oven and open carefully as the steam will be hot. If you leave them in the packet they will continue cooking. Move fish to a serving platter or individual plates, drizzling some of the cooking liquid from inside the packets over the top.

NOTE You can put two fillets in one packet if desired.

SOURCE FOR FLAVORED OLIVE OILS AND VINEGARS
evoomarketplace.com

VARIATION Place prepared packets in foil on a preheated grill over medium heat and cook for around 10 to 15 minutes.

SEA BASS WITH A PISTACHIO CRUST

This dish comes together quickly and is delicious paired with green beans and roasted potatoes. It's a bit on the rich side, so I suggest using fillets no more than 5 ounces each. If using one large fillet, you may need to increase the cooking time by a few minutes.

While the general rule of thumb for cooking fish is 10 minutes per inch of thickness, I've included the option to cook these filets for 12 minutes per inch. I find that with the crust on top, it can take a bit longer. It's really to your taste — just remember, it will continue cooking after you take it out of the oven and let it rest.

SERVES: 6

6 (4- to 5-ounce) skinless Chilean sea bass fillets

1 cup salted, dry roasted pistachio nuts, very finely chopped (can chop in a food processor)

1/2 cup firmly packed brown sugar

3 tablespoons fresh lemon juice

1 tablespoon chopped fresh dill or 1 teaspoon dried dill

Freshly ground black pepper, to taste

Preheat oven to 400 degrees. Line a 15- by 10- by 1-inch baking pan with parchment paper.

Place sea bass fillets in prepared pan. In a small bowl, combine the nuts, sugar, lemon juice, dill and pepper. Spoon the mixture evenly over each fillet, pressing down to adhere.

Bake for 10 to 12 minutes per 1-inch of thickness of the fillet, or until fish reaches 140 to 145 degrees when measured with an instant-read thermometer. Let stand for 5 minutes before serving.

MAKE AHEAD Fish with topping can be prepared but not baked up to 4 hours in advance, covered and refrigerated.

GRILLED CITRUS SALMON

The fabulous home gourmet Cappy Shopneck gave me this scrumptious recipe that she once received from her friend Max. She describes Max as "a rancher, hunting guide and lover of good food." This salmon recipe is one of those timeless dishes — full of flavor with lemon, Dijon, garlic, cayenne pepper, capers, basil and dill. It's a flexible dish — you can grill or bake it *(see Variation below)*, and serve it hot or at room temperature, which is perfect for a buffet or family style meal. *(See menu on page 265 for a fun spring dinner party!)*

SERVES: 6 to 8

1 tablespoon butter

2 tablespoons olive oil

1 1/2 tablespoons fresh lemon juice

1 tablespoon Dijon mustard

2 teaspoons chopped garlic or shallot

1 teaspoon salt

1 teaspoon dried dill

3 tablespoons capers, drained

1 tablespoon fresh chopped basil or
   1 teaspoon dried basil

2 dashes cayenne pepper

3 pounds fresh salmon fillet (one
   large or individual pieces)

Prepare a medium-hot fire in a charcoal grill, or preheat a gas grill on high.

In a medium sauté pan, melt the butter over medium heat. Stir in the olive oil, lemon juice, mustard, garlic, salt, dill, capers, basil and cayenne pepper. Bring to a boil, reduce heat and simmer for 5 minutes.

Place salmon fillets on a large piece of heavy duty foil with the edges turned up to make a pan. Pour sauce evenly over fish. If using a gas grill, reduce all the burners to medium heat. Place fish packet on grill and close grill cover. Cook for 10 to 12 minutes or until flaky and light pink in the center. Serve with sauce spooned over the top. Can be served hot or at room temperature.

VARIATION Salmon and sauce can be wrapped in foil and baked at 350 degrees for 15 to 20 minutes.

SALMON WITH LEMON-LIME CRUMB TOPPING

One of our recipe testers said it best: "We love the way the breadcrumb mixture crisps up on top of the salmon and the lemon-lime flavor gives it a great zest". Serve with Sautéed Mushrooms over Roasted Asparagus (recipe at *www.seasonedkitchen.com*) and fingerling potoatoes.

SERVES: 6 to 8

1/2 cup chopped fresh Italian
(flat leaf) parsley

6 tablespoons grated Parmesan
cheese

1 tablespoon fresh thyme leaves

2 teaspoons chopped garlic or chives

2 teaspoons lemon zest

2 teaspoons lime zest

1 1/2 teaspoons salt

1 1/2 cups fresh bread crumbs

1/4 cup butter, melted or olive oil

1 (2 1/2 pound) salmon fillet, rinsed
and patted dry

Preheat oven to 350 degrees. Generously butter a shallow baking dish large enough to hold the salmon fillet.

In a food processor, combine parsley, cheese, thyme, garlic, zest and salt; process until well blended. Transfer to a medium bowl. Stir in breadcrumbs and melted butter, tossing until well blended.

Place salmon fillet in prepared pan and top with desired amount of breadcrumb mixture. Place any extra in a zip top bag and freeze for the next time. Bake fish for 20 to 30 minutes (about 10 minutes per 1-inch of thickness) or to desired doneness. Let sit for 5 minutes before serving.

MAKE AHEAD Crumb mixture can be made the day before but do not toss with butter. Cover and refrigerate. Toss with butter just prior to putting on fish.

MAHI MAHI WITH HERB MAYONNAISE

In this recipe, a mixture of mayonnaise, lemon juice and fresh herbs is slathered over fresh fish fillets that are then baked with a bit of white wine — I could eat this uncomplicated to prepare, moist and delish dish every night! You can use any firm white fish, and I like mahi mahi or swordfish the best. This is a good dish to make in the winter or on a rainy night when grilling can be difficult. Our recipe testers recommended serving this dish with Barley Pilaf *(page 219)* and roasted asparagus.

SERVES: 4

1 cup mayonnaise

2 tablespoons freshly squeezed lemon juice

1 teaspoon chopped garlic or chives

1 tablespoon chopped fresh basil

1 tablespoon fresh thyme

1 tablespoon chopped fresh tarragon

1 tablespoon chopped fresh dill

Salt, to taste

Freshly ground black pepper, to taste

4 (6-ounce) mahi mahi, swordfish, or marlin steaks or fillets

1/4 cup dry white wine

Dried tarragon, optional

Preheat oven to 400 degrees. Butter a baking dish large enough to hold the fish in one layer.

In a small bowl, combine the mayonnaise, lemon juice, garlic or chives, basil, thyme, tarragon and dill. Season to taste with salt and pepper. Spread about 1 tablespoon of the mayonnaise mixture on each side of the fish steaks and place in the prepared baking dish. Spoon remaining mayonnaise mixture into a serving bowl. Chill fish for at least 30 minutes.

Pour wine over the fish and bake, uncovered, 10 to 15 minutes, (or 10 minutes per 1-inch of thickness) until just cooked through). Let stand for 5 minutes before serving. Pass remaining herb mayonnaise sauce on the side.

MAKE AHEAD The herb mayonnaise can be made up to two days ahead, covered and stored in the refrigerator.

VARIATION For a prettier presentation, sprinkle dried tarragon on the top after baking the fish and run it under the broiler for a few minutes to brown the top.

SALLY'S BOUILLABAISSE

This dish is another winning creation of mom's *(photo, page 8)*, written into the margins of one of her favorite cookbooks. Mom's version is somewhat of a hybrid between bouillabaisse and cioppino. The former typically has a fish seafood-based sauce, the latter a tomato sauce. Mom's has both. Typical mom, she created a faster, easier way to make Bouillabaisse. Once you have your "mis en place" (ingredients prepped, measured and ready to go), you can have this dish on the table in less than 30 minutes. Make sure to serve with our Anise Bread *(page 224)* on the side to soak up the delicious sauce and our Arugula and Spinach Salad with Lemon Dijon Dressing *(page 83)*.

SERVES: 8

4 tablespoons butter

1 cup (1 large) chopped green bell pepper

1 cup (1/2 large) chopped onion

1 cup (about 3 large stalks) chopped celery

1 1/2 teaspoons chopped garlic

2 pounds sole or flounder fillet, cut into 1-inch pieces

1 3/4 cups chopped fresh tomatoes*

2 (15-ounce) cans tomato sauce

2 cups water 2 cups dry white wine

3/4 cup clam juice

1/2 teaspoon Worcestershire sauce

1/2 teaspoon Italian seasoning

1/2 teaspoon dried oregano

1 teaspoon cayenne pepper

1/4 teaspoon seasoned salt (such as Lawry's)

1 bay leaf

Pinch or two of saffron

1 pound fresh crabmeat, rinsed and drained

24 small hard-shelled clams, scrubbed, tossing any opened shells *(see Tip)*

24 PEI fresh mussels, scrubbed *(see Note)*

1 heaping tablespoon chopped fresh basil

When fresh tomatoes aren't in season, for more flavor substitute 1 (15-ounce) can, drained

In a large saucepan, melt the butter over medium heat. Add the bell pepper, onion, celery and garlic. Sauté 5 minutes or until pepper and onions begin to soften. Add the fish and sauté 5 minutes.

Stir in the tomatoes, tomato sauce, water, wine, clam juice, Worcestershire sauce, Italian seasoning, oregano, salt, bay leaf and saffron. Bring to a boil. Gently stir in crabmeat. Add clams and mussels, reduce heat to medium-low (a low boil, slightly above a simmer), cover and cook for 10 to 15 minutes or until shells open. Discard any shells that don't open. Stir in basil and serve immediately in shallow bowls.

NOTE PEI (Prince Edward Island) mussels are farm-raised and don't require much cleaning. Wild mussels may be muddy, with long "beards" — the tendrils that hold them on to rocks and piers. Scrub vigorously under cold water, tossing any with broken shells or that fail to close tightly.

TIP

On shellfish: Keep the clams and mussels on ice in the refrigerator until just before cooking. Make sure to check frequently and drain off any water from melting ice, as they will drown in fresh water. As you clean them, check to make sure the shells are all closed. If any are open, tap on the shell and it should close. If it doesn't close, throw it away. Also throw away any broken shells.

SEAFOOD PHYLLO BUNDLES WITH CREOLE MUSTARD SAUCE

In this dish, shrimp and crab are wrapped in a delicate phyllo pastry and topped with a tangy Creole sauce, resulting in an impressive entrée that is easy to prepare and perfect for a Mardi Gras celebration. I recommend purchasing the best quality lump crabmeat you can find.

SERVES: 4

SEAFOOD FILLING

8 sheets phyllo pastry, thawed

5 to 6 tablespoons butter, divided

1/2 cup finely chopped yellow onion

1/4 cup finely chopped green and/or red pepper

1/4 cup finely chopped celery

1/4 cup finely chopped green onion

1 teaspoon chopped garlic or chives

1/2 pound peeled and deveined shrimp, coarsely chopped

1/2 pound lump crabmeat, cleaned, rinsed and drained

4 ounces block cream cheese, at room temperature and cut into cubes

1 teaspoon Old Bay seafood seasoning

Salt, to taste

Freshly ground black pepper, to taste

Fresh lemon juice (optional)

CREOLE MUSTARD SAUCE

1/2 cup half and half or evaporated whole milk

1/3 cup Creole mustard*

2 teaspoons Dijon mustard

2 teaspoons Worcestershire sauce

1/8 to 1/4 teaspoon cayenne pepper, or more to taste

1/4 cup regular or lowfat sour cream, at room temperature

Substitute 1/4 cup coarse grain mustard if you can't find Creole

Preheat oven to 375 degrees. Line a large rimmed baking sheet with parchment paper.

Bring phyllo pastry to room temperature. In a large skillet, melt 1 tablespoon butter over medium heat. Stir in onion, pepper, celery, green onion, garlic or chives and shrimp. Cook, stirring occasionally, for 5 minutes or until shrimp is cooked and vegetables are soft. Reduce heat to low and stir in the crabmeat, cream cheese and seafood seasoning. Cook, stirring constantly, until cheese is melted and incorporated. Season to taste with salt and pepper. Add a bit of lemon juice, if desired. Set aside.

In a small saucepan, melt remaining butter. Place one sheet of phyllo on a large cutting board and brush with some of the melted butter. Cover remaining phyllo with a damp cloth to prevent drying out. Place a second phyllo sheet on top and brush with a bit more butter. Fold in half lengthwise to form a 8- by 13-inch rectangle; brush with butter.

Mound 1/4 of filling in a strip at narrow side of phyllo rectangle, leaving a 1-inch border on the sides. Fold over bottom edge of phyllo just to cover filling. Fold in edges on the long sides to cover filling and roll up. Place, seam side down, on prepared baking sheet. Repeat 3 more times to make a total of 4 bundles. Brush top and sides of each bundle with melted butter. Bake 30 to 35 minutes or until golden brown and heated through.

Prepare the Creole sauce while the seafood bundles are baking. In a small saucepan, whisk together milk, mustards, Worcestershire sauce and cayenne pepper. Cook over medium-low heat until hot. Remove from heat and whisk in sour cream. Season with salt, to taste.

Place each seafood bundle on a serving plate and top with a spoonful of Creole Sauce (or spoon sauce on the side). Leftover sauce is delicious on grilled chicken or crab cakes.

MAKE AHEAD Seafood bundles can be assembled but not baked earlier in the day, covered and refrigerated. Bring to room temperature before baking. Sauce can be made the day before, covered and refrigerated.

SCALLOPS WITH TOMATOES AND PESTO

When I lived in Amsterdam, across the street from my townhome was a fabulous Italian deli that sold the most delicious house-made pesto. Ever since returning home, I've grown basil in my garden pots and make my own pesto. I'm always experimenting with new uses, and one night decided to try it as a sauce with scallops, adding a few grape tomatoes for color and to round out the flavors. My husband Robert loves this dish! Scallops cook quickly, and since this recipe has virtually no prep involved (as long as you have pesto on hand), you can have dinner on the table in about 10 minutes. I like to serve this dish with our Lemon Rice (in *A Well-Seasoned Kitchen*®) and a tossed salad.

SERVES: 6

2 tablespoons extra virgin olive oil

1 1/2 pounds large sea scallops

1/3 cup prepared basil pesto (homemade is best)

16 grape tomatoes, cut in half

Freshly grated Parmesan cheese, to taste

Salt, to taste

Freshly ground black pepper, to taste

In a large skillet or stir fry pan, heat the olive oil over medium-high heat. Add the scallops and cook 3 to 4 minutes. Turn over and cook for an additional 1 to 2 minutes or opaque and cooked through. Remove from heat. Gently stir in pesto and tomatoes. Sprinkle with Parmesan cheese. Season to taste with salt and pepper.

VARIATION You can substitute 2 pounds of medium fresh shrimp (peeled and deveined) for the scallops.

A WELL-SEASONED INSPIRATION

UNCLE BILL *Bill, one of my mom's older brothers, —pictured here, right, with his older brother Dan — loved to cook. Always experimenting with something new, he once arrived at our house with everything to make homemade sausage, just for fun. While not in the kitchen, Uncle Bill worked for the company that supplied microwave ovens to the military and one day he sent mom one of the very first ones approved for home use. He truly inspired my love of experimenting with ingredients, gadgets and techniques!*

GRILLED SHRIMP WITH TOMATILLO-AVOCADO SAUCE

During the summers in Denver, we're fortunate to have access to freshly roasted jalapeño peppers from the farmer's markets, where they're roasted on site. I buy a bagful at the end of the summer and freeze them to have on hand year round. If you are able to do the same, then you can skip the roasting step below and make this dish in even less time. Serve with flour tortillas or rice and a Caesar Salad *(see dressing recipe on page 87)*.

SERVES: 4

1/4 cup plus 2 tablespoons freshly squeezed lime juice, divided

1/4 cup soy sauce

1/4 cup water

4 teaspoons minced garlic

4 teaspoons olive oil

1 1/2 pounds large shrimp (21 to 30 per pound), peeled and deveined (tail shells removed)

2 jalapeño peppers, seeded and halved (or purchased roasted)

6 tomatillos, husked, rinsed, dried and chopped

3/4 cup cubed avocado

1/2 teaspoon sugar

Salt, to taste

Freshly ground black pepper, to taste

Soak 8 (12-inch) long wooden skewers in water for at least 30 minutes.

In a small mixing bowl, stir together 1/4 cup lime juice, soy sauce, water, garlic and olive oil. Place in a large zip top bag. Add shrimp, seal bag and shake to coat shrimp. Marinate in refrigerator for at least 30 minutes or up to 2 hours.

On a foil-lined baking sheet, arrange raw jalapeño pepper halves, skin sides up. Broil, 5- to 6-inches from heating element, until skin is charred black. Remove from oven and place in a zip top bag until cooled. Peel and discard skin; coarsely chop *(see Tip on page 125)*.

In a food processor, combine roasted jalapeños, tomatillos, remaining 2 tablespoons lime juice, avocado and sugar. Season to taste with salt and pepper. Process until very smooth. Chill until ready to serve.

Preheat grill to high.

Remove shrimp from marinade and thread onto skewers. Oil grill rack and grill shrimp skewers, uncovered, for 2 to 4 minutes on each side or until cooked through. Do not overcook or shrimp will be tough and dry *(see Tip below)*. Remove shrimp from skewers and serve with tomatillo-avocado sauce.

TIP

Grilling shrimp: The best way to grill shrimp is on skewers, on an oiled grill rack. Put vegetable oil or olive oil in a small bowl. Soak an old dishcloth or paper towel in the oil, draining off excess oil. When the grill is hot, using grill tongs, run the oil-soaked cloth quickly over the grill surface to coat. Place skewered shrimp on the oiled surface to cook. When the shrimp no longer stick to the grill surface, they are ready to flip over.

CHIPOTLE LIME SHRIMP TACOS WITH TOMATO MANGO SALSA

I found a mango salsa recipe in mom's files after she passed away. Recognizing the handwriting on the recipe card as my cousin Beth Kidwell's, I knew it would be great. Beth is a real foodie, with a family full of gourmet cooks. In her salsa, Beth balances the sweetness of the of mango and tomato with lime juice, then adds in red onion, chile peppers, cilantro and spices. Looking for something to pair with this scrumptious and refreshing salsa, I created a grilled shrimp taco, marinating the shrimp in a chipotle-lime vinaigrette. I tested it on a few friends and it received rave reviews. You know people love it when they immediately ask for the recipe! This recipe can easily be doubled.

SERVES: 4

CHIPOTLE LIME SHRIMP

1/2 cup extra virgin olive oil

1/4 cup fresh lime juice

2 tablespoons chopped fresh cilantro

2 teaspoons puréed chipotle peppers in adobo sauce

1 teaspoon ground cumin

1/2 teaspoon chopped garlic or shallot

3/4 teaspoon sugar

1 1/2 pounds large (21 to 30 per pound) shrimp, peeled and deveined

TOMATO MANGO SALSA

2 small champagne mangos or 1 regular mango, peeled, seeded and finely chopped

2 medium ripe tomatoes, seeded and chopped

3 tablespoons chopped red onion

1 (2- to 3-inch) serrano or jalapeño pepper, seeded and chopped

1 bunch fresh cilantro, chopped

Dash ground nutmeg

Dash ground cinnamon

Salt, to taste

Freshly ground black pepper, to taste

1/4 lime

8 (5-inch) flour tortillas, warmed

Soak 15 (12-inch) long wooden skewers in water for at least 30 minutes.

To make the marinade for the shrimp: In the bowl of an electric blender, process the olive oil, lime juice, cilantro, chipotle peppers, cumin, garlic and sugar until well blended. Taste and adjust seasonings as needed. Set aside.

Thread about 6 shrimp on each skewer, piercing through the head and the tail of each shrimp so they form a "u" on the skewer. Place them in a large baking dish or rimmed baking sheet (you may need to turn them on their side to fit). Drizzle with the marinade; turn skewers, making sure each shrimp is coated. Set aside for 1 hour.

To make the salsa: In a medium mixing bowl, combine mangos, tomatoes, red onion, pepper, cilantro, nutmeg and cinnamon. Season to taste with salt and pepper. Squeeze the juice from the lime over the top; stir until well blended.

Preheat grill to high.

Oil grill rack and grill shrimp skewers, uncovered, for 3 minutes *(see Tip on page 161)*. When the shrimp no longer stick to the grill surface, flip over. Grill for an additional 2 to 4 minutes or until cooked through (watch carefully so they don't burn). Serve with warmed tortillas and the salsa.

MAKE AHEAD Marinade and salsa can be made up to 24 hours in advance, covered and refrigerated.

UNCLE BILL'S SHRIMP DE JONGHE

The dish "Shrimp de Jonghe" reportedly originated at the turn of the 20th century with Henri De Jonghe, a Belgian immigrant and owner of De Jonghe's Hotel and Restaurant in Chicago. Henri died in Tucson, Arizona in 1961 and supposedly took the secret recipe with him. Versions of it continue to be served at numerous top restaurants in the Chicago area and beyond. This version is my Uncle Bill's take on this dish, and it was one of his signatures. Bill was my mom's older brother and another fabulous home gourmet. He was always experimenting with new recipes, new ingredients and new kitchen gadgets.

SERVES: 6

1 cup unsalted butter

4 large garlic cloves, sliced

1 cup fresh or panko bread crumbs

2 pounds extra large (21 to 30 per pound) shrimp, peeled and deveined (tail shells removed)

1 tablespoon chopped fresh tarragon

1 tablespoon chopped fresh parsley

2 teaspoons fresh thyme leaves

2 tablespoons minced fresh onion

1 tablespoon plus 2 teaspoons kosher salt, divided

1/4 teaspoon fresh ground pepper

Dash nutmeg

Dash mace

1/2 cup chicken broth

8 ounces spaghettini or angel hair pasta

Preheat oven to 400 degrees. In a large pot, bring 4 quarts of water to boil.

In a large skillet, melt butter over medium heat. Add garlic and cook until just beginning to turn brown. Remove from heat. Place 2 tablespoons of garlic butter into a small mixing bowl; add breadcrumbs and mix together. Set aside.

Place the remaining butter-garlic mixture in a large mixing bowl and stir in the shrimp, tarragon, parsley, thyme, onion, 2 teaspoons salt, pepper, nutmeg, mace and chicken broth. Pour into a shallow ungreased baking dish and sprinkle breadcrumbs over the top.

Stir remaining 1 tablespoon salt into the boiling water. Drop in the pasta and cook according to package directions for 5 to 6 minutes or until al dente. Drain and set aside.

Place shrimp in oven and bake for 10 to 15 minutes or until the shrimp are pink and cooked through and the breadcrumbs are golden brown. If the shrimp are done but the breadcrumbs aren't brown, broil for 1 to 2 minutes (watch it carefully so it doesn't burn). Serve immediately.

MAKE AHEAD Shrimp can be assembled, covered and refrigerated up to 24 hours in advance. Bring to room temperature before baking.

HAM AND SHRIMP JAMBALAYA

Mom often used to write her recipe creations in the margins of cookbooks and that's where I found this one. Slightly different than most jambalaya recipes, her version calls for ham instead of sausage. I love how easy it is to prepare this dish, as well as its exceptional flavor. Starting with the traditional Cajun "trinity" of onions, celery and green pepper, mom added garlic and Old Bay seafood seasoning, white wine and Worcestershire sauce.

SERVES: 6

1/4 cup butter

2 large onions, chopped

2 large celery stalks, chopped

1 green bell pepper, cored, seeded and chopped

1/2 teaspoon chopped garlic

1 teaspoon Old Bay seafood or creole seasoning

2 cups chopped ham

1/2 cup dry white wine

3 1/2 cups chopped tomatoes*

1 (10-ounce) package frozen chopped okra (no need to thaw)

2 teaspoons bouquet garni seasoning**

1 teaspoon Worcestershire sauce

1/4 teaspoon Tabasco sauce, or more to taste

1 cup uncooked long grain white rice

3/4 pound medium (36 to 40 per pound) shrimp, peeled and deveined

*When fresh tomatoes aren't in season, for more flavor substitute 2 (14.5-ounce) cans, undrained

**Bouquet garni is available in the spice section of most grocery stores. You can substitute 1/2 teaspoon dried thyme, 1/4 teaspoon dried basil and 1/4 teaspoon paprika

In a large saucepan, melt the butter over medium heat. Add the onion, celery, bell pepper and garlic and sauté for 3 minutes. Sprinkle with seafood seasoning and continue cooking, stirring occasionally, 7 minutes or until the onions and peppers are soft. Stir in ham, wine, tomatoes, okra, bouquet garni, Worcestershire sauce and Tabasco sauce. Bring to a boil; stir in rice. Reduce heat and simmer, stirring frequently, for 20 minutes. Add the shrimp and continue cooking 5 minutes or until the rice is done and the shrimp are pink and cooked through. Serve hot.

MAKE AHEAD Jambalaya can be made earlier in the day up to the step of adding the shrimp. Cool, cover and refrigerate. Bring to a simmer before adding shrimp and finishing recipe.

Pasta

"If your mother cooks Italian food, why should you go to a restaurant?" — *Martin Scorsese, film producer and director*

Pasta…the ultimate in comfort food. My pasta recipes run the gamut from traditional to innovative, and vary in primary ingredients — some are vegetarian, others feature chicken or sausage. So, whether you are looking for a quick and satisfying lunch or a sophisticated and fun evening, we have you covered!

168 | Broccoli, Mushroom, Spinach and Cheese Pasta

169 | Zucchini Stuffed Shells

170 | Thai Peanut Shrimp over Linguine

172 | Seafood Tetrazzini

173 | Ravioli with Roasted Red Pepper Sauce

174 | Parmesan-Crusted Chicken with a Tomato Cream Sauce

176 | Angel Hair with Chicken and Artichoke-Caper Sauce

178 | Sausage, Pepper, Mushroom and Onion Fusilli

179 | Tex-Mex Chicken and Chorizo Lasagna

BROCCOLI, MUSHROOM, SPINACH AND CHEESE PASTA

This vegetarian pasta dish *(photo, page 166)* is very flexible. As indicated in the variation below, you can use a variety vegetables and cheeses to suit your taste. I love the combination of the broccoli, spinach, mushrooms, Parmesan and Fontina cheeses that are in the original recipe, but I also switch it from time to time for variety. Delicious with Anise Bread *(page 224)* and a tossed salad with avocados and tomatoes.

SERVES: 8

1 (12-ounce) package whole wheat ziti pasta

3/4 pound fresh broccoli florets

1 tablespoon unsalted butter, divided

8 ounces sliced mushrooms (button, cremini, shiitake or a mix)

2 shallots, peeled and chopped

3 cups fat free milk

1/4 cup all-purpose flour

Salt, to taste

Freshly ground black pepper, to taste

5 ounces baby spinach

1 cup (4 ounces) grated Fontina cheese

1/2 cup (2 ounces) freshly grated Parmesan cheese, divided

1/3 cup breadcrumbs

Preheat oven to 425 degrees. Butter a shallow 3-quart baking dish.

In a large stockpot, cook the ziti pasta according to package directions until almost tender but still al dente. While the pasta cooks, place broccoli in a steamer basket over boiling water. Cover and steam until crisp-tender. Drain pasta, return to pot and add the broccoli. Set aside.

In a large skillet or sauté pan, melt 2 teaspoons of the butter over medium heat. Add the mushrooms and shallots and cook 5 minutes or until tender.

In a medium mixing bowl, pour in the milk. Sift the flour over the top of the milk and whisk until well blended. Season with salt and pepper. Stir the flour mixture into the mushroom mixture and bring to a boil. Reduce heat and simmer, stirring, 5 minutes or until thickened. Stir in spinach. Remove from heat and stir in Fontina and 1/3 cup of Parmesan cheese. Add mushroom sauce to pasta mixture and toss until well blended. Place in prepared baking dish.

In a small skillet or saucepan, melt remaining 1 teaspoon of butter. Stir in breadcrumbs and remaining 2 tablespoons Parmesan cheese; sprinkle over top of pasta mixture. Bake 10 to 15 minutes or until bubbly and the top begins to brown.

MAKE AHEAD Casserole can be prepared but not baked up to three days ahead, covered and refrigerated. Cover with foil to bake and increase cooking time to 30 minutes, then uncover dish and cook for an additional 10 minutes or until beginning to brown.

VARIATION Use kale instead of the spinach, add garlic and chopped leeks instead of the mushrooms and Cheddar cheese instead of the Fontina cheese.

ZUCCHINI STUFFED SHELLS

At the end of the summer many of my friends give away bushels of zucchini from their gardens. I am always trying new ways to use it and came up with this recipe, which flavors the zucchini with onion, garlic, fresh herbs and three cheeses. It's then stuffed into pasta shells and baked with marinara sauce. It's very easy to prepare with ingredients you're likely to have on hand — especially after your friends share their zucchini! Serve with Italian Popovers *(page 227)* and Arugula and Spinach Salad with Lemon Dijon Dressing *(page 83)*.

SERVES: 4 to 6

12 jumbo macaroni shells

1 tablespoon extra virgin olive oil

1 1/2 cups finely chopped zucchini

1/3 cup finely chopped onion

2 teaspoons chopped garlic
   or shallots

Salt, to taste

Freshly ground black pepper, to taste

2 tablespoons chopped Italian parsley

4 teaspoons chopped fresh basil

1/2 teaspoon chopped fresh
   mint leaves

1 egg, beaten

1/2 cup ricotta cheese

1 cup (4 ounces) fresh mozzarella
   (packed in water), drained and
   chopped

1 cup (4 ounces) fresh grated
   Parmesan cheese, divided

2 cups marinara sauce

Preheat oven to 350 degrees. Spray or coat a 2-quart (8- by 8-inch) baking dish with olive oil.

Cook shells according to package directions; drain and set aside.

In a large nonstick sauté pan or skillet, heat the olive oil. Add the zucchini, onion and garlic (or shallots); cook 10 to 15 minutes or until softened and water is rendered out of zucchini. Stir in parsley, basil and mint. Season to taste with salt and pepper. Remove from heat and set aside.

In a large mixing bowl, whisk together the egg and ricotta. Stir in the mozzarella and 1/2 cup Parmesan cheese. Fold in the zucchini mixture. Season with salt and pepper to taste. Fill cooked shells with the zucchini mixture and arrange, filled side up, in prepared baking dish. Pour marinara sauce over the top. Sprinkle remaining 1/2 cup Parmesan cheese over the top. Bake, covered, 30 to 40 minutes or until hot and bubbly.

MAKE AHEAD Shells can be prepared but not baked earlier in the day, covered and refrigerated. Bring to room temperature before baking.

THAI PEANUT SHRIMP OVER LINGUINE

The peanut, sesame and ginger flavors in this recipe are wonderful with the shrimp. This dish can be a bit salty, so if you are sensitive to salt, I suggest you use low sodium soy sauce and chicken broth. The coconut milk rounds out the flavor, but I have listed it as "optional" since you only need a few tablespoons, and if you don't regularly use coconut milk, you may not want to buy some just for this recipe.

SERVES: 6

16 ounces linguine

4 tablespoons dark or toasted sesame oil, divided

1 1/2 pounds large shrimp, peeled and deveined (remove tail shells)

2/3 cup chopped green onion (white, light green and some dark green part)

1 heaping tablespoon chopped fresh ginger

2 to 3 teaspoons chopped garlic

1/2 cup regular or low sodium soy sauce

1/2 cup regular or low sodium chicken broth

1/2 cup creamy peanut butter

2 tablespoons honey

1 tablespoon lime juice

1 1/2 teaspoons cornstarch

1/4 to 1/2 teaspoon crushed red pepper, or to taste

3 tablespoons light coconut milk (optional)

Salt, to taste

Freshly ground black pepper, to taste

In a large pot, cook pasta according to package directions until tender but still slightly firm. Rinse, drain and transfer to a large serving bowl; add 3 tablespoons sesame oil and toss to coat.

In a large pot, cook shrimp in boiling water 5 minutes or until they turn pink. Drain and pat dry; add to pasta and toss. Set aside.

In a large skillet or sauté pan, heat remaining 1 tablespoon sesame oil over medium heat. Add green onion, ginger and garlic and sauté 3 to 5 minutes or until onions are soft.

Whisk in soy sauce, chicken broth, peanut butter, honey, lime juice, cornstarch and red pepper. Cook, stirring constantly, 2 to 3 minutes or until thickened. Stir in coconut milk, if desired, and season to taste with salt and pepper. Add sauce to linguine and shrimp mixture, tossing well, and serve immediately.

SEAFOOD TETRAZZINI

This recipe came from Dorothy Hartwell's recipe box, my childhood best friend Katey Hartwell's mom. Dorothy was a great cook; she just had a different style than my mom. She loved lobster and her original version of this recipe called for lobster meat. Since cooked lobster meat isn't consistently available in Colorado and I don't always have the time to cook and shell a lobster, I tend to make this dish with crabmeat. Both are equally delicious — you can also use a mixture of the two. Serve with Spinach Salad with Curry Dressing *(page 82)* and Blueberry Peach Custard Pie *(page 232)*.

SERVES: 6 to 8

2 chicken bouillon cubes

4 cups boiling water

8 ounces thin spaghetti or spaghettini

2 tablespoons butter

2 tablespoons all-purpose flour

1/2 teaspoon salt

1/2 teaspoon freshly ground black pepper

1/4 teaspoon cayenne pepper

1 cup milk

1 cup sour cream

1 cup cottage cheese

8 ounces sliced fresh mushrooms

1/4 cup chopped fresh parsley

2 tablespoons grated onion

2 cups cooked lump crabmeat or lobster meat (or a mixture), rinsed and drained

Salt, to taste

Freshly ground black pepper, to taste

1/2 cup panko breadcrumbs

1/2 cup (4 ounces) shredded mild Cheddar cheese

1/2 cup (4 ounces) shredded Gruyère cheese

Preheat oven to 350 degrees. Lightly grease or spray a 13- by 9-inch baking dish with olive oil spray.

In a large pot, bring water to a boil. Add bouillon cubes, stirring occasionally until dissolved. Add pasta; cook 5 to 6 minutes or until al dente. Drain, rinse, drain again and set aside.

In a large skillet or sauté pan, melt butter over low heat. Whisk in flour, salt, pepper and cayenne and cook for 3 minutes over low heat. Whisk in milk and cook over medium heat, stirring until it begins to thicken.

Remove from heat and stir in sour cream, cottage cheese, mushrooms, parsley and onion. Fold in crab or lobster meat. Season to taste with salt and pepper. Stir in cooked pasta and spoon into the prepared baking dish.

In a small mixing bowl, stir together the breadcrumbs and grated cheeses; sprinkle over the top. Bake 35 to 45 minutes or until bubbly and golden brown.

MAKE AHEAD Tetrazzini can be prepared but not baked up to 24 hours in advance, covered and refrigerated. Bring to room temperature before baking.

RAVIOLI WITH ROASTED RED PEPPER SAUCE

Virtually any type of pasta would be complemented by the vibrant, flavorful sauce in this dish. I love roasted red peppers but don't always have time to roast them myself. This recipe is fabulous with pre-roasted and jarred peppers and I think the brine on the peppers adds more depth to the flavor of this sauce. The sun-dried tomatoes add another layer of flavor, accented by fresh basil, garlic and red wine vinegar. Delicious with Sautéed Mushrooms with Roasted Asparagus (recipe at *www.seasonedkitchen.com*) and garlic bread.

SERVES: 4 to 6

24 ounces prepared ravioli (cheese, or chicken and cheese works well)

1 tablespoon olive oil

1 cup oil-packed sun-dried tomatoes, drained and chopped

1 (7- or 7.25-ounce) jar roasted red peppers, drained, chopped

1 cup cream, half and half or heavy whipping cream

2 tablespoons chopped fresh basil leaves

2 teaspoons chopped garlic

1/4 teaspoon dried red pepper flakes, or more to taste

2 teaspoons red wine vinegar

Freshly grated Parmesan cheese

In a large pot, cook ravioli al dente according to package directions. Drain, reserving 1/2 cup pasta water.

In a medium saucepan, heat oil over medium heat. Add sun-dried tomatoes, red peppers, cream, basil, garlic and red pepper flakes. Bring to a boil, reduce heat and simmer for 4 to 5 minutes. Stir in red wine vinegar. Remove from heat and purée with an immersion blender or cool slightly and transfer to a blender and purée. Stir in reserved pasta water.

Divide ravioli between individual serving bowls. Top evenly with sauce and sprinkle with Parmesan cheese. Serve immediately.

MAKE AHEAD Sauce can be made up to 24 hours in advance, cooled, covered and refrigerated. Rewarm over medium-low heat before serving.

PARMESAN-CRUSTED CHICKEN
WITH A TOMATO CREAM SAUCE

Years ago, a restaurant in Denver — Sfuzzi's — served a chicken and pasta dish with a tomato sauce that was divine. After it closed I set out to create my own version. Although it took several tries to get the flavor of the sauce just right — even my husband Robert, the king of the red pasta sauce (in our house) thinks it's scrumptious! This dish is especially pretty if you use green (spinach) linguine.

SERVES: 6

TOMATO CREAM SAUCE

1/4 cup butter

1 1/2 cups (around 2 to 3) diced carrot

1/2 cup chopped yellow onion

1 large celery stalk, chopped

2 teaspoons chopped garlic

2 pounds chopped fresh Italian or plum tomatoes*

3 tablespoons chopped fresh basil

2 tablespoon chopped fresh parsley

1 1/2 teaspoons dried oregano

1/2 teaspoon dried red pepper flakes (optional)

1/2 teaspoon sugar (optional)

1/2 to 1 cup heavy cream or half and half

Kosher salt, to taste

Freshly ground black pepper, to taste

When fresh tomatoes aren't in season, for more flavor substitute 1 (28-ounce) can whole or chopped Italian tomatoes, undrained

PARMESAN-CRUSTED CHICKEN

1 cup dry or panko breadcrumbs

1 cup (4 ounces) freshly grated Parmesan cheese, divided

1 heaping teaspoon Italian seasoning

To make the sauce: In a large sauté or saucepan, melt butter over medium heat. Add chopped carrot, onion, celery and garlic and sauté 10 minutes or until soft. Add tomatoes, basil, parsley, oregano and red pepper flakes, if desired. Add sugar (it may not be necessary, depending on sweetness of tomatoes). Bring to a boil, reduce heat and simmer, stirring occasionally, for about 15 minutes or until vegetables are tender. Start preparing chicken while sauce simmers.

To make the chicken: In a small, shallow bowl combine breadcrumbs, 1/2 cup Parmesan cheese, Italian seasoning, garlic powder and pepper. In another shallow bowl, whisk together egg and buttermilk. Pound the chicken breasts to an even thickness. Butterfly larger pieces and cut in half *(see Tip on page 104).* Season with salt and ground pepper. Set aside the breading bowls and the chicken breasts.

The sauce should be done simmering by now. Remove from the heat and set aside to cool.

Preheat oven to 375 degrees. Coat a baking sheet with olive oil spray or line with parchment paper.

Back to the chicken: Dip each chicken breast into the egg mixture and then dredge in the breadcrumb mixture, coating both sides well. Place on prepared baking sheet and refrigerate about 15 minutes to allow the coating to set.

Place the cooled sauce in a blender or food processor and purée until there are no large chunks of vegetables or herbs. Return to its original saucepan and stir in 1/2 cup cream; season to taste with kosher salt and fresh ground pepper. Add more cream as needed to taste (depends on how creamy you want the sauce). Set aside.

Bake chicken for 25 to 30 minutes or until golden brown and cooked through (if not brown on top, run under the broiler for a few minutes). While the chicken bakes, cook linguine according to package directions. Drain; toss with olive oil and keep warm.

1/4 teaspoon garlic powder

1/4 teaspoon freshly ground black pepper

1 large egg

2 tablespoons buttermilk

4 boneless, skinless chicken breast halves

Salt, to taste

1 (12-ounce) package wheat or spinach linguine

1 tablespoon extra virgin olive oil

Around 5 minutes before the chicken is done, bring the sauce to a simmer over medium heat. Place a single serving of linguine on each dinner plate (or one large platter). Cut each chicken breast into diagonal slices and arrange on top of the linguine. Spoon sauce across middle of chicken and onto pasta on either side. Sprinkle top with remaining 1/2 cup grated Parmesan cheese.

MAKE AHEAD Sauce and breaded chicken can be prepared earlier in the day, covered separately and refrigerated. Rewarm sauce over medium heat. Bring chicken to room temperature before baking.

ANGEL HAIR WITH CHICKEN AND ARTICHOKE-CAPER SAUCE

Warning: This light and healthy pasta is heavy on the garlic! You can leave it out, but personally I love garlic and the extra dimension it adds to this dish. I recommend not using a nonstick pan, as the browned bits that stick to the bottom during cooking add flavor to the sauce. In this recipe you'll do something called "deglazing" the pan, which naturally removes those bits, making clean up easier — so no need for that nonstick surface. I like to serve this with Avocado Mushroom Salad with Chutney Dressing *(page 78)*.

SERVES: 6 to 8

6 to 8 ounces angel hair pasta, preferably whole wheat

1/4 cup all-purpose flour

1/2 teaspoon dried oregano

1/2 teaspoon paprika

1/2 teaspoon dried parsley

Salt, to taste

Freshly ground black pepper, to taste

1 pound boneless, skinless chicken breasts, cut into 2- by 1/2-inch strips

2 to 3 tablespoons olive oil

2 garlic cloves, cut into quarters

3 tablespoons white wine

2 cups chicken broth

1 (14-ounce) canned artichoke hearts in water, drained and quartered

1/4 cup capers, drained

1 tablespoon butter

1/4 cup (1 ounce) freshly grated Parmesan cheese (optional)

Garnish: chopped fresh parsley

In a large pot, bring salted water to boil for the pasta *(see Tip, page 178)*.

Place flour in a shallow dish and whisk in oregano, paprika and parsley; season liberally with salt and pepper. Dredge chicken in flour mixture, coating both sides and shaking off excess.

In a large skillet, heat 2 tablespoons of olive oil over medium-low heat. Add garlic and cook just until garlic begins to turn a light brown. Using a slotted spoon, remove garlic from oil and set aside. Increase heat to medium-high, add chicken to oil in pan and cook 6 to 8 minutes, or until golden brown on both sides, adding additional olive oil if needed. Remove chicken from pan, place on plate and keep warm (don't clean out the pan).

Add the wine to the pan, reduce heat to medium-low (wine should be at a simmer), scraping up any browned bits from the bottom of the pan. Add the chicken broth and bring to a boil; reduce to a simmer and cook 7 to 10 minutes or until reduced by half.

Place pasta in boiling salted water and cook 3 to 4 minutes, according to package directions. Drain and set aside (don't rinse).

Chop cooked garlic slivers; stir into the wine-broth mixture. Stir in artichokes and capers. Cook for 1 to 2 minutes, or until thoroughly heated. Stir in chicken and any juices that may have accumulated on the plate. Bring to a low boil, remove from heat and stir in butter. If pasta isn't done yet, keep sauce warm over very low heat. Spoon chicken and sauce over pasta; sprinkle with freshly grated Parmesan cheese and garnish with chopped parsley, if desired.

SAUSAGE, PEPPER, MUSHROOM AND ONION FUSILLI

Most of Robert's recipes are Italian inspired, which I attribute to the fact that his mother was Italian. While his mom wasn't the greatest cook, his Aunt Susie and Uncle Billy hosted large family dinners at their house on Sundays. Robert picked up some of Aunt Susie's Italian cooking style and techniques, and today one of his favorite dishes to prepare is sausage with peppers, onions and mushrooms. This is his recipe — and I love it as much as he does.

SERVES: 4 to 6

2 tablespoons extra virgin olive oil, divided

5 to 6 Italian sausages, mild or hot (or a mixture)

1/2 large yellow onion, chopped

1/2 large green pepper, seeded and chopped

8 ounces sliced mushrooms

1 teaspoon Italian seasoning

1/2 teaspoon chopped garlic

12 ounces fusilli (corkscrew) pasta

Salt, to taste

Freshly ground black pepper, to taste

Freshly grated Parmesan cheese, to taste

In a large skillet or sauté pan, heat 1 tablespoon olive oil over medium heat. Add sausage and brown on all sides. Transfer to a plate; cool slightly and slice. Set aside.

In the same skillet, heat remaining 1 tablespoon olive oil. Add onion, green pepper, mushrooms, Italian seasoning and garlic. Cook until vegetables are soft and onions are lightly brown. Add sliced sausage to pan. Reduce heat to low and simmer while pasta cooks.

In a large pot, cook the fusilli al dente according to package directions *(see Tip below)*. Drain the pasta and place on a serving platter or divide between individual serving plates. Season the sausage mixture with salt and pepper to taste and place on top of the cooked pasta. Serve with Parmesan cheese on the side.

MAKE AHEAD Sausage, onions, peppers and mushrooms can be cooked up to 2 days ahead, covered and refrigerated. Reheat over medium heat.

TIP

On cooking pasta: One of the keys to good, flavorful pasta is putting enough salt in the cooking water. It seasons the pasta from the inside out as it cooks. So don't skimp on the salt — add 1 to 2 tablespoons of kosher salt to a large pot of boiling water when cooking your pasta. To prevent sticking, always stir your pasta once or twice during the first few minutes of cooking. Never add oil — that just makes the sauce slip off the noodles!

TEX-MEX CHICKEN AND CHORIZO LASAGNA

This lasagna is very hearty with lots of flavorful ingredients. My recipe calls for Mexican chorizo, not Spanish. Mexican chorizo is an uncooked, ground meat sausage (similar in form to Italian sausage), whereas Spanish chorizo is cured, ready to eat and in link form (similar to salami). Delicious served with a Caesar Salad *(dressing recipe, page 87)*.

SERVES: 8 to 10

2 cups chopped tomatoes*

1/4 cup butter

1/4 cup all-purpose flour

2 cups chicken broth

1 cup half and half

1/8 teaspoon ground nutmeg

Salt, to taste

Freshly ground black pepper, to taste

8 ounces bulk chorizo sausage

8 ounces lean ground beef

1 cup chopped green pepper

1 cup chopped onion

1 tablespoon chopped garlic

3 cups sliced mushrooms

A few dashes hot sauce

A few dashes Worcestershire sauce

1 cup sliced black olives

12 no-boil lasagna noodles

2 cups shredded or chopped
   cooked chicken

3 cups (12 ounces) shredded sharp
   Cheddar cheese

1/2 cup (2 ounces) grated
   Parmesan cheese

When fresh tomatoes aren't in season, for more flavor substitute 2 cups canned diced tomatoes, drained

In a nonstick saucepan, cook tomatoes over medium-low heat, stirring occasionally, for around 30 minutes or until they are reduced to 1 1/2 cups.

In a large saucepan, melt the butter over low heat. Whisk in the flour and cook, whisking for 3 minutes. Slowly whisk in the chicken broth. Bring to a simmer and cook, stirring, 10 minutes or until thickened. Stir in cream, nutmeg and cooked tomatoes. Season to taste with salt and pepper. Set aside.

Preheat oven to 375 degrees. Butter a large 13- by 9-inch baking dish.

In a large nonstick skillet, cook chorizo and ground beef over medium-high heat until the meat is no longer pink, stirring and breaking up meat into small pieces. Drain off any excess grease. Stir in green pepper, onion, garlic and mushrooms and cook until the vegetables are soft. Stir in tomato mixture, hot sauce, Worcestershire sauce and olives. Season to taste with salt and pepper.

Place 4 lasagna noodles on the bottom of the prepared baking dish. Sprinkle 1/2 of the shredded chicken evenly over noodles. Top chicken with 1/3 of the meat-tomato mixture. Cover with 1/3 of the Cheddar cheese. Repeat one more time (lasagna noodles, chicken, meat-tomato mixture, Cheddar). Top with remaining 4 lasagna noodles, remaining meat-tomato mixture and remaining Cheddar cheese. Sprinkle top with Parmesan cheese. Bake for 30 to 40 minutes or until hot, bubbly, and golden brown. Let stand for 10 minutes (up to 30 minutes) before serving.

MAKE AHEAD Lasagna can be prepared up to 24 hours in advance, without the Parmesan cheese and without baking. Cover and refrigerate. Bring to room temperature, sprinkle with Parmesan cheese and bake.

Mediterranean Quinoa Stuffed Sweet Peppers | 186

Vegetarian Main Dishes

"You can't taste the beauty and energy of the earth in a Twinkie."
— *Astrid Alauda, humorist*

Not long ago, a meal wasn't considered complete without chicken, fish or meat. Today, thanks to inspiration from sources around the globe, fresh vegetables are playing the starring role in many a main course. With our recipes, the carnivores in your house won't even know what's missing!

182 | Green Chiles Stuffed with Goat Cheese

183 | Stuffed Eggplant

184 | Roasted Root Vegetable Pot Pie

186 | Mediterranean Quinoa Stuffed Sweet Peppers

188 | Individual Fontina Cheese and Broccoli Soufflés

190 | Tempura Vegetable Fondue

192 | Peruvian Artichoke Tart

194 | Vegetable Curry

196 | Roasted Butternut Squash Risotto

GREEN CHILES STUFFED WITH GOAT CHEESE

My Aunt Bobbie grew up in Tucson, Arizona and loves Mexican food. She is particularly partial to chile rellenos — delicious little bundles of roasted green chiles stuffed with cheese, battered and deep-fried. This recipe came from Bobbie's recipe box and it combines the main ingredients of chile rellenos — lots of cheese and green chiles — into a dish that is baked instead of fried. It's delicious with fresh-roasted green chiles if you want to roast your own or have access to purchasing them. *(See our Mexican Fiesta Dinner menu on page 266!)*

SERVES: 8 to 10

1 (8-ounce) Neufchatel (low fat) cream cheese

4 ounces goat cheese, crumbled

9 large eggs, divided

2 tablespoons chopped fresh sage

1 clove garlic, chopped

3 tablespoons chopped green onion, white, light green and some dark green part

About 15 large roasted whole green chiles *(see Tip, page 38)**

1/2 cup all-purpose flour

1/4 teaspoon salt

1/4 cup (1 ounce) freshly grated Parmesan cheese

Prepared salsa

Can substitute 1 (27-ounce) can whole green chiles, drained

Preheat oven to 375 degrees. Butter a 3-quart shallow baking dish.

In a food processor or blender, combine the Neufchatel cheese, goat cheese, 1 egg, sage, garlic and green onion and process until well blended.

Slit the chiles, removing seeds for a less spicy dish, if desired, and pat dry. Place half of the chiles on the bottom of the prepared pan. Cover with cheese mixture. Top with remaining chiles.

In a food processor or blender, combine remaining 8 eggs, milk, flour, salt and Parmesan cheese and process until smooth. Pour evenly over chiles. Bake 45 to 55 minutes or until lightly browned and a toothpick inserted in the center (not in the cheese) comes out clean. It should feel solid when touched in the center. Let stand about 5 minutes. It will settle slightly on sitting. Serve with salsa on the side.

MAKE AHEAD Chiles can be stuffed with the cheese mixture but not covered with the custard, covered and refrigerated up to 24 hours ahead. Bring to room temperature before continuing with recipe.

STUFFED EGGPLANT

One evening I had an eggplant and some other veggies in the refrigerator that needed to be used and came up with this scrumptious recipe. Meaty eggplant is sautéed with garlic, onion, green pepper and mushrooms and then combined together with a creamy sauce of basil, parsley and Romano cheese. The vegetable mixture is then placed into eggplant shells and topped with chopped tomatoes and cheese for baking. A dash of cayenne adds some spice. For a non-vegetarian option, add 1 pound cooked ground turkey or turkey sausage. Serve it with a light side dish like angel hair pasta tossed with a garlic-white wine sauce.

SERVES: 4

1 large eggplant

2 tablespoons extra virgin olive oil

1 1/2 cups chopped yellow onion

1 large green pepper, seeded and chopped

8 ounces fresh mushrooms (white, cremini or shiitake), chopped

1 1/2 teaspoons chopped garlic

Salt, to taste

Freshly ground black pepper, to taste

2 tablespoons butter

2 tablespoons all-purpose flour

1 cup milk (whole or skim)

1/4 teaspoon cayenne pepper

1/8 teaspoon ground nutmeg

1 1/4 cups (5 ounces) freshly grated Romano cheese, divided

1/4 cup chopped fresh Italian parsley

1/2 cup chopped fresh basil

1 large tomato, seeded and chopped

Preheat oven to 350 degrees. Grease a baking dish large enough to hold the eggplant when cut in half lengthwise.

Cut eggplant in half lengthwise; remove pulp, leaving a 1/4-inch thick shell. Set the shells aside; chop the pulp in to small pieces. In a large sauté pan or skillet, heat the olive oil over medium heat. Add the chopped eggplant, onion, green pepper, mushrooms and garlic; cook, stirring occasionally, 3 to 4 minutes or until the mixture begins to soften. Cover and cook on low heat for 15 minutes, stirring occasionally. Season to taste with salt and pepper.

While the vegetables are cooking: In a small saucepan, melt the butter over low heat. Whisk in the flour and cook, whisking constantly, for 3 minutes. Whisk in the milk until smooth and well blended. Bring the mixture to a slow boil, stirring constantly, until thickened. Whisk in the cayenne pepper, nutmeg and 3/4 cup of the cheese.

Stir 1/2 cup of the sauce into the vegetable mixture. Add additional sauce as needed. You may not need much more; it depends on the size of the eggplant. Stir in 1/4 cup of the cheese, parsley and basil. Season to taste with salt and pepper (needs a fair amount of salt). Season the eggplant shells with salt and pepper. Fill shells with the vegetable mixture and place in prepared baking dish. Sprinkle with chopped tomato and remaining 1/4 cup cheese. Bake, uncovered, for 45 to 50 minutes or until bubbly hot and cheese is golden brown. Cut each eggplant shell in half crosswise and serve.

MAKE AHEAD Eggplant can be stuffed but not baked earlier in the day, covered and refrigerated. Bring to room temperature before baking.

ROASTED ROOT VEGETABLE POT PIE

As a fan of all root vegetables, I love to make this dish on a cold winter night. When prepared properly, root vegetables are delicious — and good for you too! In this recipe, roasting enhances the sweetness of the carrots, turnips and celery root. The caramelized root vegetables are then blended with a tangy Parmesan cheese sauce spiked with fresh herbs, and topped off with a layer of puff pastry. Beautiful to look at and satisfying to eat — what more could you ask for? Well, maybe a piece of our Sticky Ginger Cake *(page 248)* with whipped cream, to finish off the meal.

SERVES: 8

1/2 cup unsalted butter, divided

2 medium shallots, halved

2 teaspoons sugar

2 large carrots, peeled and cut into 1/2-inch square pieces

1 turnip, peeled and cut into 1/2-inch square pieces *(see Tip)*

1 celery root, peeled and cut into 1/2-inch square pieces

Olive oil cooking spray

1/3 cup all-purpose flour

2 1/2 cups milk (whole, 2 percent or skim)

2/3 to 1 cup (3 to 4 ounces) grated Parmesan cheese

2 teaspoons fresh thyme leaves

1/3 cup chopped fresh Italian parsley

Salt, to taste

Freshly ground black pepper, to taste

1 large egg, lightly beaten

1 sheet frozen puff pastry, thawed

TIP

On buying turnips: Turnips are best when young, when their flavor is sweetest. Older turnips can actually be tough and bitter. So, smaller is better. They should be firm, blemish-free, creamy colored with purple rings around the top. If the greens are attached, they should look fresh.

Preheat oven to 400 degrees.

In a large skillet, melt 1/4 cup butter over medium-low heat. Add shallots, cover and cook, stirring occasionally for 15 to 20 minutes or until tender. Increase heat to medium; add sugar and continue cooking, stirring, for 6 to 8 minutes or until caramel-colored. Watch carefully so they don't burn. Place in a large deep-dish pie pan. Set aside.

While the shallots are cooking, place the carrots, turnip and celery root in a shallow roasting pan and spray with olive oil; toss. Roast, stirring occasionally, for 30 to 35 minutes or until tender when pierced with a fork. Add to the pie dish with the shallots.

In a medium saucepan, melt the remaining 4 tablespoons butter over low heat. Whisk in flour and continue cooking for 3 minutes. Gradually whisk in milk. Bring to a slow boil over medium heat, stirring constantly; cook for 6 to 8 minutes or until thickened. Add Parmesan cheese, stirring until melted. Stir in thyme and parsley; season to taste with salt and pepper. Pour into the pie dish and stir well.

Brush the edges of the pie dish with beaten egg. Cover with the pastry, trimming excess (using scraps to decorate the top, if desired). Push down on the edges to adhere to the pan. Brush top of pastry with egg and cut a slit or two in the center to allow steam to escape. Place on a baking sheet and bake for 25 to 30 minutes or until pastry is golden brown. Cover edges if they start to burn. Remove from oven and cool 5 minutes before serving.

MAKE AHEAD Pot pie can be assembled (but not baked) earlier in the day, covered and refrigerated. Bring to room temperature before baking.

VARIATION Add 1 to 1 1/4 cups chopped ham (preferably country ham). Stir in with the thyme and parsley.

MEDITERRANEAN QUINOA STUFFED SWEET PEPPERS

This delicious, full-of-flavor recipe *(photo, page 180)* comes from my cousin Beth's daughter Becca Kidwell. The Kidwells are all foodies — and fabulous cooks. Becca is a professionally trained chef who ran her own catering company for several years before starting an organic edible gardening business with her sister Sarah, called *myfarmyard.com*. In addition to assisting homeowners with the design, installation and maintenance of their home vegetable gardens, Becca and Sarah run their own CSA (Community Supported Agriculture). When I was looking for a new and unique vegetarian entrée recipe, I knew Becca would have the perfect dish. Even your meat-eating friends will be pleased with this recipe, featuring sweet bell peppers stuffed with rosemary and garlic-infused quinoa, onions, tomatoes, Serrano peppers, garbanzo beans, fresh cheeses and herbs. For a pretty presentation, I like to use orange or red bell peppers, adding a "pop" of color on the plate.

| SERVES: 6 |

1/2 cup quinoa

1 teaspoon minced fresh rosemary

1/2 teaspoon garlic powder

1 cup vegetable stock

4 large sweet orange or red bell peppers, halved, seeded and divided

Salt, to taste

Freshly ground black pepper, to taste

3 tablespoons extra virgin olive oil, plus more for drizzling

1/2 sweet yellow onion, diced small

3 cloves garlic, chopped finely

2/3 pint multi-colored cherry tomatoes, quartered

2 tablespoons diced fresh Serrano chile pepper, or to taste

1 (15-ounce) can chickpeas or garbanzo beans, drained and rinsed

1 cup (4 ounces) cubed fresh mozzarella

Preheat oven to 375 degrees.

In a small saucepan, combine quinoa, rosemary, garlic powder and vegetable stock and bring to a boil. Cover, reduce heat to low and simmer until all liquid evaporates and grain is soft. Set aside to cool.

Place 6 bell pepper halves in a 13- by 9-inch baking dish. With a sharp knife, pierce the bottom of the peppers a couple of times and drizzle with extra virgin olive oil and season liberally with salt and fresh black pepper. Set aside.

Slice the remaining 2 bell pepper halves into thin strips; quarter pieces and transfer to a large mixing bowl. Stir in the onion, chopped garlic, tomatoes, chile pepper, garbanzo beans and mozzarella. Stir in 1/2 cup of the Parmesan cheese, lemon juice, basil, parsley and 3 tablespoons of olive oil. Season with salt and black pepper to taste (around 1 to 1 1/2 teaspoons of salt should do it). Stir in the cooled quinoa and mix well.

1 cup (4 ounces) freshly grated
   Parmesan cheese, divided

1 teaspoon fresh lemon juice 3
   tablespoons chopped fresh basil

3 tablespoons finely chopped fresh
   Italian parsley

3/4 cup (3 ounces) shredded
   Monterey Jack cheese

Spoon a heaping amount of quinoa stuffing into each pepper half and transfer to baking dish. Any leftover stuffing can be sprinkled in the pan or tucked into corners of the dish. Top each pepper with approximately 1 tablespoon of Parmesan and 2 tablespoons of Monterey Jack cheese. Bake about 35 to 45 minutes, until bubbly, hot and the cheese on top is golden brown. Let stand about 10 minutes before serving.

MAKE AHEAD Peppers can be assembled, but not baked, earlier in the day, covered and refrigerated. Bring to room temperature before baking, or increase cook time by around 10 minutes.

A WELL-SEASONED INSPIRATION

THE KIDWELL FAMILY *My cousin Beth Kidwell and her family (husband Jim and daughters Becca and Sarah) taught me the importance of cooking with fresh, flavorful, and most importantly, the best quality ingredients. Jim would happily drive 45 minutes across town to purchase a certain feta cheese or perfect cut of bison. Fresh is the operative word at the Kidwells — cooking with lemons picked from trees in their yard, fresh eggs from their coop and vegetables from their own garden.*

INDIVIDUAL FONTINA CHEESE AND BROCCOLI SOUFFLÉS

I love creating new dishes with broccoli, as simply steaming or roasting can get boring. One night I was feeling inspired and made a soufflé! If you have family or friends who aren't broccoli fans, substitute chopped zucchini and this dish will still be delicious. These delectable soufflés are perfect for a lunch, light dinner entrée when served with our Avocado Mushroom Salad with Chutney Dressing *(page 78)* or for brunch, and can easily be doubled and/or made in one large soufflé dish *(see Variation on the next page)*.

SERVES: 4

2 tablespoons butter

3 tablespoons freshly grated
    Parmesan cheese

2 cups chopped raw broccoli florets
    (1/2-inch pieces)

Juice from 1/2 lemon

1 tablespoon extra virgin olive oil

1/2 cup chopped onion

2 tablespoons all-purpose flour

1 1/4 cups milk (whole or low fat)

1 teaspoon Dijon mustard

1/2 teaspoon lemon zest

1/2 heaping teaspoon salt

Freshly ground black pepper, to taste

1/2 cup (2 ounces) shredded Fontina
    cheese (aged is better)

3 large eggs, separated

2 large egg whites

1/4 teaspoon cream of tartar

Preheat oven to 375 degrees.

Butter 4 individual (8-ounce) soufflé dishes. Dust evenly with Parmesan cheese. Prepare a buttered foil collar for each dish *(see Tip on the next page)*. Place prepared soufflé dishes in a large roasting pan with 2-inch high sides.

Place broccoli in a steamer basket over boiling water with juice from 1/2 lemon added to the water. Cover and steam until broccoli is tender. Set aside.

In a large saucepan, melt remaining 1 tablespoon butter together with the olive oil over medium heat. Add onion and cook until soft. Whisk in flour, reduce heat to medium-low and cook, whisking constantly, for 3 minutes. Whisk in the milk, mustard, lemon zest, salt and a few grinds of the pepper.

Bring to a slow boil, stirring constantly, and cook 2 to 3 minutes or until thickened. Remove from heat and gradually add Fontina cheese, stirring after each addition, until cheese is melted. Add egg yolks and stir until well combined. Stir in the cooked broccoli.

Tear off a large sheet of foil long enough to wrap around the soufflé dish with at least 3 inches of overlap on the end. Fold in half lengthwise and grease one side with butter. Wrap foil, butter side in, around the side of the dish to make a collar around 2 to 3 inches above the rim of an 8-ounce soufflé dish (or 3 to 4 inches above the rim of a 1 or 2 quart dish). Fold over overlapping ends to secure. If necessary, secure by tying a string around the outside of the collar, just below the top of the dish.

With an electric mixer, beat the 5 egg whites until soft peaks form. Add the cream of tartar and continue beating until stiff peaks form. Gently stir one-quarter of the whipped egg whites into the milk mixture. Carefully fold in the remaining egg whites. Transfer to prepared dishes and place in roasting pan. Pour 2 cups of hot water into the pan surrounding the soufflé dishes. Bake 10 to 12 minutes or until puffed, firm to the touch and lightly browned on top. Serve immediately.

HIGH ALTITUDE Beat egg whites with the cream of tartar just until soft peaks form and stop beating.

VARIATION Soufflé can be baked in one 16-ounce soufflé dish.

TEMPURA VEGETABLE FONDUE
WITH A SOY-GINGER DIPPING SAUCE

Fondue was a family favorite growing up — cheese, beef and tempura style. It's great fun for kids as it's so active. Dad was always stealing everyone else's food out of the fondue pot! Mom loved it because there is so little prep involved — just a bit of chopping, and everyone cooks their own meal, while together. This recipe is very flexible — you can add and subtract vegetables based on what is available or in season. In addition, you can add peeled and deveined shrimp for the non-vegetarians in your family. This works best with an electric fondue pot for controlling the temperature of the oil. Serve with brown or fried rice. You might want to cover your table with an oilcloth or vinyl tablecloth as this fondue can be messy!

SERVES: 4

1/2 cup soy sauce

1/4 cup rice vinegar

2 tablespoons grated fresh ginger

2 tablespoons chopped green onion

1 teaspoon chopped garlic

2 teaspoons sugar

1 teaspoon dark (toasted) sesame oil

Vegetable oil for fondue pot

1 cup tempura batter mix (see Tip below to make your own)

3/4 cup cold water (or sparkling water for a lighter consistency)

1 medium zucchini, sliced 1/2-inch thick

1 medium yellow squash, sliced 1/2-inch thick

1 large carrot, peeled and sliced 1/2-inch thick

1/2 medium onion, sliced 3/4 to 1-inch thick wedges

16 ounces small to medium whole mushrooms, cleaned and stemmed (I like baby bellas)

2 red, green and/or yellow peppers, cut into 1-inch pieces

1 bunch asparagus, tough ends removed and cut into 1-inch pieces

In a medium mixing bowl, stir together the soy sauce, vinegar, ginger, green onion, garlic, sugar and sesame oil. Divide equally between 4 small bowls or ramekins; set aside.

Pour oil in the fondue pot about 2 inches (or more) deep. Cook over medium-high heat until oil reaches 375 degrees.

While oil heats, whisk together the batter mix and cold water. Divide batter between 4 additional small bowls or ramekins. Set aside.

Place the chopped vegetables in bowls on the table. Give each person a plate, 1 to 2 fondue forks and their own bowl of batter and bowl of dipping sauce. Carefully place the pot of hot oil on the fondue burner. Instruct everyone to put 1 to 2 vegetables on a fondue fork, dip in the batter and then place in the hot oil to cook until golden brown. It doesn't take long, just a minute or two! Remove vegetables from oil, let cool slightly and then dip into dipping sauce. Using a candy or instant-read thermometer, maintain the oil temperature so it doesn't fall below 370 degrees, otherwise tempura can get greasy. Also, don't let it get too hot or it might self-ignite.

TIP

To make your own tempura batter mix, sift together 3/4 cup all-purpose flour, 1/4 cup cornstarch, 1/4 teaspoon baking soda and 1/2 teaspoon baking powder.

PERUVIAN ARTICHOKE TART

When good friends Evie Haskell and Paul Maxwell returned from a trip to Peru with their daughter Cody, they hosted a dinner party featuring Peruvian dishes. I was asked to bring an appetizer. After doing some research, I created my own version of the Peruvian dish Tarta de Alcachoras — or Artichoke Tart — which is sort of like a cheesy artichoke quiche. Everyone loved it! Note the "Variation" on the next page that includes directions on how to serve this dish as a passed appetizer instead of a plated first course or main dish.

SERVES: 8 as a main dish or 12 as a side dish

CRUST

1 1/2 cups all-purpose flour

1/2 teaspoon salt

12 tablespoons unsalted chilled butter, cut into small cubes

1 egg yolk

3 to 4 tablespoons cold water

FILLING

1 tablespoon olive oil

3 tablespoons butter

1/2 cup chopped onion

1/2 teaspoon chopped garlic

3 tablespoons flour

3/4 to 1 cup (3 to 4 ounces) freshly grated Parmesan cheese

2 (14-ounce) cans artichoke bottoms packed in water, drained, dried and chopped

Salt, to taste

Freshly ground black pepper, to taste

2 cups milk

1 cup half and half

4 large eggs, lightly beaten

1 tablespoon Dijon mustard

Prepare crust: In a food processor fitted with the steel chopping blade, combine the flour and salt; process to mix. Sprinkle cubed butter evenly over the flour mixture and process until mixture resembles coarse crumbs. With the machine running, add the egg yolk. Add the cold water, one tablespoon at a time, until the mixture forms a dough (you might not need all the water). Shape into a flat disc, wrap in plastic wrap and refrigerate for at least 30 minutes.

Preheat oven to 350 degrees.

On a lightly floured surface, roll out the dough to fit the bottom and up the sides of a 9-inch tart pan with removable sides. Place rolled dough in tart pan, folding dough over the on the sides to reinforce. Prick all over the bottom of crust with a fork, line with foil and add pie weights. Place on a rimmed baking sheet and bake for 15 minutes. Remove the weights and foil and continue cooking for another 5 minutes. Prick the bottom with a fork if it starts to expand with air. Set aside to cool. (Leave the oven on.)

In a large sauté or saucepan, heat the olive oil and butter over medium heat. Add the onion and garlic; cook until the onion is soft and translucent. Reduce the heat to low and whisk in the flour. Continue cooking, whisking, for 3 minutes. Slowly whisk in the milk and cream. Increase heat to medium and cook, stirring, 12 to 15 minutes or until thickened.

Remove from heat and add Parmesan cheese, stirring until melted. Stir in chopped artichoke bottoms; season to taste with salt and pepper. Cool slightly; stir in the beaten eggs. Brush the pre-baked crust with the Dijon mustard. Pour filling into the crust (it will be fairly full). Place on a baking sheet and bake for 35 to 40 minutes or until set (firm to the touch) and lightly browned on top. Cool, cut into wedges and serve.

MAKE AHEAD Crust pastry can be made up to one month ahead, well wrapped and frozen. Thaw in the refrigerator before rolling. Tart can be made and cooked earlier in the day, covered and refrigerated. Bring to room temperature before serving.

PASSED APPETIZER VARIATION Cut cooled tart into 1-inch squares and place on a platter.

> **TIP**
>
> *Brushing the crust of a savory tart, pie or quiche with Dijon mustard before adding the filling not only layers in flavor, it prevents the crust from getting soggy.*

VEGETABLE CURRY

I am a sucker for pretty much any dish with curry in it! I am especially fond of the combination of the curry, ginger and coconut milk in this dish. The three flavors together complement perfectly the butternut squash, cauliflower, zucchini, chickpeas, spinach and bell pepper.

Make sure to chop all the vegetables in this dish into 1/2- to 1-inch pieces.

SERVES: 8

1 tablespoon olive oil

1 large yellow onion, chopped

2 tablespoons chopped fresh ginger

1 teaspoon chopped garlic

1 1/2 cups vegetable broth

1 cup coconut milk (light or regular)

1 tablespoon curry powder

1 1/2 teaspoons ground cumin

3/4 teaspoon ground turmeric

1/4 teaspoon cayenne pepper (optional)

2 cups chopped butternut squash or sweet potato

2 cups chopped cauliflower

1 cup chopped red bell pepper

1 cup chopped carrot

1 medium zucchini, chopped

1 (15-ounce) can chickpeas (garbanzo beans), drained and rinsed

5 cups (about 6 to 7 ounces) fresh baby spinach

1/4 cup chopped fresh cilantro (optional)

2 tablespoons lemon juice

Salt, to taste

Freshly ground black pepper, to taste

3 cups cooked brown rice or brown rice-quinoa mixture

In a 5- to 6-quart Dutch oven, heat the oil over medium-low heat. Add the onion, ginger and garlic; cook, stirring occasionally, 8 minutes or until onion is soft and beginning to brown. Stir in the vegetable broth, coconut milk, curry powder, cumin, turmeric and cayenne. Bring to a boil, reduce heat and simmer for 10 minutes.

Stir in the butternut squash, cauliflower, bell pepper, carrot and zucchini. Bring to a boil, reduce heat and simmer, covered, 20 minutes or until all the vegetables are tender. Stir in the chickpeas, spinach, cilantro and lemon juice; cover and continue cooking until the spinach has wilted and the chickpeas are heated through. Season to taste with salt (may need a fair amount depending on how salty your vegetable broth is). Serve over the brown rice or brown rice-quinoa mixture.

MAKE AHEAD Curry can be prepared earlier in the day, covered and refrigerated. Reheat over medium heat.

ROASTED BUTTERNUT SQUASH RISOTTO

I love the sweet, earthy and slightly nutty flavor of butternut squash, especially when it's been roasted. Now that most major grocery stores — including Costco — offer peeled and cubed fresh butternut squash, cooking with it is even easier (if it's not available prepped and ready to go in your area, directions for peeling and cubing are provided in the Tip on opposite page). After enjoying butternut squash risotto at several different restaurants around the country, I decided to take a stab at creating my own. I have served it to Robert and at a few dinner parties to rave reviews. My version is a bit on the rich side, so I suggest keeping the portion size smaller than other risottos.

SERVES: 6 to 8

6 cups peeled and cubed butternut squash (from a 2 to 2 1/2 pound squash)

2 tablespoons olive oil, divided

1 heaping teaspoon chopped fresh rosemary

Kosher salt, to taste

Freshly ground black pepper, to taste

7 cups vegetable broth

1/2 large onion, cut into 1-inch pieces

10 peppercorns

1 bay leaf

1 teaspoon maple syrup (optional)

2 tablespoons butter, divided

1 tablespoon walnut or vegetable oil

1 medium to large leek, white and pale green parts only, cleaned and chopped

1 3/4 cups Arborio rice

1/2 cup dry white wine

1 tablespoon chopped fresh sage

1/3 cup chopped fresh mozzarella cheese (buffalo or burrata)

1/2 cup (2 ounces) grated Parmesan cheese, divided

Preheat oven to 450 degrees.

If starting with a whole squash, peel, seed and chop it into 3/4-inch pieces. In a large roasting pan, toss squash with 1 tablespoon of the olive oil and the rosemary. Season with kosher salt and fresh ground pepper. Bake, stirring occasionally, for 25 minutes or until tender. Remove from oven and coarsely mash. Set aside.

While the squash is roasting: In a large saucepan, combine the vegetable broth, onion, peppercorns, bay leaf and maple syrup (if using). Bring to a boil, reduce heat and simmer about 20 to 25 minutes. Strain out solids and return seasoned broth to the same pan; keep at a low simmer.

In a large sauté pan or skillet, melt 1 tablespoon butter over medium heat. Stir in the remaining 1 tablespoon olive oil and when hot, stir in the leeks. Cook 2 to 3 minutes until beginning to soften. Stir in the rice and cook for 5 minutes. Stir in the wine and cook, stirring, until the wine is absorbed.

Stir in about 2 cups of the hot broth, reduce heat to medium-low and continue cooking, stirring occasionally, until broth is absorbed. Continue adding broth, about 1/2 to 3/4 cup at a time, letting each addition completely absorb before adding more broth. Rice should be creamy and al dente (still somewhat firm). This risotto shouldn't look like porridge nor should it be soupy. It will take around 15 to 25 minutes to cook and may or may not use all of the broth. You should stir it frequently while cooking, but you don't need to stir it constantly.

Stir in the remaining 1 tablespoon butter and the mashed squash. Cook 1 to 2 minutes or just until heated through (add a bit more broth or hot water if it starts to get too thick). Remove from heat and stir in the sage, mozzarella cheese and 1/4 cup of the Parmesan cheese. Season to taste with salt and pepper. Spoon into bowls and sprinkle top with remaining 1/4 cup Parmesan cheese.

TIP

Tip on how to peel and cube butternut squash: First, pierce the squash in several places with a fork and then microwave it for 1 minute (this softens it a bit and makes it easier to cut). Remove from microwave and cut off the ends, then cut in half across the middle, near the top of the fat part (where it starts to narrow). The round part is where most of the seeds are, and by cutting there you should be able to see all the seeds. Scrape out all the seeds and membrane (I like to use a grapefruit spoon). You can peel both pieces of squash with a vegetable peeler, but I like to set the round piece flat on the counter and cut off the peel in strips, cutting from top to bottom. Then I take the remaining longer piece of squash, cut it into two pieces and do the same. Now it's ready to slice, then cube.

Side Dishes

"Dining is and always was a great artistic opportunity."
— *Frank Lloyd Wright, architect*

Side dishes, like supporting actors, shouldn't be dull, while walking the line between enhancing the main dish and being the star. When selecting side dishes to prepare for a meal, I like to keep in mind not just complementary flavors, but also colors and textures.

VEGETABLES

200 | Prosciutto Wrapped Asparagus

201 | Shredded Brussels Sprouts with Bacon

202 | Stuffed Tomatoes with Olives and Prosciutto

203 | Zucchini and Yellow Squash Ribbons

204 | Roasted Zucchini with Crumb Topping

206 | Broccoli with Curry-Mayonnaise Sauce

207 | Cauliflower with Parmesan Sauce

208 | Lemon-Dijon Green Beans with Caramelized Shallots

210 | Corn and Prosciutto Salad

POTATOES

211 | New Potatoes with Lemon-Caper Sauce

212 | Golden Potatoes

214 | Brandied Sweet Potato Soufflé

RICE, GRAINS & RELISH

213 | Cheese Grits Soufflé

216 | Saffron Cilantro Rice

217 | Portobello Mushrooms, Sundried Tomatoes and Rice

218 | Baked Spinach Risotto

219 | Barley Pilaf

220 | Couscous with Dried Cranberries and Pecans

222 | Cranberry and Golden Raisin Relish

BREADS

223 | Nama's Buttermilk Biscuits

224 | Anise Bread

226 | Anna Mae's Freezer Rolls

227 | Italian Popovers

PROSCIUTTO WRAPPED ASPARAGUS

The Denver Post ran a feature article on one of my cooking classes at the Denver Botanic Gardens, which included this asparagus recipe. Called "Appetite for Seduction," the class had a Valentine's Day theme and provided a turnkey menu for a romantic dinner *(see Menu, page 264)*. Both easy and elegant, this asparagus *(photo, page 198)* is the perfect make ahead side dish you can pop in the oven 10 minutes before serving.

SERVES: 8

24 to 32 asparagus spears, tough ends removed *(see Tip)*

Extra virgin olive oil

Kosher salt, to taste

8 thin slices of prosciutto

Freshly grated Parmesan cheese (optional)

Toasted bread crumbs (optional)

Preheat oven to 425 degrees.

Toss the asparagus spears with olive oil to coat and sprinkle with kosher salt. Divide asparagus into 8 bundles of 3 to 4 spears each. Tie a piece of prosciutto around each bundle. Place on a rimmed baking sheet.

Bake 10 minutes or until asparagus is crisp-tender. Sprinkle top with Parmesan cheese and/or breadcrumbs, if desired.

MAKE AHEAD Prepare the asparagus but don't bake it earlier in the day. Cover and store at room temperature.

TIP

Asparagus spears have a tough end to them that needs to be removed before cooking. Grab the tough end with one hand (between your thumb and first finger). Grab the tip with your other hand and gently bend the tip end downward, holding the tough end still. The spear will snap in two at the right point, where the tough part stops. Discard tough ends.

SHREDDED BRUSSELS SPROUTS WITH BACON

I adore Brussels sprouts, always have. Robert, not so much, so I've had to experiment with various preparations in order to get him to eat them. I found a winner: in this dish the sprouts are shredded, sautéed with shallots in a bit of bacon drippings, then combined with lemon, Parmesan cheese, pecans and bacon crumbles. Albeit begrudgingly, he admits that he loves this dish. I think it's the bacon that won him over.

SERVES: 6

16 ounces fresh Brussels sprouts

2 to 3 ounces (about 3 slices) bacon

1 tablespoon olive oil

1/3 cup sliced shallots

3/4 to 1 teaspoon lemon zest

1 tablespoon fresh lemon juice

1 1/4 cup (1 ounce) freshly grated
    Parmesan cheese

2 tablespoons chopped toasted
    pecans or pine nuts

Salt, to taste

Freshly ground black pepper, to taste

Peel and discard the outer leaves of the Brussels sprouts and cut off the stems. Using the 2mm slicing disc of your food processor (or shredding disc if you have one), finely shred the sprouts. Set aside.

Preheat the oven to 350 degrees.

In a large skillet or sauté pan, fry the bacon over medium heat until crispy. Remove and drain on paper towel, reserving the drippings in the pan.

Add the olive oil to the bacon drippings. Add the shallots and cook over medium heat for 4 minutes or just until tender. Add the shredded sprouts and cook, stirring occasionally, for 8 to 10 minutes, or just until the sprouts are tender and starting to brown. Remove from heat and stir in the lemon zest, lemon juice, Parmesan cheese, pecans and crumbled cooked bacon. Season to taste with salt and pepper. Transfer to a 1-quart baking dish and bake for 5 to 7 minutes or just until the cheese melts.

MAKE AHEAD Sprouts can be assembled (but not baked), cooled, covered and refrigerated. Uncover and bring to room temperature before baking; increase cook time about 5 minutes.

STUFFED TOMATOES WITH OLIVES AND PROSCIUTTO

My best friend Katey Hartwell's mom, Dorothy Hartwell, had a recipe box brimming with impressive recipes. This is one of my favorites. Look for tomatoes that are still on the vine, usually in bunches of around 4 or 5 — they'll be the perfect size for this recipe. Even with just a few ingredients, these tomatoes are full of flavor and an excellent complement to our Feta Chicken *(page 105)*, Lemon-Rosemary Swordfish en Papillote *(page 150)* or Wild Bill's Bison with Shiitake Bourbon Sauce *(page 132)*.

SERVES: 6

6 medium tomatoes

1 (4.25-ounce) can chopped black olives

12 ounces prosciutto, trimmed of fat and chopped

1/4 cup chopped fresh Italian (flat leaf) parsley

1/4 chopped fresh basil, or more to taste

1/2 cup mayonnaise

Salt, to taste

Freshly ground black pepper, to taste

Preheat oven to 350 degrees. Lightly oil a baking dish large enough to hold 12 tomato halves in one layer.

Cut tomatoes in half and remove the seeds with a small spoon (I like to use a grapefruit spoon). Place the tomatoes, cut side up, in the prepared baking dish.

In a medium mixing bowl, stir together the olives, prosciutto, parsley, basil and mayonnaise. Season to taste with salt and ground pepper. Fill the hollow tomato cavities with the olive mixture. Bake for 15 to 20 minutes or until heated through.

MAKE AHEAD Tomatoes can be stuffed earlier in the day, covered and kept at room temperature. Bake before serving.

ZUCCHINI AND YELLOW SQUASH RIBBONS

After reading several blogs with recipes for squash "ribbons," I decided to try my hand at making my own. I've experimented with a mandolin, a sharp knife, and a vegetable peeler — and the peeler wins by a landslide, making beautiful, long, thin slices.

Note that the prepared zucchini needs to stand at room temperature for at least 30 minutes before serving.

SERVES: 8

1 pound small to medium zucchini

1 pound small to medium yellow squash

1/4 cup lemon-flavored olive oil

1/2 cup chopped fresh herbs, such as chives, basil, tarragon, thyme and/ or parsley

1/4 cup toasted pine nuts

Red pepper flakes, to taste

Salt, to taste

Freshly ground black pepper, to taste

Cut the ends off of the zucchini and yellow squash, and using a vegetable peeler, thinly slice lengthwise, until you reach the center where the seeds make ribbons rough and uneven. Turn the zucchini or squash over and slice until you reach the same place on the other side.

Discard the seedy middle section (or save for another recipe). Place squash and zucchini ribbons in a large mixing bowl. Toss with oil, herbs, pine nuts and pepper flakes. Season to taste with salt and pepper. Let stand at room temperature for at least 30 minutes before serving.

MAKE AHEAD Zucchini can be prepared but not baked earlier in the day, covered and stored at room temperature.

ROASTED ZUCCHINI WITH CRUMB TOPPING

Zucchini is very easy to grow and therefore abundant and easy to find at the end of the summer. It's an incredibly versatile vegetable that tastes great steamed, roasted, grilled, stuffed, baked — just about any way you prepare it. Growing up, mom made a delicious zucchini baked with cheese. She never wrote the recipe down and I didn't get it from her before she passed away. This is my recreation of her delicious and easy zucchini topped with grated Cheddar cheese mixed with crushed crackers and herbs. I think adding a bit of lime juice to the zucchini brings out its flavor.

SERVES: 4 to 6

Cooking spray

2 large zucchini, sliced 1/8-inch thick

1 tablespoon extra virgin olive oil

1 tablespoon fresh lime juice

Kosher salt, to taste

Freshly ground black pepper, to taste

1/2 cup (2 ounces) grated Cheddar cheese

5 large crackers, crushed (I like Milton multigrain)

1/4 cup chopped fresh Italian parsley

1 tablespoon fresh thyme leaves

2 to 3 tablespoons chopped red onion

Preheat oven to 400 degrees. Coat a 7-by-11 inch baking dish with nonstick cooking spray.

In a large mixing bowl, toss zucchini with the olive oil and lime juice. Arrange in layers in the prepared baking dish. Season with kosher salt and fresh ground pepper. Set aside.

In a small mixing bowl, stir together the cheese, crackers, parsley and thyme. Sprinkle over top of zucchini; sprinkle chopped onion over the top. Bake 20 to 25 minutes or until squash is tender and crumbs are light brown.

MAKE AHEAD Zucchini can be prepared but not baked earlier in the day, covered and stored at room temperature.

BROCCOLI WITH CURRY-MAYONNAISE SAUCE

One night when Robert and I were camping in our Airstream, I tried this favorite recipe of mom's to serve with grilled sirloin steak. We both savored it. You can roast the broccoli instead of steaming it if you like, it's equally delicious both ways.

Note that the sauce needs to be refrigerated for at least 30 minutes.

SERVES: 4

1/2 cup mayonnaise

1/3 cup sour cream

1 teaspoon curry powder, or more to taste

1 pound fresh broccoli

1/2 lemon

Salt, to taste

Freshly ground black pepper, to taste

Red pepper flakes (optional)

In a small mixing bowl, stir together the mayonnaise, sour cream and curry powder. Cover and refrigerate at least 30 minutes, to allow the flavors to blend.

Cut broccoli into florets and place in a steaming rack over boiling water; cover and steam 10 to 15 minutes or until crisp-tender. Place broccoli on a serving platter or individual dinner plates. Squeeze fresh lemon over the top. Season to taste with salt and fresh ground pepper. Spoon some sauce over the top, passing remaining sauce on the side. To spice it up a bit, sprinkle a few red pepper flakes over the top.

MAKE AHEAD Sauce can be made up to 2 days in advance, covered and refrigerated.

CAULIFLOWER WITH PARMESAN CHEESE SAUCE

This is another dish inspired while camping, where most of what I cook is outside on our portable gas grill. One snowy winter night at home, I had a craving for this dish but Robert didn't want to dig the grill out of the snow. I tried broiling the cauliflower instead, and it is equally delicious both ways *(see Variation below)*.

SERVES: 3 to 4

3 tablespoons sour cream

3 tablespoons mayonnaise

1 heaping teaspoon Dijon mustard

3 tablespoons freshly grated
   Parmesan cheese

Fresh lemon juice, to taste

1 head cauliflower

2 to 3 tablespoons extra virgin
   olive oil

Salt, to taste

Freshly ground black pepper, to taste

Preheat the grill to medium heat.

In a small mixing bowl, whisk together the sour cream, mayonnaise, mustard, cheese and lemon juice to taste.

Slice the cauliflower head into 1/2 to 3/4-inch thick slices *(see Tip below)*. Brush one side of cauliflower with olive oil. Place on a grill pan, oiled side down, cover and grill about 5 to 7 minutes or until starting to brown. Turn over and brush top with oil, then top with Parmesan sauce. Cover and grill for an additional 5 to 6 minutes or until the cauliflower is crisp-tender. Season to taste with salt and pepper and serve immediately.

VARIATION Preheat broiler with rack 5 to 6 inches from heating element. Spray a large rimmed baking sheet with nonstick cooking spray (for easy clean up, line pan with aluminum foil). Place cauliflower slices on sheet in a single layer and brush top with olive oil. Broil for 10 minutes or until starting to brown. Turn over, brush with oil and broil an additional 5 minutes. Spread Parmesan sauce over the top and continue broiling 5 minutes or until sauce is bubbly and starting to brown. Season to taste with salt and fresh ground pepper and serve immediately.

TIP

Remove the outer leaves from the cauliflower and cut the stem so that it is flat and flush with the base of the crown. Place the cauliflower, the stem side down, on a work surface. Cut down through the head, cutting 1/2 to 3/4-inch thick slices.

LEMON-DIJON GREEN BEANS
WITH CARAMELIZED SHALLOTS

The deep, rich sweetness of caramelized onions are the perfect match for these roasted green beans tossed in a light sauce of olive oil, lemon juice and Dijon mustard. The beauty of this dish is it can be served hot or at room temperature, making it perfect for buffets, potlucks or picnics. Delicious with our Asian Pork Tenderloin *(page 139)*, Scallops with Tomato and Pesto *(page 160)* and Parmesan-Onion Breaded Chicken Breasts *(page 111)*.

SERVES: 6

2 tablespoons butter

4 ounces (about 2 to 3 large) shallots

1 teaspoon sugar

Kosher salt, to taste

Freshly ground black pepper, to taste

1 1/2 pounds fresh green beans, trimmed and broken into 1- to 2-inch pieces

4 tablespoons extra virgin olive oil, divided

2 to 3 teaspoons fresh lemon juice

1 1/2 teaspoons Dijon mustard

In a medium skillet, melt butter over medium-low heat. Peel shallots, cut in half and thinly slice. Using your hands, break slices into individual pieces. Sauté shallots in butter, stirring occasionally, about 10 to 12 minutes or until very soft. Stir in sugar and continue cooking, stirring occasionally, about 3 minutes or until golden brown. Season to taste with salt and pepper. Set aside.

Preheat oven to 400 degrees.

Place beans on a large rimmed baking sheet. Drizzle with 2 tablespoons olive oil, tossing to coat. Season with salt. Roast for 10 to 12 minutes or crisp-tender.

In a medium mixing bowl, whisk together the lemon juice, mustard and remaining 2 tablespoons olive oil. Add cooked beans and toss. Season to taste with salt and pepper. Serve hot or at room temperature with caramelized shallots sprinkled over the top.

MAKE AHEAD Shallots can be caramelized up to 24 hours in advance, covered and refrigerated. Sauce can be made up to 24 hours ahead, covered and refrigerated. Bring shallots and sauce to room temperature before serving.

VARIATION Green beans can be steamed instead of roasted.

CORN AND PROSCIUTTO SALAD

One of my favorite foods in summer is fresh corn. Here in Colorado, we have wonderful corn from the town of Olathe — sweet, juicy and tender. This fast, delicious recipe from good friend Kathy Soter is my new favorite way to fix fresh corn. Cut the corn off the cob and sauté it with onion and prosciutto (or with bacon, as in Kathy's original recipe), then top it off with chopped fresh chives. So simple and fresh — and so scrumptious! *(photo, page 10)*

SERVES: 4 to 6

4 large ears fresh corn, shucked (preferably from Olathe, Colorado)

3 teaspoons extra virgin olive oil, divided

3 large, thin slices prosciutto*

1/2 large yellow onion, chopped

2 tablespoons chopped fresh chives

Salt, to taste

Freshly ground black pepper, to taste

Substitute 4 slices bacon for the prosciutto, if desired; omit the olive oil, and pour off some of the bacon grease

Cut the corn kernels off the cob *(see Tip below)* and place in a medium bowl. Set aside.

In a large skillet, heat 2 teaspoons olive oil over medium heat. Add prosciutto and cook until crisp. Remove prosciutto from pan, reserving drippings. Crumble and set aside.

Add remaining 1 teaspoon olive oil to drippings in skillet over medium heat. Add onion and sauté until slightly softened. Stir in about 2 teaspoons of water, scraping up any brown bits stuck to the bottom of the pan. Continue cooking until onions are soft.

Stir in corn; cook 5 minutes or until heated through and the corn is crisp-tender. Remove from heat. Stir crumbled prosciutto and chopped chives into corn mixture. Season to taste with salt and pepper. Best if served hot or at room temperature.

TIP

On cutting corn kernels off the cob: Place a small bowl upside down in the middle of a large mixing bowl. Set the cob of corn on top of the small bowl, flat side down (break off the end if needed). Starting at the top of the cob, slightly angle a sharp knife toward the cob and cut downward, scraping the kernels off. The larger bowl will catch the kernels and keep them from flying all over the counter.

NEW POTATOES WITH LEMON-CAPER SAUCE

Another great recipe from my childhood friend Katey Hartwell's mom, Dorothy. Dorothy was not a "gourmet" cook, but still a great home cook. I loved going to the Hartwell house for dinner because Dorothy's style was different than my mom's — more focused around comfort foods. Still, she did make some more creative dishes, like these potatoes, from time to time. I love the tang of the lemon and capers in this super quick and impressive side dish that can be served with just about anything! These potatoes can easily be doubled.

SERVES: 4

1 pound medium red-skinned
   new potatoes, cut into eighths (or
   quarters if small)

1/4 cup butter

2 tablespoons fresh lemon juice

1 tablespoon capers, with 1/2
   teaspoon liquid from jar

1 tablespoon grated onion

1 tablespoon chopped fresh parsley

2 tablespoons freshly grated
   Parmesan cheese

Salt, to taste

Freshly ground black pepper, to taste

Place potatoes in a steamer basket over boiling water. Cover and steam potatoes 10 to 15 minutes or until fork tender.

About 5 minutes before the potatoes are done, melt the butter in a medium saucepan over medium heat. Stir in the lemon juice, capers and liquid, onion and parsley. Stir in cheese. Reduce heat to low and cook, stirring occasionally, until well blended.

Remove potatoes from oven and toss with desired amount of sauce. Season to taste with salt and pepper.

A WELL-SEASONED INSPIRATION

ANNA MAE WATKINS *Anna Mae — pictured here with me on my first day of kindergarten — worked for the Clayton family for over 30 years, and was one of the most influential women in my life. She kept our house clean and organized, and made it possible for my parents to host frequent dinner parties. Anna Mae easily earned respect from those around her and taught me the value of quiet strength, determination, tact, and most importantly, a sense of humor. She also taught me how to make her delicious rolls (page 226)!*

GOLDEN POTATOES

This recipe, from family friend (and excellent cook) Charlene Clinton, features all the ingredients in twice-baked potatoes, but with a much easier preparation. See Variation below to bake in individual ramekins for a more elegant presentation. I like to serve these with Cajun Meatloaf *(page 122)* or Roasted Hoisin Pork Tenderloin *(page 138)*; any leftovers are great reheated for breakfast.

SERVES: 6

1 1/2 pounds (about 2 large) Idaho (russet) potatoes

2 to 3 teaspoons extra virgin olive oil, divided

Salt, to taste

Freshly ground black pepper, to taste

Cooking spray

3 tablespoons butter, divided

1 cup (4 ounces) shredded reduced fat sharp Cheddar cheese

1 cup light sour cream

1/4 to 1/3 cup green onions, chopped (white, light green and some dark green part)

1/2 cup panko bread crumbs

Paprika, to taste

Preheat oven to 400 degrees.

Peel the potatoes and pierce them in several places with a fork. Tear off a piece of aluminum foil large enough to wrap around each potato. Place 1 potato in the middle of one piece of foil. Pull up the edges of the foil around the potato, but do not completely cover. Drizzle with 1 teaspoon olive oil. Season with salt and pepper. Wrap the potato completely. Repeat with the remaining potato.

Place potatoes in the oven on the middle rack and bake for 25 minutes. Rotate potatoes and continue cooking for an additional 25 minutes or until fork tender but not soft. Cool and coarsely chop the potatoes by hand or shred in a food processor. Set aside.

Reduce heat to 350 degrees. Butter or spray a 7-by-11 inch baking dish with cooking spray.

In a large saucepan over low heat, melt 2 tablespoons of the butter. Add the grated cheese and cook, stirring, until almost melted. Remove from the heat and stir in sour cream, onions, 3/4 teaspoon salt and 1/8 teaspoon pepper. Add potatoes and stir lightly. Turn into prepared dish.

Melt the remaining 1 tablespoon butter and mix with breadcrumbs. Sprinkle on top of potato mixture, then sprinkle lightly with paprika, and bake for 30 minutes or until golden brown and heated through.

MAKE AHEAD Potatoes can be prepared, but not baked, earlier in the day, covered and refrigerated. Bring to room temperature before baking.

VARIATION Spoon prepared potato mixture into 6 (6-ounce) greased ramekins. Sprinkle top with buttered breadcrumbs. Reduce baking time by 5 minutes.

CHEESE GRITS SOUFFLÉ

A Kentucky native, my mother Sally loved grits. What good Southerner doesn't? My favorite grits recipes include some variety of cheese as a key ingredient. My cousin Beth Kidwell's daughter Sarah created this delicious Cheese Grits Soufflé. Lighter than traditional cheese grits, it's still full of flavor — and pretty enough to serve at a dinner party. Mom would have loved it!

SERVES: 6

Butter, for greasing the soufflé dish

1 cup quick 5-minute grits

2 cups milk (whole or 2%)

2 cups water

1 teaspoon chopped garlic

1 1/2 teaspoons salt

1/2 teaspoon ground white pepper

1/4 teaspoon hot sauce

1 teaspoon Worcestershire sauce

2 1/2 cups shredded sharp Cheddar cheese

4 egg yolks

6 egg whites

Preheat oven to 350 degrees.

Butter a deep 2-quart soufflé dish or 2 1/2-quart round baking dish. Create a collar for the soufflé dish using foil *(see Tip on page 189)*. Place prepared dish in a deep roasting pan with 2-inch high sides.

Prepare grits according to package instructions using the grits, milk and water. When fully cooked, stir in the garlic, salt, pepper, hot sauce, Worcestershire sauce and cheese. Set aside for 5 minutes to slightly cool.

Beat egg yolks with a fork and stir them into the cooked and cooled grits. Whisk or beat the egg whites with an electric mixer until soft peaks form and fold into the grits mixture. Pour batter into the prepared dish and put in the oven. Pour water to depth of 1-inch around soufflé dish in roasting pan.

Bake 30 minutes or until well puffed and just starting to brown. Reduce temperature to 275 degrees. Bake 20 to 30 minutes or until it is firm to touch in the middle (not very jiggly) and golden brown on the top.

MAKE AHEAD See Tip on page 214.

BRANDIED SWEET POTATO SOUFFLÉ

Get ready for another showstopper out of mom's files. I serve this on Thanksgiving as a side dish, but it also makes a wonderful dessert too. There's no sugar needed in this recipe. The flavor of the sweet potatoes is enhanced by roasting, then adding in brandy, milk, butter, nutmeg and a bit of lemon zest. The end result is the perfect amount of sweetness.

SERVES: 6

1 to 2 tablespoons fine, dry bread crumbs

2 very large sweet potatoes, peeled and cut into 1-inch cubes

2 teaspoons olive oil

Kosher salt, to taste

1/2 cup whole milk

4 tablespoons butter, softened

1/4 cup brandy

1/8 teaspoon cayenne

1/4 teaspoon ground nutmeg

1/2 teaspoon salt, or more to taste

1 generous teaspoon lemon zest

4 eggs, separated

Preheat oven to 400 degrees.

Butter a 1-quart soufflé dish and coat inside with fine bread crumbs, tilting and turning dish to coat sides completely.

Place sweet potato cubes in a roasting pan; toss with olive oil and sprinkle with kosher salt to taste. Roast, stirring occasionally, about 30 to 35 minutes or until very soft. Cool slightly, then transfer to a food processor. Pureé until smooth to yield 2 cups. Freeze extra pureé and save for other uses.

In a small saucepan or glass bowl in the microwave, heat the milk until hot but not boiling. In the bowl of an electric mixer, beat together the hot milk, mashed sweet potato, butter and brandy, mixing until smooth. With machine running, add the cayenne, nutmeg, salt, lemon zest and 4 egg yolks.

In a clean bowl, beat the 4 egg whites until stiff peaks form (do not overbeat). Fold egg whites into sweet potato mixture; pour into prepared soufflé dish. Bake for 25 to 30 minutes or until well puffed and browned on top. Serve immediately.

VARIATION 2 more beaten egg whites can be added for a lighter soufflé.

TIP

On making a soufflé ahead: If making the day before serving, make the base but don't beat the egg whites. Cover and refrigerate. The day of serving, bring to room temperature, beat the egg whites, fold in to base and bake as directed. If making the day of serving (up to 4 hours ahead), the soufflé can be prepared through folding in the egg whites. Add a pinch of cream of tartar to the egg whites when whipping them. Cover and refrigerate. Bring to room temperature before baking. With these methods, the soufflé won't rise quite as much, but will still be delicious.

SAFFRON CILANTRO RICE

This flavorful rice complements any Asian or Southwestern dish and also pairs beautifully with grilled meat. I don't recommend using low sodium or no sodium broth; if you do, plan on adding a fair amount of salt when it says to season with salt and pepper. Since saffron can be very expensive, I've offered a variation below, using cumin as a substitute for the saffron, which makes for an equally delicious version of this rice. Serve with our Asian Pork Tenderloin *(page 139)* or the cumin version with our Steak Enchiladas with Roasted Tomatillo-Green Chile Salsa *(page 124)*.

SERVES: 6

1/4 cup extra virgin olive oil, divided

1/2 cup chopped yellow onion

Salt, to taste

Freshly ground black pepper, to taste

2 cups uncooked long grain white rice

4 cups chicken or vegetable broth (not low sodium)

Pinch or 2 of saffron threads

1 cup packed fresh cilantro leaves, or more to taste

1 teaspoon chopped garlic

1/2 cup chopped green onion, chopped (white, light green and some dark green part)

2 to 3 tablespoons fresh lime juice

2 tablespoons toasted pistachios *(see Tip)*

In a large heavy saucepan, heat 1 tablespoon of the oil over medium heat. Add the onion and a pinch of salt and pepper and cook, stirring occasionally, 5 minutes or until tender.

Stir in the rice and a pinch of salt and pepper. Cook, stirring frequently, 3 to 4 minutes. Add the broth, saffron and another pinch of salt. Bring to a boil; reduce heat, and simmer, covered, for 20 minutes or until desired tenderness. Watch carefully to make sure it doesn't overcook and get mushy. Let stand 5 minutes or until all the broth is absorbed.

In a food processor, combine the remaining 3 tablespoons olive oil, cilantro, garlic, green onion and lime juice; process until well blended. Fluff cooked rice with a fork and stir in the cilantro sauce. Stir in the pistachios. Season to taste with salt and fresh ground pepper. Serve immediately.

MAKE AHEAD The cilantro mixture can be made up to 24 hours in advance, covered and stored in the refrigerator. Bring to room temperature before using.

VARIATION Use 2 teaspoons cumin in place of the saffron and toasted, slivered (not sliced) almonds or pine nuts instead of the pistachios.

TIP

To toast nuts: Bake at 350 degrees on a rimmed baking sheet, stirring occasionally, for 6 to 8 minutes, or until golden brown.

PORTOBELLO MUSHROOMS, SUNDRIED TOMATOES AND RICE

Earthy Portobello mushrooms are paired with bright sun-dried tomatoes, Parmesan cheese and fresh basil in this unusual rice side dish. Pine nuts or almonds are added for a bit of crunch and sour cream for tangy creaminess. Serve with Spicy Pork Chops with Argentine Chimichurri Sauce *(page 140)*, Grilled Rosemary-Dijon Chicken Breasts *(page 102)* or grilled beef tenderloin.

SERVES: 6 to 8

1 tablespoon extra virgin olive oil

1 (8-ounce) package Portobello, baby bella or cremini mushrooms, coarsely chopped

1/2 cup chopped yellow onion

1 cup long grain white rice

2 1/2 cups chicken broth

3/4 cup sun-dried tomatoes (not packed in oil), chopped

Dash red pepper flakes

Salt, to taste

Freshly ground black pepper, to taste

1/4 cup sour cream

1/4 cup (1 ounce) freshly grated Parmesan cheese

1/4 cup chopped fresh basil

1/4 cup toasted pine nuts or slivered almonds

In a large saucepan, heat the olive oil over medium heat. Add mushrooms and onion and cook, stirring occasionally, about 10 minutes or until tender. Add the rice and cook, stirring constantly, for 1 minute.

Stir in the broth, tomatoes and red pepper flakes. Add a dash of salt and pepper. Bring to a boil, reduce heat and simmer, covered, over low heat for 20 to 25 minutes or until the rice is tender. Stir in sour cream, Parmesan cheese and chopped basil. Season to taste with salt and pepper. Spoon into serving dish or onto dinner plates; sprinkle with nuts.

BAKED SPINACH RISOTTO

Making risotto is easy with this dish — eliminating the need to stand by the stove, stirring the entire cooking time. With just a few minutes on the cooktop at the beginning, you then pop it in the oven to finish for 20 minutes before serving. The spinach gives it a pretty green color. Simple and delicious! Serve with Balsamic-Honey Pork Tenderloin *(page 138)* or Grilled Citrus Salmon *(page 154)* and Anise Bread *(page 224)*.

SERVES: 6 to 8

1 tablespoon extra virgin olive oil

1 teaspoon chopped garlic

1 cup chopped yellow onion

1 1/8 cups Arborio rice

3/4 cup dry white wine

2 1/4 cups chicken or vegetable stock

1 (5-ounce) container fresh spinach, chopped

1 cup (4 ounces) freshly grated Parmesan cheese, divided

Dash nutmeg

Salt, to taste

Freshly ground pepper, to taste

Preheat the oven to 375 degrees.

Grease an 8-by-8 inch baking dish. In a large skillet or sauté pan, heat the olive oil over medium heat. Add the garlic and onion and cook 5 minutes or until onion is tender. Stir in the rice, reduce heat to low and cook, stirring constantly for 2 to 3 minutes.

Stir in wine and bring to a boil; reduce heat and simmer, stirring, until the wine is absorbed. Stir in the stock and bring to a boil. Reduce heat and simmer, stirring occasionally, for 6 to 8 minutes.

Remove from heat; Stir in chopped spinach, 1/2 cup of Parmesan cheese and nutmeg (place in a large mixing bowl if your sauté pan isn't big enough to add the other ingredients). Season to taste with a generous amount of salt and fresh ground pepper.

Spoon mixture into the prepared baking dish and sprinkle evenly with remaining 1/2 cup Parmesan cheese. Cover and bake for 20 to 25 minutes or until bubbly hot and rice is cooked.

MAKE AHEAD The risotto can be prepared earlier in the day (not baked), covered and refrigerated. Bring to room temperature before baking, adding more chicken stock if necessary.

BARLEY PILAF

When cooked, barley is a high fiber, low fat grain with a chewy, almost pasta-like texture and nutty flavor. It makes an unusual, delicious and impressive side dish that comes together easily. Make sure to use pearled or polished barley, otherwise you'll need a lot more water (3+ cups), and a longer cook time. Serve with our Mahi Mahi with Herb Mayonnaise *(page 156)*, Balsamic-Honey Pork Tenderloin *(page 138)* or Feta Chicken *(page 105)*.

SERVES: 6 to 8

1 1/2 cups pearled or polished barley (not hulled)

6 tablespoons butter

1 teaspoon chopped garlic

1 chicken bouillon cube, crushed or 1 1/2 teaspoons chicken broth granules

3 green onions, chopped (white, light green and some dark green part)

1/3 cup chopped fresh Italian or flat leaf parsley

Salt, to taste

Freshly ground black pepper, to taste

Preheat oven to 350 degrees.

In a large saucepan, combine barley and 5 cups water. Bring to a boil; cover, reduce heat to low, and simmer 25 to 30 minutes or until tender (barley will still be slightly chewy).

While the barley cooks, melt the butter in a shallow ovenproof baking dish over medium heat. If you don't have an ovenproof dish that you can use on the cooktop, follow directions in variation below. Stir in garlic and cook for one minute. Remove from heat and stir in 3/4 cup hot water, bouillon cube or granules, onion and parsley. Drain barley and stir into mixture. Season to taste with salt and pepper. Cover and bake for around 25 to 30 minutes. Serve immediately.

MAKE AHEAD Barley can be cooked earlier in the day, covered and refrigerated. Bring to room temperature before stirring into onion-parsley mixture and baking.

VARIATION In baking dish, melt butter in microwave. Add garlic and cook in microwave for 10 to 15 seconds. Follow remaining directions as outlined.

COUSCOUS WITH DRIED CRANBERRIES AND PECANS

Couscous is a wonderful alternative to rice or potatoes as a side dish. A coarse, ground pasta — the granules are made from crushed durum wheat. It takes only minutes to prepare, provided you're using the instant variety (most packaged couscous is). The grain itself doesn't have much flavor on its own and needs to be prepared with herbs, spices and other ingredients including nuts, dried fruits and/or sautéed vegetables. In this dish, we combine couscous with sautéed onion and celery, along with dried cranberries, toasted pecans, herbs and spices. It's a perfect side dish for Thanksgiving, served alongside roast turkey or our Rolled Turkey Breast with Roasted Red Pepper Stuffing *(page 118)*.

SERVES: 8 to 10

9 cups water

6 cups plain couscous (instant)

2 tablespoons butter

1 large onion, finely chopped

2 celery stalks, finely chopped

1 cup dried cranberries

Zest of 1 large orange

1 teaspoon cinnamon

2 tablespoons fresh thyme leaves

1 tablespoon chopped fresh sage

Salt, to taste

Fresh ground pepper, to taste

1 cup chopped pecans, toasted

In a large saucepan, bring the water to a boil. Stir in couscous; cover and remove from heat. Let stand for 5 to 10 minutes. Uncover and fluff with a fork.

Meanwhile, melt butter in a large skillet or sauté pan over medium heat. Add onion and celery; cook, stirring occasionally, until soft. Stir into couscous. Add cranberries, orange zest, cinnamon, thyme and sage and toss to combine. Season to taste with salt and pepper. Just before serving, stir in chopped pecans.

CRANBERRY AND GOLDEN RAISIN RELISH

This recipe is from my Aunt Bobbie, who found it in one of her favorite cookbooks, Fancy Pantry by Helen Witty. It's the best cranberry relish I have ever had! One Thanksgiving, while celebrating with our friends Jeanne and Dick Saunders, I made this relish — and now Jeanne's daughters insist she make it every year.

Note that the relish needs to sit overnight (or longer) before serving.

MAKES: 2 1/2 to 3 cups

3/4 cup golden raisins

1 (12-ounce) bag fresh or frozen and thawed cranberries

3 tablespoons chopped red onion or shallots

3/4 cup currant jelly

1/3 cup sugar

1 1/2 teaspoons salt

1/8 teaspoon ground ginger

Generous pinch of cayenne pepper

3 tablespoons fresh lemon juice

If raisins are not soft, soak in warm water to cover for 5 to 10 minutes or until tender and pliable. Drain and coarsely chop by hand or in a food processor; transfer to a medium mixing bowl and set aside.

Pick over berries, removing any shriveled or discolored ones and rinse under cold water; drain. Coarsely chop in a food processor. Add cranberries and chopped onion to raisins, stirring to combine. Set aside.

In a small saucepan, combine together the jelly, sugar, salt, ginger and cayenne pepper. Cook over medium heat, stirring, until sugar and salt dissolve and mixture is smooth and quite hot (it doesn't have to boil). Pour hot mixture over berry mixture, stirring until blended. Stir in lemon juice and mix well. Scrape into a jar, cover and refrigerate at least overnight before serving.

MAKE AHEAD Relish can be made up to 2 weeks in advance and stored, covered, in the refrigerator.

VARIATION Add around 1 teaspoon well-drained horseradish per cup of berry mixture. Taste and add more if desired. This zesty relish is especially good with leftover turkey and cold meats.

NAMA'S BUTTERMILK BISCUITS

Nama was my maternal grandmother and a fabulous home gourmet. She taught all of her children (mom, Uncle Dan and Uncle Bill) to love cooking and entertaining. Nama's biscuits are famous for their light, flaky and buttery deliciousness. A wonderful accompaniment to any main dish, the recipe also makes a perfect topping for my Chicken Pot Pie *(page 116)*. One of our recipe testers, Laura Parker, suggested they would be delicious as a base for strawberry shortcake.

MAKES: about 20 (2-inch) biscuits or about 32 (1 1/2-inch) biscuits

2 cups all-purpose flour, plus more for rolling and cutting

2 teaspoons baking powder

1/2 teaspoon baking soda

1/2 teaspoon salt

1/2 teaspoon sugar

1/4 cup cold unsalted butter, cut into small squares

1 cup buttermilk *(see Note)*

2 tablespoons butter, melted

TIP

On cutting out biscuits (scones or rolls, too): Push the biscuit cutter straight down and don't twist it! If needed, move it sideways to separate the cut out biscuit from the rest of the dough. If you twist, your biscuits will rise uneven.

Preheat oven to 450 degrees.

In the bowl of an electric mixer using the whisk attachment, combine the flour, baking powder, baking soda, salt and sugar. Add butter to flour mixture and mix on medium speed, just until butter is incorporated (it should resemble course meal).

Switch the whisk to the dough hook and with the machine running, add buttermilk all at once and mix just until the dough begins to form a ball on the hook.

Turn the dough out onto a heavily floured work surface (dough will be very wet). Sprinkle flour over the top and flour your hands, then pat the dough to 1/2- to 3/4-inch thick disk. Use a round cutter to cut into rounds *(see Tip below)*. Gently combine the scraps together and cut out more biscuits. Place the biscuits on a buttered baking sheet, or in a buttered 9-inch cake pan or 7-by-11 inch baking dish. (The baking sheet biscuits will have crusty sides, the ones cooked in the dishes will be tender.)

Brush top of biscuits with melted butter. Bake 10 minutes, or until the biscuits are light golden brown on the bottom.

MAKE AHEAD Prepare biscuits, place on a cookie sheet and freeze (don't bake). When frozen, place in a zip top bag and return to freezer. Biscuits will keep for up to 1 month. To serve, place frozen biscuits on a baking sheet and bake, increasing baking time to 15 to 18 minutes.

NOTE Recipe also works with powdered buttermilk. If using, mix the powder in with the other dry ingredients and add the water when the recipe calls for the buttermilk.

VARIATION For a more rustic looking biscuit, instead of cutting the dough, drop the dough by heaping spoonfuls onto the buttered baking sheet.

ANISE BREAD

Growing up, mom often served Anise Bread at dinner parties. When she and I were writing our first cookbook, *A Well-Seasoned Kitchen*®, we wanted to include the recipe, but by the time we thought of it, mom's memory was going and she just couldn't remember where she put it. I searched high and low, but wasn't able to find it. Last year I started experimenting, trying to recreate the recipe based on what I remembered it looked and tasted like. My brother Jim and I think that this version is pretty close to mom's original bread, and our recipe testers approved! It has just the right amount of flavor to make it interesting, without overwhelming the other dishes it's served with. The anise (licorice) flavor is very mild — I don't like licorice and I love this bread.

MAKES: 2 loaves

1 cup whole milk

4 tablespoons butter

3 tablespoons sugar

1 1/4 teaspoons salt

1 (.25-ounce) package active dry yeast

1/4 cup warm water

3 to 4 cups all-purpose flour, divided

1 large egg, beaten, divided

1 tablespoon anise seed

Sesame seeds, for sprinkling on top

In a medium saucepan, heat milk and butter over medium-high heat, stirring occasionally, until the butter melts. Stir in sugar and salt. Remove from heat and let cool to no higher than 110 degrees.

Dissolve yeast in warm (100 to 110 degrees) water. Set aside. Put cooled milk mixture in a large mixing bowl and using whisk attachment on an electric mixer, blend in 1/2 cup flour; blend in 1/2 beaten egg, anise seed and then the yeast.

Using a dough hook and keeping machine on speed 2, add just enough flour to blend in, 1/2 cup at a time, to form dough. Beat for 2 additional minutes or until dough clings to the hook and cleans sides of the bowl. Knead an additional 2 minutes on speed 2 or until the dough is smooth and elastic (dough will be sticky).

Remove dough from bowl and turn out onto a lightly floured surface. Knead a few times by hand to confirm texture is correct (it should feel like your earlobe or a baby's bottom).

Transfer dough to a large greased bowl, turning once to coat surface. Cover with a clean dish towel and let rise in a warm place (85 degrees) about 45 to 60 minutes or until doubled in bulk.

Preheat oven to 350 degrees. Butter two 8-by-4-inch loaf pans.

Punch down dough and knead briefly to push out additional air. Divide dough in half and shape each half into an oblong loaf that will fill the prepared pans; put in pans. Brush tops with remaining beaten egg and sprinkle with sesame seeds. Bake about 35 minutes or until golden brown and loaves sound hollow when tapped on top. Remove from pan and cool completely on a wire rack.

ANNA MAE'S FREEZER ROLLS

Anna Mae Watkins worked for my family for around 30 years. She helped raise my brother Jim and me and pretty much ran the household on the days she spent with us. She frequently made these rolls for mom to serve at her dinner parties, to glowing reviews. They can be made ahead and frozen, making them super convenient. I've also included directions at the end of this recipe for making and baking them without freezing.

During recipe testing for this book, my final round tester, culinary-trained chef Bailey Jeann Ruskus, suggested adding toppings to these rolls. After brushing tops with the egg wash, simply sprinkle on sesame seeds, garlic powder and/or dried herbs for added flavor.

MAKES: around 3 dozen

5 1/2 to 6 cups unsifted all-purpose flour, divided

1/2 cup sugar

1 1/2 teaspoons salt

2 (.25-ounce) packages active dry yeast

1 1/4 cups water

1/2 cup plus 2 tablespoons whole milk, divided

1/3 cup butter

3 large eggs, at room temperature, divided

In a medium mixing bowl or the bowl of a stand mixer, whisk together 2 cups of the flour, the sugar, salt and yeast. Set aside.

In a medium saucepan, heat water, 1/2 cup milk and butter over low heat until liquids are very warm — between 120 and 130 degrees (butter does not need to melt completely).

Directions with a hand mixer or stand mixer without a dough hook:
Gradually add warm liquids to the flour mixture and beat for 2 minutes at medium speed. Add 2 eggs and 1/2 cup flour. Beat at medium speed for 2 minutes, scraping bowl occasionally. Beat in enough additional flour to make soft dough. Turn out onto a lightly floured surface and knead dough about 8 to 10 minutes or until smooth and elastic.

Directions using a standing mixer with a dough hook:
With mixer on speed 2, gradually add warm liquids to the flour mixture, beating for 1 to 2 minutes. Add 2 eggs and another 1/2 cup flour. Beat on speed 2 until blended. Continue adding flour, 1/2 cup at a time, until mixture forms a soft dough. Beat about 2 minutes, until dough clings to hook and starts to pull from sides of bowl. (Note: Dough doesn't always clean the sides of the bowl.) Knead on speed 2 for another 2 minutes or until dough is smooth and elastic.

Transfer dough to a large greased bowl, turning to coat top. Cover with plastic wrap, then a towel and let rest in a warm, dry place (85 degrees) for 45 minutes.

Punch down to expel air; roll or pat dough 1/2-inch thick and cut out rolls with a 2 1/4-inch circle. Place on greased baking sheets and cover with plastic wrap. Let rise for 30 minutes. Cover with foil, sealing well and refrigerate for 2 hours, then freeze until firm. Transfer to zip top bags and store in the freezer for up to 4 weeks.

To bake, preheat oven to 350 degrees. Remove rolls from freezer and place on greased baking sheets. Cover and let rise about 2 hours or until close to doubled in size. Whisk together remaining 2 tablespoons milk and 1 egg. Brush tops of rolls with egg wash was and bake about 15 minutes or until golden brown. Serve immediately.

VARIATION Brush unfrozen rolls with egg wash and let rise 30 minutes. Bake immediately for about 15 minutes or until golden brown.

ITALIAN POPOVERS

Another recipe from mom's files — prosciutto and Fontina cheese baked into puffy popovers — yum! Her notes said, "serve with hearty soups." I think these popovers are wonderful with most any soup or vegetarian pasta. I serve them with our Butternut Squash Soup *(page 59)* and Broccoli, Mushroom, Spinach and Cheese Pasta *(page 168)*. Robert insists on eating them with butter; they're so moist I think they are good just plain.

SERVES: 8

2 large eggs

1 cup all-purpose flour

1 cup whole milk

1/4 teaspoon salt

2 ounces prosciutto, chopped

1/2 cup (2 ounces) packed shredded
   Fontina cheese

2 tablespoons chopped green onion

Preheat oven to 375 degrees. Heavily butter 8 (2- to 2 1/2-inches wide) popover or muffin cups.

In a blender, mix together the eggs, flour, milk and salt. Pour into a mixing bowl and stir in prosciutto, cheese and onion. Immediately pour batter evenly into prepared cups — they will be very full. I like to use a 1/2-cup measure to make sure I put some of the cheese and prosciutto in each cup. Fill any empty muffin cups halfway with water to prevent burning.

Bake about 40 to 45 minutes or until popovers are golden brown and firm to the touch. Let popovers sit for a minute or two in the pan before removing. Serve hot.

MAKE AHEAD Popovers can be baked earlier in the day, cooled and covered on the kitchen counter. Reheat before serving.

Banana Raspberry Cake with Lemon Frosting | 246

Desserts

"Research shows, 14 out of any 10 individuals like chocolate."
— *Sandra Boynton, author of "Chocolate: The Consuming Passion"*

The last thing your guests will remember, dessert, should be inspired, just like the recipes you'll find here. After all, it's the perfect way to complete any (and every) meal!

PIES AND TARTS

230 | Grandma Clarice's Cinnamon Apple Pie

231 | Key Lime Pie with Ginger Whipped Cream

232 | Blueberry Peach Custard Pie

234 | Frozen Strawberry Pie

235 | Frozen Lemon Velvet

236 | Individual Plum Tarts

238 | White Chocolate and Lime Tart with Strawberries

239 | Rum Pumpkin Tart

MOUSSES

240 | Rum Pumpkin Pots de Crème

242 | Mint Chocolate Mousse

CAKES

243 | Chocolate Biscuit Cake

244 | Pear Kuchen

246 | Banana Raspberry Cake with Lemon Frosting

247 | Nantucket Cranberries

248 | Sticky Ginger Cake

FRUIT & ICE CREAM

249 | Sea Salt Caramel Apple Slices

250 | Fresh Fruit with Brandy Custard Sauce

252 | Peach Ice Cream

COOKIES & BROWNIES

253 | Bea's Pecan Crispies

254 | Chocolate Pecan Toffee Bars

256 | Almond-Cocoa Wedding Cookies

257 | Chocolate Oatmeal Cookies

257 | Chocolate Peanut Butter Bars

258 | Ginger Spice Cookies

259 | Pecan Shortbread Bars with Butter-Rum Glaze

260 | Lemon Ginger Brownies

261 | Blonde Brownies

GRANDMA CLARICE'S CINNAMON APPLE PIE

Shortly after our first cookbook, *A Well-Seasoned Kitchen*®, was published, I received an email from a woman who shared my passion for collecting and sharing family recipes. She included a tasty recipe from her Grandma Clarice — this apple pie. Touched by the email, I had to share the recipe for such a scrumptious pie. Grandma Clarice said it was best served warm with vanilla ice cream, and I agree.

SERVES: 8

2 1/4 cups all-purpose flour, sifted

3/4 teaspoon salt

1/4 cup plus

1 tablespoon ice cold water, divided

3/4 tablespoon apple cider vinegar

3/4 cup solid vegetable shortening or butter, softened

5 cups peeled, cored and thinly sliced (1/8-inch thick) Golden Delicious or Cortland apples

1/2 cup granulated sugar

1/2 cup firmly packed dark brown sugar

1 teaspoon ground cinnamon

1/8 teaspoon ground nutmeg

1/4 teaspoon apple pie spice

1/4 teaspoon ground coriander

1/4 teaspoon mace

Pinch salt

1 large egg

Preheat oven to 400 degrees.

In a large bowl, combine sifted flour and salt. Remove 1/3 cup of flour mixture and place in a small bowl. To the 1/3 cup mixture, add 1/4 cup ice cold water and the vinegar; mix together with a fork to form a paste. Place in the refrigerator while continuing to make the crust.

Using an electric mixer on low (or with a pastry cutter or two knives) cut shortening into remaining flour mixture. Stir in paste with fork. (Dough will be thick.) Divide dough in half. On a lightly floured work surface, roll one half of dough into a 12-inch circle. Fit pie crust in a 9-inch pie plate. Beat together egg and remaining 1 tablespoon water; brush crust with egg mixture.

In a large bowl, stir together apples, sugars, cinnamon, nutmeg, apple pie spice, coriander, mace and salt. Place the apple filling inside the crust.

Roll remaining half of dough into a 12-inch circle. Moisten the edges of the bottom crust with water, then place dough over filling. Fold the edges of the top crust over the lower one and pinch to seal. Mold the edges into a fluted rim; cut 4 to 5 slits in top crust to allow steam to escape.

Bake for 45 to 50 minutes. Cover crust edges with foil or a pie crust shield if browning too quickly.

MAKE AHEAD Pie can be prepared earlier in the day, covered and kept at room temperature.

KEY LIME PIE WITH GINGER WHIPPED CREAM

Back in the 90's, I was lucky enough to spend several spring breaks in Key Largo, Florida with my college roommate Cynthia Ballantyne and her two youngest boys. It was then that I came to love Key Lime Pie, and just recently discovered how easy it is to prepare. It can even be made ahead of time! To take it up a notch, I add ginger whipped cream. For a simpler variation (without piping the whipped cream as directed below), just serve a dollop of it on top of each slice. Either way, it's delicious!

Note that the crust needs to be refrigerated for at least 30 minutes, and the prepared pie for at least 1 hour.

SERVES: 8

1 cup graham cracker crumbs

1/4 cup ground almonds or macadamia nuts, toasted

1/4 cup sugar

5 tablespoons butter, melted

1 (14-ounce) can sweetened condensed milk

3 egg yolks

Zest from 1 large lime, divided

1/2 cup key lime juice*

1/2 cup whipping cream

1 to 2 tablespoons powdered sugar, or more to taste

1 tablespoon ginger liqueur (such as Canton), or more to taste

Dash vanilla

If you are lucky enough find fresh key limes in your area, that is best. If not, I like to use the Nellie & Joe's brand of bottled key lime juice

Preheat oven to 350 degrees.

In a medium mixing bowl, stir together the graham cracker crumbs, nuts and sugar. Drizzle with melted butter and stir until evenly blended (I like to use my hands). Press into the bottom and sides of a 9-inch pie plate. Refrigerate at least 30 minutes.

Using an electric mixer with the whisk attachment, blend together the milk, egg yolks, 1/2 of the lime zest and lime juice. Place pie pan with crust on a baking sheet. Pour filling into the pie crust. Bake for 15 minutes. Cool about 10 to 15 minutes, then refrigerate for at least 1 hour.

Using an electric mixer with the whisk attachment, whip the cream until soft peaks form. Add the sugar, ginger liqueur, vanilla and remaining 1/2 of lime zest; beat until firm peaks form. Cut the corner off a zip top bag (can also use a pastry bag) and fit a large star tip in the corner. Fill the bag with the whipped cream. Pipe 1-inch stars around the border of the pie and put one larger one in the center. Cover and refrigerate until ready to serve.

MAKE AHEAD Pie can be prepared and refrigerated earlier in the day.

BLUEBERRY PEACH CUSTARD PIE

This delicious recipe came from my dear friend Catherine Petros. Recipe testers loved how the tangy, creamy flavor of the custard complemented the peach and berries. Many people fear the challenge of pie making, but this one is especially easy — and rewarding.

Note that the pie takes around 7 to 10 minutes longer to cook when using 2% milk instead of skim.

SERVES: 8 to 10

1 cup sugar

3/4 cup skim or 2% milk

3/4 cup nonfat, plain Greek-style yogurt

2 large eggs

1/4 teaspoon almond or vanilla extract

2 tablespoons all-purpose flour

2 teaspoons cornstarch

Pinch of salt

1 prepared pie crust*

1 heaping cup fresh blueberries

1 heaping cup peeled, sliced, pitted fresh peaches

*My favorite pie crust recipes are on our website, www.seasonedkitchen.com. Refrigerated pie crust also works well (preferably organic)

Position rack in lower third of the oven and preheat to 400 degrees. Spray a 9-inch pie pan with nonstick cooking spray.

In medium bowl, whisk together the sugar, milk, yogurt, eggs and vanilla until well blended. Whisk in the flour, cornstarch and salt until smooth and set aside.

On a lightly floured surface, roll pie crust into a 12-inch circle. Place crust in the pie pan and trim so it overhangs edge evenly by about 1 inch. Fold edges under and crimp or flute. Place the pie pan on a baking sheet.

Arrange blueberries in the bottom of the crust and top evenly with the sliced peaches. Pour the filling on top (the fruit will float but this won't affect the final results). Bake for 25 minutes, remove from oven and cover edges of the crust with foil or a pie crust shield (see Tip below) to help prevent over-browning.

Reduce heat to 350 degrees and return pie to the oven. Bake 20 to 25 minutes (for a total cook time of 45 to 50 minutes) or until a knife inserted at the center of the pie comes out clean. Let cool for 1 1/2 hours. Pie will settle during cooling. Serve warm or chilled.

TIP

For no-burn pie crust edge: To prevent the edges of a pie crust from overbrowning before the pie center is done, simply cover it with a pie crust shield. I like the brand "Mrs. Anderson" — it's easier and more reliable than covering the edge with foil.

TIP

For no-soggy crust: If you want to make this, or any pie ahead of time, brush the bottom of the crust with an egg wash (1 egg beaten with 1 tablespoon water) before baking. This magically forms a barrier between the crust and the filling.

FROZEN STRAWBERRY PIE

Nothing tastes better on a warm summer day than a cool, frozen dessert. Mom's Frozen Strawberry Pie brings back fond childhood memories of summer days spent playing outside. I loved coming home to enjoy a piece of mom's delicious pie, a refreshing treat to beat the heat. This pie is a great end to warm weather dinner parties, because it can be made up to 2 months ahead — another great trick mom taught me about cooking and entertaining.

SERVES: 16

1 cup all-purpose flour

1/2 cup chopped walnuts

1/4 cup firmly packed light brown sugar

1/2 cup butter, melted

2 cups chopped fresh strawberries*

1 cup granulated sugar

Pinch salt

2 egg whites

2 tablespoons fresh lemon juice

1 cup whipping cream

Can substitute 1 (10-ounce) package frozen and reduce granulated sugar to 2/3 cup

Preheat oven to 350 degrees.

In a food processor, combine the flour, walnuts and brown sugar and process until well blended and nuts are finely chopped. Stir in the melted butter. Press 3/4 of mixture into the bottom of 2 (9-inch) pie pans (or one 13- by 9-inch baking pan) and place remaining 1/4 of mixture into a shallow baking dish. Bake crusts and topping, stirring the latter often, 15 to 20 minutes, or until golden brown. Set aside to cool.

In a large mixing bowl, combine strawberries, granulated sugar, salt, egg whites and lemon juice. Beat with an electric mixer on medium speed for 20 minutes (yes, 20 minutes — this isn't a typo!).

In a large bowl, whip cream with an electric mixer until stiff peaks form and fold into strawberry mixture. Spread on top of crust in pan(s). Sprinkle top with remaining crumb mixture. Freeze for at least 24 hours. Place in refrigerator to soften before serving.

MAKE AHEAD Pie can be made up to 2 months ahead and kept frozen.

FROZEN LEMON VELVET

Smooth as velvet, this timeless make-ahead recipe from mom's collection is another crowd pleaser. Mom took a basic cheesecake recipe, added layers of lemon flavor (zest and juice) and then froze it, resulting in a deliciously cool and creamy dish, perfect for a warm summer night. I like to serve this with fresh berries or our Blueberry Balsamic Sauce *(page 40)*.

Note that the completed dish needs to be frozen overnight.

SERVES: 12

1 (12-ounce) can evaporated milk

1 1/2 cups graham cracker crumbs

2/3 cup butter, melted

2 (8 ounce) packages cream cheese, softened

1 cup sugar

2 tablespoons lemon zest

2 tablespoons fresh lemon juice

Fresh blueberries (optional)

Butter a 13- by 9-inch baking dish.

Place evaporated milk in a metal bowl and freeze about 1 hour.

In a small mixing bowl, combine the graham cracker crumbs with the melted butter. Set aside 3 tablespoons; press remaining crumbs into the bottom of the prepared baking dish.

In a large mixing bowl, beat together the cream cheese, sugar, lemon zest and lemon juice with an electric mixer until smooth.

Remove evaporated milk from freezer and beat about 5 minutes with an electric mixer until stiff peaks form. Fold into cheese mixture and then pour into graham cracker crust. Sprinkle top with remaining 3 tablespoons of graham cracker mixture. Freeze overnight. Cut into squares and serve with blueberries, if desired.

MAKE AHEAD Can be made up to 2 months ahead and kept frozen.

INDIVIDUAL PLUM TARTS

My husband Robert and I often venture to Mexico to spend time with my childhood friend Katey Hartwell. One evening, a neighbor brought a simple and delicious dessert that combined rich buttery puff pastry with perfectly ripe plums in a rustic galette. Every last bite was delicious. When we returned home, I refined the recipe a bit, including transferring it from one large galette into individual tarts. This way, guests get a perfect little something all their own. While these tarts look like they take more effort to make, they don't. Beautiful and delectable, these tarts make for an impressive, easy to pull together dessert.

SERVES: 6

1 (17.3-ounce) package (2 sheets) frozen puff pastry, thawed *(see Tip on page 22)*

1/4 cup butter, melted

6 ripe but slightly firm plums

2 tablespoons sugar

2 tablespoons chopped fresh mint, plus whole leaves for garnish

3 teaspoons fresh lemon zest

1/4 teaspoon ground cinnamon

1/3 cup apricot jam

Vanilla Ice Cream (optional)

Preheat oven to 325 degrees.

On a lightly floured surface, roll out 1 puff pastry sheet until very thin. Cut into 3 (6-inch) circles. Pierce the bottom all over with a fork. Repeat with remaining pastry sheet; you will have a total of 6 rounds. Place on ungreased cookie sheets and brush with melted butter. Set aside.

Pit plums and cut each into 16 slices (around 1/4-inch thick). In a medium mixing bowl, combine plums, sugar, mint, lemon zest and cinnamon. Arrange on top of the pastry, placing the plum slices on their side, forming a pinwheel. Fold over edges of the pastry up to (but not over) the plums, to form a small rim.

In a small saucepan, melt the jam over medium heat, stirring. Remove from heat; brush lightly over the top of the plums with a basting brush. Bake about 30 minutes or just until the crusts are done and the fruit is starting to bubble and get juicy (watch carefully so they don't get overdone). Serve at room temperature, placing a small scoop of vanilla ice cream in the center. If desired, garnish with whole mint leaves.

MAKE AHEAD Tarts can be made earlier in the day, cooled, covered and kept at room temperature.

WHITE CHOCOLATE AND LIME TART WITH STRAWBERRIES

My mom Sally received this recipe *(photo, page 6)* from a friend in Vancouver. The tartness of the lime is balanced by the white chocolate's sweetness and together they form a wonderful base for the strawberries. Make sure to make this dish when strawberries are in season and full of flavor. It's delicious served after one of our salmon dishes or Uncle Bill's Shrimp de Jonghe *(page 164)*.

SERVES: 6

CRUST

3/4 cup all-purpose flour

1/3 cup whole almonds

1/3 cup powdered (confectioners) sugar

1/4 teaspoon salt

6 tablespoons chilled butter, cut into pieces

2 teaspoons chilled water

FILLING

1/4 cup fresh lime juice

1/2 teaspoon unflavored gelatin

3/4 cup heavy whipping cream, divided

5 ounces white chocolate, chopped

1 teaspoon grated lime zest

2 tablespoons sugar

2 tablespoons sour cream

TOPPING

3 cups sliced fresh strawberries

2 tablespoons currant jelly

To make the crust: In a food processor, combine the flour, almonds, powdered sugar and salt and process until nuts are ground. Add butter; pulse until mixture resembles corn meal. Slowly blend in water until mixture begins to clump. Gather mixture into a ball in your hands, then press dough over the bottom and up the sides of a 9-inch tart pan with a removable bottom. Freeze for 30 minutes or until firm.

Preheat oven to 375 degrees. Bake crust for 15 minutes or until golden brown, shielding edges with pie shields or aluminum foil if browning too quickly. Cool on a wire rack.

To make the filling: In a small bowl, pour in lime juice and sprinkle with gelatin. Let soften for 10 minutes.

In a medium saucepan, bring 1/4 cup whipping cream to a simmer. Reduce heat to low, add white chocolate and stir until melted. Remove from heat and stir in gelatin mixture. Stir in lime zest. Transfer to a mixing bowl and refrigerate 35 to 40 minutes or until cold and just beginning to thicken.

In a mixing bowl, beat the sugar, sour cream and remaining 1/2 cup whipping cream with an electric mixer to medium-stiff peaks. Fold whipped cream mixture into chilled white chocolate mixture; spread evenly over crust. Cover and refrigerate at least 3 hours or until set.

Before serving, arrange sliced berries decoratively on top. In a small saucepan or bowl in the microwave, melt jelly over low heat and brush over top of berries.

MAKE AHEAD The tart can be made up to 24 hours ahead, covered and stored in the refrigerator.

RUM PUMPKIN TART

One Thanksgiving I decided to create a new pumpkin dessert. I started with the basic ingredients in our Fluffy Pumpkin Pie recipe (in *A Well-Seasoned Kitchen*® cookbook) and added crystallized ginger and rum. The result is delicious and beautiful!

SERVES: 10

1 1/2 cups (9 to 10 ounces) gingersnap cookie crumbs

4 tablespoons butter, melted

4 to 5 tablespoons good quality golden or dark rum, divided

3 tablespoons chopped crystallized ginger

1 teaspoon unflavored gelatin powder

7 1/2 ounces (about 1 cup) pumpkin purée (can use canned)

1 egg yolk

1/4 cup firmly packed light brown sugar

5 tablespoons sugar, divided

Zest from 1/2 large navel orange

5/8 teaspoon ground cinnamon, divided

1/8 teaspoon ground nutmeg

1 3/4 teaspoons vanilla, divided

1 3/4 cups whipping cream, divided

Preheat oven to 350 degrees. Line the bottom of a 9-inch tart tin with a circle of parchment paper or grease a 9-inch pie pan.

In a medium mixing bowl, combine cookie crumbs with the butter and 2 tablespoons of the rum. Press into the bottom and up the sides of the prepared pan. Place pan on a baking sheet and bake for 10 minutes or until set. Sprinkle crystallized ginger over the top of the crust and set aside to cool.

Pour remaining 2 to 3 tablespoons rum in the top of a double boiler (don't put it over simmering water yet). Sprinkle the gelatin over the top and let soften about 8 to 10 minutes (it will start to solidify but that's okay).

While the gelatin softens, in a large mixing bowl whisk together the pumpkin, egg yolk, brown sugar, 1/4 cup sugar, orange zest, 1/4 teaspoon cinnamon, nutmeg and 3/4 teaspoon of the vanilla.

Place top of double boiler with rum mixture over simmering water and heat just until the gelatin melts (the rum will be clear). Whisk into the pumpkin mixture.

In a large mixing bowl, whisk 3/4 cup of the whipping cream with an electric mixer until soft peaks form; fold into pumpkin mixture. Spread evenly over crystallized ginger on cookie crust. Refrigerate for about 1 hour or until set.

In a large mixing bowl, whisk the remaining 1 cup whipping cream, remaining 1 tablespoon granulated sugar, remaining 1 teaspoon vanilla and remaining 3/8 teaspoon cinnamon with an electric mixer until stiff peaks form. Spread evenly over top of pumpkin mixture. You can set aside around 1/3 cup of the whipped cream mixture to pipe a decorative edge on top of the whipped cream. Cover and refrigerate until ready to serve. Tart can also be frozen and served partially frozen.

MAKE AHEAD Can be made up to 24 hours in advance, covered and refrigerated, or can be frozen for up to 1 month.

RUM PUMPKIN POTS DE CRÈME

I collect pots de crème and have for years. While I haven't really counted them, I think there must be 50 or more in our china closet. This recipe, a deconstructed pumpkin pie with crystallized ginger and rum, is a fun and delicious way to show off the collection. If you don't have pots de crème, use wine glasses or ramekins. I use the same filling for my Rum Pumpkin Tart *(page 239)*.

SERVES: 6

20 gingersnap cookies

3 tablespoons plus 1 teaspoon chopped crystallized ginger

7 tablespoons good quality golden or dark rum, divided

1 teaspoon unflavored gelatin powder

7 1/2 ounces (about 1 cup) pumpkin purée (can use canned)

1 egg yolk

1/4 cup firmly packed light brown sugar

5 tablespoons sugar, divided

Zest from 1/2 large navel orange

5/8 teaspoon ground cinnamon, divided

1/8 teaspoon ground nutmeg

1 3/4 teaspoons vanilla, divided

1 3/4 cups heavy whipping cream, divided

In a heavy-duty plastic zip top bag, crush the gingersnap cookies with a rolling pin or meat mallet (don't smash into fine crumbs; cookie pieces should be around 1/2-inch in size). Divide cookie pieces evenly in the bottom of each pots de crème. Sprinkle evenly with chopped crystallized ginger. Measure out 1/4 cup of the rum and set aside. Sprinkle remaining rum over the cookies and ginger (around 1 to 1 1/2 teaspoons per cup). Set aside.

Put the reserved 1/4 cup rum in the top of a double boiler (don't put it over simmering water yet). Sprinkle the gelatin over the top and let soften for about 8 to 10 minutes (it will start to solidify but that's okay).

While the gelatin softens, in a large mixing bowl whisk together the pumpkin, egg yolk, brown sugar, 1/4 cup sugar, orange zest, 1/4 teaspoon cinnamon, nutmeg and 3/4 teaspoon of the vanilla.

Place top of double boiler with rum mixture over simmering water and heat just until the gelatin melts (the rum will be clear). Whisk into the pumpkin mixture.

In a large mixing bowl, whisk 3/4 cup of the whipping cream with an electric mixer until soft peaks form; fold into pumpkin mixture. Carefully spoon into pots de crème; smooth the top. Refrigerate about 1 hour or until set. In a large mixing bowl, whisk the remaining 1 cup whipping cream, remaining 1 tablespoon granulated sugar, remaining 1 teaspoon vanilla and remaining 3/8 teaspoon cinnamon until stiff peaks form. Pipe or spoon onto top of pots de crème. Cover and refrigerate until ready to serve.

MAKE AHEAD Can be made up to 24 hours in advance, covered and refrigerated

MINT CHOCOLATE MOUSSE

With my expansive collection of pots de crème (those little cups, often with lids, used for serving individual puddings and mousses), I'm always inspired to create new recipes to show them off. In this recipe, I add a bit of peppermint to a dark chocolate-based mousse, and for texture, add a crust of cookie crumbs and nuts tossed with brandy on the bottom. The peppermint-brandy combination is a throw back to my après ski cocktail of choice during college — the Stinger. You can serve the mousse in ramekins or wine glasses if you don't have pots de crème. The number of servings in any one batch depends on what vessel you put it in. Case in point: a wine glass will typically hold a bit more than a pot.

SERVES: 6 to 8

2 ounces unsweetened chocolate

3/4 cup chocolate cookie crumbs (see Tip below)

1/4 cup chopped pecans, toasted (see Tip on page 216)

2 to 3 tablespoons good quality brandy

1/2 cup butter, softened

1 cup powdered (confectioners) sugar

2 large eggs

1/2 teaspoon peppermint extract

1 teaspoon vanilla extract

1/2 cup heavy whipping cream

Garnishes: whipped cream, chocolate curls

In the top of a double boiler set over a pan of simmering water, melt chocolate. Remove top pan and set aside to cool.

In a small mixing bowl, stir together the cookie crumbs, nuts and brandy. Divide evenly between 6 wine glasses or 8 pots de crème or ramekins. Pat down. Set aside.

In a large mixing bowl, cream butter and sugar with an electric mixer on medium speed. Add the melted chocolate, eggs, peppermint extract and vanilla extract and beat until smooth and well blended.

In a medium mixing bowl, whip the cream with an electric mixer until stiff peaks form. Fold into the chocolate mixture. Carefully spoon into glasses, cups or ramekins to fill. Cover and refrigerate. Garnish with whipped cream and/or chocolate curls.

ALCOHOL-FREE VARIATION Can substitute 2 to 3 tablespoons melted butter for the brandy.

MAKE AHEAD Mousse can be made ahead and frozen. I recommend doing this either in ramekins or one large dish.

SERVING VARIATION Mixture can be prepared in one large, pretty serving dish, preferably glass so you can see the layers.

TIP

On making chocolate cookie crumbs: In a food processor, process around 1/2 of a 9-ounce box of Nabisco Chocolate Wafers until the consistency of fine breadcrumbs. Some stores also carry prepared chocolate cookie crumbs.

CHOCOLATE BISCUIT CAKE

This cake is very well known in Britain — in fact, there are several different versions. Prince William even selected this cake to be served at his wedding reception in 2011! The royal version was made by the British McVitie Cake Company and included their butter biscuits as a key ingredient. So, when creating my own version, I included McVities "biscuits" (cookies in the US). I also include raisins, dried cherries, nuts and lots of dark chocolate — as most British versions feature these ingredients. To top it off, I added some brandy and orange zest. If you can't find the McVities, substitute butter cookies or graham crackers.

SERVES: 12

4 cups broken McVities digestives (or biscuits) with dark chocolate coating (pieces should be around the size of an almond, or smaller)*

1/4 cup raisins

1/4 cup chopped toasted walnuts or almonds

1/4 cup chopped toasted pistachios

1/8 cup dried cherries

1/2 cup butter, sliced

5 bars (3.5 ounce) dark chocolate (50 to 60% cacao), broken into pieces, divided

1 cup whipping cream, divided

1/4 cup Lyle's Golden Syrup*

1 teaspoon orange zest

1 teaspoon brandy

Available in specialty food stores, at Cost Plus World Market and in the specialty food aisle of most grocery stores. Can substitute butter cookies or graham crackers for the McVities

Spray a 9-inch spring form pan with nonstick cooking spray. Line the bottom with parchment paper.

In a large mixing bowl, stir together the broken biscuits, raisins, walnuts (or almonds), pistachios and dried cherries. Set aside.

In the top of a double boiler, melt butter and 3 bars (around 10 ounces) of the chocolate, stirring constantly. Stir in 3/4 cup cream, golden syrup, orange zest and brandy. Pour over biscuit mixture and stir until well blended and all the biscuit pieces are coated with chocolate. Place in prepared spring form pan, pressing down and smoothing out the top as much as possible (it will be lumpy, but this will be the bottom of the cake so it's okay). Refrigerate at least 3 hours.

In the top of a double boiler, stir together remaining 1/4 cup cream and 2 bars chocolate (around 7 ounces) until melted and well blended. Set aside to cool until slightly thickened to the consistency of cake frosting, around 10 to 15 minutes.

While icing is cooling, remove cake from the refrigerator. Release the spring on the side of the pan and slowly remove ring. You may need to use a knife to separate the cake from the sides of the pan. Invert cake onto a cake platter or other serving dish. Remove the bottom of the pan, and then carefully peel off the parchment paper. Using a paper towel, wipe off any liquid remaining from the nonstick cooking spray. Spread icing over the top and sides of the cake to cover. Put in the refrigerator for around 1 hour or until chocolate icing hardens.

MAKE AHEAD Cake can be made up to 2 days ahead, covered and refrigerated – either iced or not. Cake, un-iced, can also be wrapped in foil and frozen for up to 1 month. Thaw before icing.

PEAR KUCHEN

When mom and dad were first married, they lived in a fifth floor walk-up in the Boston area. Mom would tell stories about a lovely German woman who lived on the fourth floor, a wonderful cook who helped her when she was first learning her way around the kitchen. Mom was just 23 when she and dad married — living miles away from their families, she couldn't easily turn to her own mom for help (the way I did). Since *kuchen* is the German word for cake, I think Mom's recipe just might have come from that lovely woman who taught mom so much in her early cooking days.

SERVES: 8

1 1/2 cups all-purpose flour, divided

1/2 cup unsalted butter, chilled and cut into 6 pieces

1/3 cup plus 3 tablespoons whipping cream, divided

3 tablespoons light brown sugar, divided

1/2 teaspoon ground ginger

1/4 teaspoon ground nutmeg

1/4 teaspoon plus pinch salt, divided

3/4 cup granulated sugar

3 egg yolks

1 teaspoon fresh lemon juice

1 teaspoon vanilla extract or vanilla bean paste

2 to 3 large firm, ripe pears (D'Anjou or Bartlett), peeled, cored and cut into 1/2-inch slices*

Whipped cream, melted dark chocolate for garnish

This recipe works best with pears that are firm but not rock hard. They should be ripe enough to have flavor, but not so ripe that they turn to mush when baked

Preheat oven to 375 degrees. Butter a 9-inch spring form pan and line bottom with parchment paper.

In a food processor fitted with the steel blade, combine 1 1/4 cups flour, butter, 3 tablespoons whipping cream, 1 tablespoon light brown sugar, ginger, nutmeg and 1/4 teaspoon salt. Process just until mixture resembles coarse crumbs (do not over mix). Set aside 1/2 cup; press remainder of the crumb mixture onto bottom and around 1 inch up the sides of the prepared pan. Bake for 15 minutes. Remove from oven and let cool for around 10 to 15 minutes.

Reduce oven temperature to 350 degrees.

In a food processor, combine the granulated sugar, remaining 1/3 cup whipping cream, remaining 1/4 cup flour, egg yolks, lemon juice, vanilla and pinch salt. Process for 30 seconds and pour into baked crust. Arrange pear slices on top in a circular pattern; the point of each slice toward the center. Fit slices tightly together, overlapping them. Combine remaining 2 tablespoons brown sugar with the reserved crumb mixture and sprinkle over top of the pears. Bake 40 to 50 minutes or until golden brown on top and set (I lightly press down on the top to see if it's firmed up). Let stand at room temperature for 10 minutes before removing the sides. Serve warm or at room temperature with freshly whipped cream and/or melted dark chocolate.

MAKE AHEAD Crust can be prepared and baked up to 24 hours in advance. Cover crust and reserved crumbs and store at room temperature. Bring both to room temperature before using.

TIP

Buying and storing fresh pears (and peaches): Make sure to purchase pears that are firm and let them ripen at room temperature. Look for pears that are not bruised, shriveled or discolored. This way, the only person poking them to see if they are ripe is you, minimizing bruising. Refrigerating pears will reduce their flavor.

BANANA RASPBERRY CAKE WITH LEMON FROSTING

This beautiful, delicious cake recipe comes from my cousin Barb's daughter Mindy Newlin. Surprisingly easy to prepare, the buttermilk and bananas keep the cake super moist and the lemon-cream cheese frosting is simply divine. Don't be surprised if you find yourself licking the scraps out of the bowl and off the utensils so not to waste any of its deliciousness! Serve with your favorite ice cream — I like it with Butter Pecan or Ben & Jerry's Vanilla. *(photo, page 228)*

SERVES: 14

CAKE

1 1/2 cups sugar

1/4 cup butter, softened

3 large eggs

1 3/4 cups all-purpose flour

2 teaspoons baking powder

1/2 teaspoon salt

1 cup buttermilk

1 cup (2 medium or large) mashed
   banana

1 teaspoon vanilla extract

FROSTING

6 ounces regular or low fat cream
   cheese, softened

2 tablespoons butter, softened

2 1/2 to 3 teaspoons lemon zest
   (about 2 lemons)

1/2 teaspoon vanilla extract

Dash salt

2 1/2 cups powdered sugar, sifted

1 3/4 cups fresh raspberries, divided

To make the cake: Preheat oven to 350 degrees. Coat 2 (8-inch) round cake pans with nonstick cooking spray. Line bottoms with parchment or wax paper. Spray paper with cooking spray and dust each pan with flour.

In a mixing bowl of an electric mixer, beat the sugar and butter at medium speed for 3 minutes, or until well blended. Add eggs, one at a time, beating well after each addition.

In a medium mixing bowl, whisk together the flour, baking powder and salt. In a small mixing bowl, stir together the buttermilk, banana and vanilla. With mixer running, add the flour mixture and banana mixture alternately with the sugar mixture, beginning and ending with the flour mixture. Beat just until combined (do not overmix).

Divide batter equally between the prepared pans and bake for 25 to 30 minutes or until a toothpick inserted into the middle comes out clean. Cool in pans 12 minutes on a wire rack. Remove from pans, peel off paper, and cool completely on wire rack.

To make the frosting: In the bowl of an electric mixer, beat the cream cheese, butter, lemon zest, vanilla and salt at high speed until light and smooth. With mixer on low speed, gradually add the powdered sugar, beating until well blended.

To assemble, place one cake layer on serving plate and spread 1/3 cup frosting over the top. Arrange 1 1/4 cups of the raspberries in a single layer over the frosting, placing the raspberries on their side. Place second cake layer on top of the raspberries. Spread remaining frosting on the top and sides of the cake. Decorate the top with remaining raspberries. I like to put a single row of raspberries along the outside edge. Store in refrigerator until just before serving

HIGH ALTITUDE No adjustments necessary.

MAKE AHEAD Cake layers and frosting can be made and stored in the refrigerator the day of serving.

NANTUCKET CRANBERRIES

Another fabulous and easy-to-prepare dessert from good friend Catherine Petros. Fresh cranberries and walnuts are sprinkled with sugar and then topped with a moist yellow cake batter. This dessert takes only around 10 minutes to prepare and is super tasty and colorful when cut. Mom would have loved this one!

SERVES: 8 to 10

2 cups fresh or frozen and thawed cranberries

1 1/2 cups sugar, divided

1/2 cup chopped walnuts

3/4 cup butter, melted

2 large eggs

1 cup all-purpose flour

1 teaspoon almond extract

Whipped cream or vanilla ice cream

Preheat oven to 325 degrees. Grease a 10-inch pie pan.

Wash and dry cranberries and place in prepared pie pan. Sprinkle 1/2 cup sugar and nuts over cranberries.

In a large mixing bowl, beat butter and remaining 1 cup sugar with an electric mixer until light in color. Add eggs, flour and almond extract. Mix just until blended; pour batter over berries. Bake for 40 minutes or until a tester inserted the middle comes out clean. Can be served warm or at room temperature, with ice cream or whipped cream.

MAKE AHEAD Cake can be prepared earlier in the day, covered and stored at room temperature. It can also we wrapped and frozen for up to 1 month. Thaw overnight in the refrigerator.

STICKY GINGER CAKE

Who doesn't love gingerbread? This version of the traditional dish comes from my cousin Beth Kidwelll, wife of Jim and mother of Becca and Sarah — all fabulous cooks (with innovative, delicious recipes in this book!).While many gingerbread recipes call for lemon curd on top (or on the side), Beth's version has a scrumptious lemon glaze. Using the variation below, you can make these into mini-bites, perfect for passing at a cocktail party or taking on a picnic.

SERVES: 8

1/2 cup butter

1/2 cup firmly packed dark brown sugar

1/2 cup molasses (can use sorghum according to taste)

1/2 cup maple syrup

1 cup 2% milk

1 large egg

1 1/2 cups all-purpose flour

1 teaspoon baking soda

1 teaspoon baking powder

1 teaspoon ground ginger

1 teaspoon ground cinnamon

1/2 teaspoon ground allspice

1 tablespoon grated fresh ginger

1 cup powdered (confectioners) sugar

4 to 6 teaspoons fresh lemon juice

Preheat oven to 350 degrees. Line the bottom of a 9- by 9-inch pan with parchment paper.

In a medium saucepan, melt the butter over medium heat. Stir in the brown sugar, molasses and maple syrup and cook just until the mixture begins to bubble. Remove from heat and let cool for 10 minutes.

In a small bowl, whisk together the milk and egg.

In a large mixing bowl, whisk together the flour, baking soda, baking powder, ground ginger, cinnamon, allspice and fresh ginger. Make a well in the middle and whisk in the milk mixture. Add the cooled butter mixture and stir just until incorporated. Pour into prepared baking dish and bake for 30 to 40 minutes or until a toothpick inserted in the middle comes out clean. Cool in pan for about 5 minutes, then transfer to a wire rack to finish cooling.

In a small bowl, stir together powdered sugar and 4 teaspoons lemon juice until well blended. Mixture should be fairly thick, yet thin enough to drizzle. If too thick, add more lemon juice. Drizzle over the top of the cake (I like to put it in a squeeze bottle and drizzle it in lines).

HIGH ALTITUDE No adjustements necessary.

VARIATION FOR MINI CAKES Pour the batter into 32 greased mini-muffin cups and bake for 9 to 11 minutes. Double the glaze.

SEA SALT CARAMEL APPLE SLICES

I love the flavors of caramel and apple together. Actually, I like caramel with just about anything! One fall night I was craving what, as kids, we called a "candy apple" and after experimenting a bit, I came up with this recipe. The sauce is actually somewhere in between a traditional caramel sauce and a butterscotch sauce, but closer in flavor to the former, hence the name.

SERVES: 4 to 5

6 tablespoons butter

3 tablespoons granulated sugar

1/2 cup firmly packed dark brown sugar

3/4 cup heaving whipping cream

Pinch of salt

3 large or 4 medium Granny Smith or other apples, cored and sliced into 1/2-inch wedges

1/4 cup toasted slivered or coarsely chopped almonds

Garnishes: Melted dark chocolate or chocolate sauce, large flake sea salt

In a heavy, deep saucepan, melt the butter over medium heat, stirring constantly. Add the sugars, whisking until well blended. Whisk in the cream and pinch of salt and bring to a low boil. Reduce heat to medium-low and continue cooking the mixture at a low boil for 6 to 7 minutes, stirring frequently.

Stir in the apple slices and continue cooking at a low to medium boil for around 10 to 12 minutes, stirring frequently, until the apples are tender when pierced with a fork. Remove from heat and stir in almonds. Let stand at room temperature for around 10 to 15 minutes, allowing the sauce to cool and thicken. Spoon into individual dessert bowls. To garnish, drizzle with melted chocolate and sprinkle with sea salt.

MAKE AHEAD Can be made the day before, covered and refrigerated. Heat over low heat just until warmed through before serving. Can also be reheated in the microwave.

FRESH FRUIT WITH BRANDY CUSTARD SAUCE

A light and delicious dessert, this dish is perfect for warm summer nights. The custard sauce is based on a traditional French crème anglaise, flavored with brandy. I like to serve this dish together with our Blonde Brownies *(page 261)* or Bea's Pecan Crispies *(page 253)*. Make sure to use fresh fruit!

Note that the brandy sauce needs to be refrigerated for several hours.

SERVES: 6

2 cups whole milk

2 egg yolks

1/3 cup sugar

2 tablespoons cornstarch

1 1/2 teaspoons vanilla extract

3 tablespoons brandy

6 cups mixed fresh fruit such as raspberries, blueberries, peaches, pears and/or plums, peeled and chopped

Garnishes: ground cinnamon and fresh mint leaves

In a medium saucepan, whisk together the milk and egg yolks; whisk in the sugar and cornstarch. Place over medium-high heat and cook, whisking constantly, just until the mixture boils and thickens. Remove from the heat and whisk in the vanilla and brandy. Transfer to a medium bowl. Cool slightly, then press plastic wrap onto the surface of the custard sauce and place in the refrigerator for several hours.

Divide fruit among 6 martini glasses or glass bowls. Spoon custard sauce over fruit. Sprinkle with cinnamon and garnish with mint leaves.

MAKE AHEAD Custard sauce can be made up to 1 day ahead and stored, covered, in the refrigerator.

PEACH ICE CREAM

Growing up, my brother Jim and I always looked forward to those summer days when mom would get out the ice cream maker and whip up something wonderful. One of our favorites was her Peach Ice Cream. She'd make it with fresh peaches from Palisade, Colorado, ripe and in season. While we weren't able to find mom's recipe before she passed away, our friend Stan Hitchcock, a talented cook from Tennessee, was willing to share his famous peach ice cream recipe with us. It tastes just like mom's recipe — simply divine!

SERVES: 6

4 very ripe peaches, peeled, pitted and chopped

1 cup plus 2 tablespoons sugar, divided

Juice from 1/2 lemon, preferably Meyer lemon

Dash salt

2 cups whole milk

1 teaspoon honey

4 egg yolks, beaten

1 teaspoon vanilla extract

1 cup half and half

1 cup heavy whipping cream

1/2 (14-ounce) can sweetened condensed milk

In a nonreactive bowl, combine chopped peaches, 2 tablespoons sugar, lemon juice and dash of salt. Cover and place in the refrigerator.

In a large saucepan, stir together the whole milk and remaining 1 cup sugar. Cook over medium-low heat, stirring, until the sugar melts. Stir in the honey. Remove from heat.

Place beaten egg yolks in a small bowl and very slowly whisk in about half of the milk mixture. Pour the egg-milk mixture back into the saucepan with the rest of the milk and continue cooking over medium-low to medium heat, stirring, until thickened (don't let it boil). Remove from heat and stir in vanilla, half and half, cream and condensed milk. Let cool, then refrigerate for at least 1 1/2 hours.

Stir peach mixture into the milk mixture until well blended. Place in ice cream maker and process according to manufacturer's directions until firm.

TIP

If you accidentally cook the eggs a bit: Pour the milk mixture through a strainer to remove any cooked egg before putting it in the refrigerator.

BEA'S PECAN CRISPIES

I found this recipe from Mrs. Bevard, or Bea, as we called her, in mom's recipe box after she passed away. Bea babysat for me and my brother Jim until I was around 4 years old. While I don't remember much about her, I do remember that we adored her...I'm sure in part because she baked these fabulous cookies. They have a wonderful molasses flavor, stemming from the brown sugar in the recipe.

MAKES: 5 1/2 dozen cookies

2 1/2 cups all-purpose flour

1/2 teaspoon baking soda

1/2 teaspoon salt

1/2 cup shortening

1/2 cup butter

2 1/2 cups firmly packed light brown sugar (can also use dark brown sugar for more molasses-like flavor) — *see Tip below*

2 large eggs

1 teaspoon vanilla extract

1 cup chopped pecans

Preheat oven to 350 degrees. Butter 3 large baking sheets.

In a large mixing bowl, sift together the flour, baking soda and salt. Set aside.

In the bowl of an electric mixer, cream together the shortening, butter and brown sugar until fluffy. With mixer running, beat in eggs one at a time; beat in vanilla. Add the flour mixture and slowly beat just until blended. Stir in chopped pecans (if dough is very thick, turn it out onto the counter and fold in the pecans by hand).

Using a small, spring-release ice cream scoop (about 1-inch in diameter), scoop the dough into balls and place on the prepared baking sheets, about 1 1/2 to 2 inches apart. Bake for 10 to 14 minutes or until golden brown and cookies are starting to get crisp on top. Remove to rack to cool.

TIP

For storing brown sugar: Put brown sugar in a zip top bag and place it in the refrigerator, in the crisper drawer. It will keep for months without turning hard or getting those little hard pieces in it.

CHOCOLATE PECAN TOFFEE BARS

Toffee has always been a favorite in the Clayton household. Mom was famous for her toffee candy (find the recipe in *A Well-Seasoned Kitchen*®). She packaged it in pretty boxes and gave it to friends and family at Christmas. Such an anticipated gift, if mom ran behind schedule with the deliveries, her friends would call me asking if they'd been dropped from her list. When mom became ill and could no longer make it, I took over the tradition. When a toffee craving hits and I don't have time to make mom's recipe, I simply whip up a batch of these flavorful and faster to prepare toffee cookies to satisfy my hunger.

MAKES: about 6 dozen cookies

1 cup butter, softened

1 cup firmly packed light brown sugar (*see Tip on page 253*)

1 egg yolk

1 teaspoon vanilla extract

1/4 teaspoon salt

2 cups all-purpose flour

8 ounces milk chocolate (such as Hershey brand), broken into pieces

1/2 cup chopped roasted pecans

Preheat oven to 350 degrees. Lightly grease ad 15- by 10-inch rimmed baking sheet.

In a large mixing bowl, beat the butter and sugar with an electric mixer until well mixed and light in color. With the mixer running, add the egg yolk and vanilla; beat until blended. Add the salt and flour and beat just until blended. Spread in prepared pan and top with a piece of waxed paper. Push down on the paper to spread the dough evenly in the pan. Remove the paper and bake for 20 minutes.

In a small glass bowl, melt chocolate using the microwave oven (do not overheat or it can turn white). Remove cookie base from oven and immediately spread chocolate over top. Sprinkle with chopped pecans, pressing down lightly to make sure they adhere to the chocolate. Let cool until the chocolate hardens (I put it in the refrigerator). Cut into bars and serve.

Chocolate Oatmeal Cookies, Almond-Cocoa Wedding Cookies, Chocolate Pecan Toffee Bars

ALMOND-COCOA WEDDING COOKIES

These cookies are so addictive; it's virtually impossible to sneak one without leaving a trail of powdered sugar in your wake! I once brought a tin-full as a hostess gift to our friends Melinda and John Couzens. Midway through their cocktail party, a server (who'd clearly tried one) began sharing them with the guests — this was not supposed to happen! By the time Melinda discovered my hostess gift had become fair game for all, the cookies were gone. Naturally, I made another batch the next day and dropped them off for our friends to enjoy…sans guests. Don't say I didn't warn you! *(photo, page 255).*

MAKES: about 4 dozen

1 1/4 cups all-purpose flour

1/2 cup unsweetened cocoa

1/2 cup butter, softened

1/2 cup unsalted butter, softened

1/2 cup sugar

1 tablespoon vanilla extract

1 1/2 cups almonds, finely ground and toasted

1 cup powdered (confectioners) sugar

1 teaspoon ground cinnamon

Preheat oven to 325 degrees. Line 2 large baking sheets with parchment paper.

In a medium mixing bowl, whisk together the flour and the cocoa. Set aside.

In a large mixing bowl, beat together the butters and sugar with an electric mixer until light and fluffy. Add the vanilla and beat until blended. Add one-third of the flour mixture at a time, mixing just until blended after each addition. Beat in the ground almonds (do not over mix).

Using a small spring-release scoop (about 1 inch in diameter), scoop the dough into balls and place 2 to 3 inches apart on the prepared baking sheets.

Bake for 22 minutes until cookies feel medium-firm to the touch. They will firm up as they cool. Cool completely on baking sheets.

Combine the powdered sugar and cinnamon in a shallow bowl. Roll the cooled cookies in the sugar mixture, one at a time. Repeat with cookies and sugar mixture. Store in an airtight container.

CHOCOLATE OATMEAL COOKIES

Here's another wonderfully delicious recipe from the recipe box at the Gordon Ranch in Wyoming, where my family spent a few weeks each summer. The orange zest is a refreshing and unusual addition to these oatmeal cookies *(photo, page 255)*.

MAKES: about 4 dozen

1/2 cup butter, softened

1 cup firmly packed light brown sugar, packed *(see Tip on page 253)*

Zest from 1 large orange

1 large egg, beaten

1/4 teaspoon salt

1 teaspoon vanilla extract

1 1/2 cups quick-cook oatmeal

1/2 cup all-purpose flour

8 ounces semi-sweet chocolate chips

Preheat oven to 375 degrees. Line 2 large baking sheets with parchment paper.

In a large mixing bowl, cream together the butter and sugar with an electric mixer. Add orange zest, egg, salt and vanilla and beat until well mixed. In a small mixing bowl, stir together the oatmeal and flour; add to butter mixture and beat just until mixed. Stir in chocolate chips. Using a small spring-loaded scoop, place balls of dough on prepared baking sheets about 1 inch apart.

Bake for 10 to 12 minutes, remove from oven and cool on baking sheets about 5 minutes; remove cookies to a wire rack to cool completely.

CHOCOLATE PEANUT BUTTER BARS

These amazing cookies take me back to my childhood with each bite. Naturally it makes sense, because the original recipe came to mom from Jean O'Donnell, a neighbor and good friend who lived across the street. For as long as I can remember, these delectable cookies were always a favorite treat for my brother Jim and me as children — and still are today. There's something magical about the combination of chocolate and peanut butter, don't you think?

MAKES: about 3 dozen

Coconut oil, for greasing the pan

10 graham cracker rectangles (4 crackers each)

1 1/2 cups powdered (confectioners) sugar

1 cup butter, melted

1 cup smooth or crunchy peanut butter

Dash kosher salt

1 (12-ounce) package (2 cups) semi-sweet chocolate chips

Preheat oven to 325 degrees. Grease a 13- by 9-inch glass baking dish with coconut oil.

In a food processor, process graham crackers until they resemble fine crumbs. Transfer to a large mixing bowl; add the sugar, butter, peanut butter and salt, stirring until well blended. Pat into prepared baking dish and bake for 15 minutes (it will be lightly browned and bubbly on top).

Remove from oven and let stand for 5 minutes. Sprinkle chocolate chips over the top and carefully spread into a smooth, even layer. Let cool, then cut into 1 1/2 inch bars.

GINGER SPICE COOKIES

I'm a big fan of ginger, which is probably quite obvious now that you've seen it in many of my recipes. Each yummy bite of these cookies packs a flavorful punch of ginger enhanced with cinnamon, cloves and nutmeg. The molasses and brown sugar add richness and depth. These Ginger Spice Cookies are even more wonderful served with our Peach Ice Cream *(page 252)*!

MAKES: about 2 1/2 to 3 dozen

2 cups all-purpose flour

1 teaspoon baking powder

1/4 teaspoon salt

1 teaspoon ground ginger

1 teaspoon ground cinnamon

1/2 teaspoon ground cloves

1/4 teaspoon nutmeg

3/4 cup butter, softened

1 cup firmly packed light brown sugar

1 large egg

1/4 cup unsulphured molasses

1/4 cup granulated sugar

Preheat oven to 350 degrees. Lightly spray 2 large baking sheets with cooking spray; wipe off excess with paper towel.

In a medium bowl, sift together the flour, baking powder, salt, ginger, cinnamon, cloves and nutmeg. Set aside.

Using an electric mixer, beat together the butter and brown sugar until creamy and well blended. Add the egg and molasses, mixing well. With the mixer running, slowly add the flour mixture and beat just until well blended.

Place sugar in a shallow bowl. Using a small, spring-release scoop (around 1 inch in diameter) scoop the dough into balls, roll in the sugar and place 2 inches apart on the prepared baking sheets (you should be able to get 18 cookies on each sheet). Bake for 10 to 12 minutes or until cookies are brown on the edges. Place on wire rack to cool.

A WELL-SEASONED INSPIRATION

GORDON RANCH *For almost 40 years, several weeks each summer were spent at the Gordon Ranch in Wyoming. Friends of my parents since the early 50's, our families built fond memories together at the ranch, many centered around meals. Most of what we ate came from the ranch — freshly laid eggs, milk, homemade churned butter, ranch-raised beef, vegetables and herbs from the garden. At the Gordon Ranch, I truly learned how delicious cooking with fresh, locally sourced ingredients can be! (left to right: Mark Gordon, me, and my brother Jim)*

PECAN SHORTBREAD BARS WITH BUTTER-RUM GLAZE

These delectable cookies have the flavor of a pecan pie, but in a shortbread cookie. This recipe comes from my childhood friend Mark Gordon (of the Gordon Ranch). There is just a hint of rum flavor in the glaze. You can add more rum if you like, but may need to also add more sugar to keep the right consistency for the glaze.

MAKES: about 3 dozen

BARS

3/4 cup butter or shortening

3/4 cup powdered (confectioners) sugar

1 1/2 cups plus 2 tablespoons all-purpose flour, divided

3/4 cup firmly packed light brown sugar

1/2 teaspoon baking powder

1/4 teaspoon salt

2 large eggs

1/2 teaspoon pure vanilla extract

1 cup chopped pecans

GLAZE

2 tablespoons butter, melted

1 tablespoon rum

1 cup powdered (confectioners) sugar

Preheat oven to 350 degrees.

To make the bars: In a large mixing bowl, cream butter and powdered sugar using an electric mixer with the whisk attachment, until mixture is light colored and well blended. On low speed, add 1 1/2 cups flour, blending just until combined. Press mixture into the bottom of an ungreased 9- by 13-inch baking dish. Bake for 12 to 15 minutes.

In a medium mixing bowl, combine the remaining 2 tablespoons flour, brown sugar, baking powder and salt. In a small bowl, whisk together the eggs and vanilla. Add pecans to the egg mixture and then stir into brown sugar mixture. Spread carefully over hot crust. Return dish to oven and bake 15 minutes or until lightly browned. Cool slightly while you make the glaze.

To make the glaze: Stir together the butter, rum and sugar; spread evenly over the cookies. Cool until firm, then cut into 1 1/2-inch bars.

LEMON GINGER BROWNIES

My good friend Katey Hartwell called one day from her home in Malinalco, Mexico, asking me to recreate the brownies she had just tasted at a dinner party. She described them as very chocolaty, chewy, gooey and flavored with lemon and ginger. In response, I took my favorite dark chocolate brownie recipe and added some lemon zest and crystalized ginger. According to my husband Robert (and Katey), the resulting brownies are "amazing!"

MAKES: about 16

2 ounces unsweetened chocolate, coarsely chopped

1/2 cup (1 stick) unsalted butter, softened

1 cup sugar

1 tablespoon fresh lemon zest (from 2 lemons)

3 tablespoons chopped crystalized ginger

1/2 teaspoon vanilla extract

2 large eggs, beaten

1/4 cup all-purpose flour

1/4 teaspoon salt

Powdered (confectioners) sugar

Preheat oven to 325 degrees. Grease and flour an 8- by 8-inch baking dish.

In the top of a double boiler, melt the chocolate and butter over simmering water, stirring often. Remove from heat, cool slightly (so you don't cook the eggs) and stir in 1 cup sugar. Add the lemon zest, ginger, vanilla and eggs; stir until well blended.

In a small bowl, stir together the flour and salt. Add to the chocolate mixture and stir just until blended; do not over mix. Pour batter into the prepared pan and bake for 30 to 35 minutes or until a toothpick inserted in the center comes out clean. Remove from oven and cool on a wire rack. Sift powdered sugar over the top. Serve at room temperature.

HIGH ALTITUDE No adjustments necessary.

MAKE AHEAD The brownies can be baked and frozen for up to 3 months.

BLONDE BROWNIES

Mom loved blonde brownies, mostly because they taste like butterscotch, one of her favorite flavors. Here's a quick and easy recipe for blonde (butterscotch-like) brownies from her recipe box, one you're sure to enjoy!

MAKES: about 4 dozen

2 cups all-purpose flour

1 1/2 teaspoons baking powder

1/4 teaspoon salt

10 tablespoons butter, softened

2 cups firmly packed light brown sugar *(see Tip on page 253)*

2 large eggs

2 teaspoons vanilla extract

1 cup semi-sweet chocolate chips (optional)

3/4 cup chopped walnuts

Preheat oven to 350 degrees. Butter and flour a 13- by 9- by 2-inch baking dish.

In a medium bowl, sift together the flour, baking powder and salt. Set aside.

Using the whisk attachment of an electric mixer, cream together the butter and sugar. Add the eggs, one at a time, beating after each addition; beat in the vanilla. Add flour mixture, beating just until blended (do not overmix). Stir in the chocolate chips and walnuts.

Spread the batter evenly in the prepared pan (batter will be very thick) and bake for 30 to 35 minutes, or until the brownies begin to pull away from the sides of the pan and a toothpick inserted in the middle comes out clean. Cool completely before cutting into 1-inch squares.

HIGH ALTITUDE Reduce baking powder by 1/8 to 1/4 teaspoon. Brownies may need another 5 to 10 minutes cooking time.

Menus

"A hostess must be like a duck: calm and unruffled on the surface, and paddling like hell underneath." — *Anonymous*

I've been hosting dinner parties since I was a teenager, and over the years, I've learned how to create a good menu. While all of my tips for stress-free entertaining are on our website (*www.seasonedkitchen.com*), here are some highlights for designing a menu:

- Don't stretch yourself — delicious over impressive works every time.

- Ask about guests' dietary restrictions.

- Think about the setting (Buffet? At a table?).

- Pair flavors that work well together.

- Vary food colors; we eat with our eyes first.

- Think about texture.

- Don't overdo an ingredient.

- Prepare as much as possible ahead of time!

COCKTAIL PARTY

Featured Drinks

34 | Robert's Perfect Martini

35 | Robert's Perfect Manhattan

Passed Hors d'oeuvres:

16 | Chorizo, Cheese and Jalapeño Turnovers

22 | Prosciutto, Fig and Goat Cheese Tarts

26 | Tomato Shortbread with Olive Tapenade

Plated Hors d'oeuvres:

17 | Goat Cheese, Pesto and Tomato Crostini

21 | Hot Onion Soufflé

20 | Mushroom Paté

   | Mixed nuts (on the bar)

Sweets

254 | Chocolate Pecan Toffee Bars

248 | (Mini) Sticky Ginger Cakes

VALENTINE'S DAY DINNER
(OR OTHER CELEBRATION DINNER)

32 | Champagne Cocktail

82 | Spinach Salad with Curry Dressing

148 | Halibut with Celery Root Purée and Tomato Garnish

200 | Prosciutto Wrapped Asparagus

242 | Mint Chocolate Mousse

EASTER BRUNCH

38 | Southwestern Chile-Cheese "Soufflé"

42 | Banana Caramel Baked French Toast

43 | Spiced Bacon Twists

48 | (Mini) Toasted Bagels with Egg Salad and Smoked Salmon

49 | Mini Sticky Pecan Rolls

53 | Mini Raspberry Nut Muffins

| Purchased Chocolate Bunnies

SPRING DINNER

30 | Hearts of Palm Dip

60 | Carrot-Ginger Soup

154 | Grilled Citrus Salmon

218 | Baked Spinach Risotto

224 | Anise Bread

235 | Frozen Lemon Velvet

MEMORIAL DAY GET TOGETHER

25 | Zesty Pimiento Cheese Spread

→ | BBQ Beef *(128)* and/or Pulled Pork Sandwiches *(144)*

84 | Dorothy's Potato Salad

Web | Coleslaw with Lemon-Mayonnaise Dressing — *recipe at www.seasonedktichen.com*

74 | Tomato and Cucumber Salad with Yogurt-Herb Dressing

234 | Frozen Strawberry Pie

→ | Ginger Spice Cookies *(258)* and/or Lemon Ginger Brownies *(260)*

CONCERT IN THE PARK PICNIC

58 | Chilled Minted Pea Soup

93 | Asian Shrimp and Brown Rice Salad

224 | Anise Bread

259 | Pecan Shortbread Bars with Butter-Rum Glaze

MEXICAN FIESTA DINNER

18 | Green Chile Canapés

62 | Puréed Black Bean Soup

124 | Steak Enchiladas with Roasted Tomatillo-Green Chile Salsa

182 | Green Chiles Stuffed with Goat Cheese

216 | Saffron Cilantro Rice (made with cumin instead saffron)

256 | Almond-Cocoa Wedding Cookies (with purchased coffee ice cream)

FRENCH LUNCH (OR LIGHT DINNER)

56 | Cucumber Leek Vichyssoise

94 | Tuna Salad Niçoise with Lemon-Tarragon Dressing

   | Purchased French Baguette

238 | White Chocolate and Lime Tart with Strawberries

CELEBRATION OF FALL

28 | Smoked Salmon Mousse

139 | Asian Pork Tenderloin

208 | Lemon-Dijon Green Beans with Caramelized Shallots

216 | Saffron Cilantro Rice

230 | Grandma Clarice's Cinnamon Apple Pie

THANKSGIVING MENU

20 | Mushroom Paté

118 | Rolled Turkey Breast with Roasted Red Pepper Stuffing

220 | Couscous with Dried Cranberries and Pecans

214 | Brandied Sweet Potato Soufflé

222 | Cranberry and Golden Raisin Relish

201 | Shredded Brussels Sprouts with Bacon

→ | Rum Pumpkin Tart (239) or Pots de Crème (240)

ELEGANT HOLIDAY DINNER

17 | Goat Cheese, Pesto and Tomato Crostini

83 | Arugula and Spinach Salad with Lemon-Dijon Dressing

114 | Coq au Vin

→ | Roasted New Potatoes (tossed with parsley) — in *A Well-Seasoned Kitchen*®

     | Purchased Sourdough Bread

247 | Nantucket Cranberries

NEW YEAR'S EVE DINNER

32 | Champagne Cocktail

22 | Prosciutto, Fig and Goat Cheese Tarts

59 | Butternut Squash Soup

132 | Wild Bill's Bison with Shiitake Bourbon Sauce

212 | Golden Potatoes

201 | Shredded Brussels Sprouts with Bacon

244 | Pear Kuchen

APRES SKI DINNER

     | Assorted Cheeses and Crackers

136 | Slow Cooker Mediterranean Meatball Ratatouille

76 | Apple, Walnut and Stilton Cheese Salad

224 | Anise Bread

     | Purchased Sea Salt Caramel Gelato

254 | Chocolate Pecan Toffee Bars

A

Almond-Cocoa Wedding Cookies, *255*, 256
Angel Hair with Chicken and Artichoke-Caper Sauce, 176, *177*
Anise Bread, 224, *225*
Anna Mae's Freezer Rolls, 226–227
Appetizers
  Canapés, Green Chile, 18, *19*
  Chicken Wings, Spicy, 24
  Crostini, Goat Cheese, Pesto and Tomato, 17
  Hearts of Palm Dip, 30
  Mushroom Paté, 20
  Pimiento Cheese Spread, Zesty, *14*, 25
  Puffs, Poppy Seed, *28*, 29
  Smoked Salmon Mousse, 28, *28*
  Soufflé, Hot Onion, 21
  Taco Salad Dip, 31
  Tarts, Prosciutto, Fig and Goat Cheese, 22, *23*
  Tomato Shortbread with Olive Tapenade, 26, *27*
  Turnovers, Chorizo, Cheese and Jalapeño, 16
Apple(s)
  Muffins, Butterscotch, *36*, 52
  Pie, Grandma Clarice's Cinnamon, 230
  Salad, Walnut, Stilton Cheese and, 76, *77*
  Slices, Sea Salt Caramel, 249
Argentine Chimichurri Sauce, Spicy Pork Chops with, 140, *141*
Arroz con Pollo, 106, *107*
Artichoke Bottoms
  Tart, Peruvian, 192–193
Artichoke Hearts
  Sauce, Angel Hair with Chicken and Caper, 176, *177*
  Topping, Baked Chicken with, 104
Arugula
  Dressing, Roasted Beet Salad with, 79
  Salad with Lemon-Dijon Dressing, Spinach and, 83
Asian
  Pork Tenderloin, 139
  Shrimp and Brown Rice Salad, 93
Asparagus
  Prosciutto Wrapped, *198*, 200
  Stir-Fried Pork and, 145
Avocado(es)
  Mexican Baked Chicken, 112, *113*
  Salad with Chutney Dressing, Mushroom and, 78
  Sauce, Grilled Shrimp with Tomatillo and, 161
  Yogurt Dressing, Layered Salmon Salad with Lime and, 90, *91*

B

Bacon
  Brussels Sprouts with, Shredded, 201
  Coq au Vin, 114–115, *115*
  Twists, Spiced, 43
Bagels with Egg Salad and Smoked Salmon, Toasted, 48
Balsamic
  Pork Tenderloin, Honey and, 138

Sauce, Cheese Blintz Soufflés with Blueberry, 40, *41*
Banana(s)
  Cake with Lemon Frosting, Raspberry, *228*, 246–247
  Caramel French Toast, Baked, 42
Barley Pilaf, 219
Bars
  Chocolate Peanut Butter, 257
  Chocolate Pecan Toffee, 254, *255*
  Pecan Shortbread, with Butter-Rum Glaze, 259
BBQ
  Beef Sandwiches, 128, *129*
  Sauce, Oklahoma, 128, *129*
Beans and Legumes
  Black Beans, Pesto Chicken with, *98*, 100
  Black Bean Soup, Puréed, 62
  Mediterranean Quinoa Stuffed Sweet Peppers, *180*, 186–187
  Vegetable Curry, 194, *195*
Bea's Pecan Crispies, 253
Beef
  Lasagna, Tex-Mex Chicken and Chorizo, 179
  Meatloaf, Cajun, *120*, 122
  Meatloaf, Hill Family, 123
  Sandwiches, BBQ, 128, *129*
  Steak, Roasted Potatoes and Tomato Salad, 88, *89*
  Steak Enchiladas with Roasted Tomatillo-Green Chile Salsa, 124–125
  Stew with Caramelized Root Vegetables, 130–131
Beet Salad with Arugula Dressing, Roasted, 79
Biscuits
  Chicken Pot Pie, 116, *117*
  Nama's Buttermilk, 223
Bison with Shiitake Bourbon Sauce, Wild Bill's, 132–133, *133*
Black Bean(s)
  Pesto Chicken with, *98*, 100
  Soup, Puréed, 62
Blintz Soufflés with Blueberry Balsamic Sauce, Cheese, 40, *41*
Blonde Brownies, 261
Blueberry
  Balsamic Sauce, Cheese Blintz Soufflés with, 40, *41*
  Pie, Peach Custard, 232, *233*
  Salad, Chicken, Mango and, 97
Bouillabaisse, Sally's, *8*, 157
Bourbon
  Grilled Pork Chops with Mushrooms Sautéed in, 142
  Sauce, Wild Bill's Bison with Shiitake, 132–133, *133*
Brandied Sweet Potato Soufflé, 214, *215*
Brandy
  Custard Sauce, Fresh Fruit with, 250, *251*
Bread
  Anise, 224, *225*
  Bagels with Egg Salad and Smoked Salmon, Toasted, 48
  Cinnamon Loaf, 50, *51*

Crostini, Goat Cheese, Pesto and Tomato, 17
  French Toast, Baked Banana Caramel, 42
  Popovers, Italian, 227
  Rolls, Anna Mae's Freezer, 226–227
  Strata, Pesto, Sausage and Parmesan Cheese, 39
Breakfast and Brunch
  Bacon Twists, Spiced, 43
  Bagels with Egg Salad and Smoked Salmon, Toasted, 48
  Biscuits, Nama's Buttermilk, 223
  Cinnamon Loaf, 50, *51*
  French Toast, Banana Caramel Baked, 42
  Frittata with Goat Cheese, Mushroom, Spinach and Onion, 47
  Huevos Rancheros, 46
  Muffins, Apple Butterscotch, *36*, 52
  Muffins, Mini Raspberry Nut, *36*, 53
  Smoked Salmon Eggs Benedict with Mustard-Dill Sauce, 44, *45*
  Soufflé, Southwestern Chile-Cheese, 38
  Soufflés, Cheese Blintz, with Blueberry Balsamic Sauce, 40, *41*
  Sticky Pecan Rolls, Mini, 49, *51*
  Strata, Pesto, Sausage and Parmesan Cheese, 39
Broccoli
  with Curry-Mayonnaise Sauce, 206
  Pasta, Mushroom, Spinach, Cheese and, *166*, 168
  Soufflés, Individual Fontina Cheese and, 188–189
Brownies
  Blonde, 261
  Lemon Ginger, 260
Brown Rice
  Salad, Asian Shrimp and, 93
  Salad, Indonesian, 86
Brussels Sprouts with Bacon, Shredded, 201
Buffalo with Shiitake Bourbon Sauce, Wild Bill's, 132–133, *133*
Butternut Squash
  Risotto, 196–197
  Salad, Mushroom Spinach and Roasted, 80, *81*
  Soup, 59
  Vegetable Curry, 194, *195*
Butter-Rum Glaze, Pecan Shortbread Bars with, 259
Butterscotch Muffins, Apple, *36*, 52

C

Caesar Salad Dressing, 87
Cajun Meatloaf, *120*, 122
Cake
  Banana Raspberry with Lemon Frosting, *228*, 246–247
  Chocolate Biscuit, 243
  Ginger, Sticky, 248
Canapés, Green Chile, 18, *19*
Caper(s)
  Sauce, Angel Hair with Chicken and Artichoke, 176, *177*
  Sauce, New Potatoes with Lemon and, 211

Sauce, Roasted Halibut with a Pine Nut, Tomato and, 149
  Sauce, Sautéed Chicken Breasts with Tomato, Olive and, 101
  Sauce, Sautéed Pork with a Mustard and, 143
Caramel
  Apple Slices, Sea Salt, 249
  French Toast, Baked Banana, 42
Carrot(s)
  Beef Stew with Caramelized Root Vegetables, 130–131
  Coq au Vin, 114–115, *115*
  Pot Pie, Roasted Root Vegetable, 184, *185*
  Soup, Ginger and, 60, *61*
Cauliflower
  with Parmesan Sauce, 207
  Vegetable Curry, 194, *195*
Celery Root
  Pot Pie, Roasted Root Vegetable, 184, *185*
  Purée, Halibut with Tomato Garnish and, 146, 148
Champagne Cocktail, 32, *33*
Cheese
  Blintz Soufflés with Blueberry Balsamic Sauce, 40, *41*
  Brussels Sprouts with Bacon, Shredded, 201
  Canapés, Green Chile, 18, *19*
  Eggplant, Stuffed, 183
  Eggplant Parmesan with Sausage, Mushroom and Olive Marinara Sauce, 137
  Enchiladas with Roasted Tomatillo-Green Chile Salsa, Steak, 124–125
  Feta Chicken, 105
  Fontina and Broccoli Soufflés, Individual, 188–189
  Goat Cheese, Green Chiles Stuffed with, 182
  Goat Cheese, Pesto and Tomato Crostini, 17
  Goat Cheese, Prosciutto and Fig Tarts, 22, *23*
  Hearts of Palm Dip, 30
  Lasagna, Tex-Mex Chicken and Chorizo, 179
  Mediterranean Quinoa Stuffed Sweet Peppers, *180*, 186–187
  Mushroom, Spinach and Onion Frittata with Goat Cheese, 47
  Parmesan-Crusted Chicken with a Tomato Cream Sauce, 174–175, *175*
  Parmesan-Onion Breaded Chicken Breasts, 111
  Pasta, Broccoli, Mushroom, Spinach and, *166*, 168
  Potatoes, Golden, 212
  Risotto, Baked Spinach, 218
  Risotto, Roasted Butternut Squash, 196–197
  Shells, Zucchini Stuffed, 169
  Soufflé, Grits, 213
  Soufflé, Hot Onion, 21
  Soufflé, Southwestern Chile-Cheese, 38
  Stilton, Apple and Walnut Salad, 76, *77*

Strata, Pesto, Sausage and Parmesan, 39
Taco Salad Dip, 31
Tart, Peruvian Artichoke, 192–193
Tetrazzini, Seafood, 172
Turnovers, Chorizo, Jalapeño and, 16

Chicken
Arroz con Pollo, 106, *107*
and Artichoke-Caper Sauce, Angel Hair with, 176, *177*
with Artichoke Topping, Baked, 104
Breasts with Tomato-Olive-Caper Sauce, Sautéed, 101
Coq au Vin, 114–115, *115*
Dijon Curry, 110
Feta, 105
Ginger-Orange, with Spicy Couscous, 108–109, *109*
Lasagna, Tex-Mex Chorizo and, 179
Mexican Baked, 112, *113*
Noodle Soup, Chinese, 69
Parmesan-Crusted, with a Tomato Cream Sauce, 174–175, *175*
Parmesan-Onion Breaded Breasts, 111
Pesto, with Black Beans, *98*, 100
Pot Pie, 116, *117*
Rosemary-Dijon Breasts, Grilled, 102, *103*
Salad, Blueberry, Mango and, 97
Wings, Spicy, 24

Chickpeas
Mediterranean Quinoa Stuffed Sweet Peppers, *180*, 186–187
Vegetable Curry, 194, *195*

Chile(s). *See* Green Chile(s)
Chimichurri Sauce, Spicy Pork Chops with Argentine, 140, *141*
Chinese Chicken Noodle Soup, 69
Chipotle Lime Shrimp Tacos with Tomato Mango Salsa, 162, *163*
Chocolate
Bars, Peanut Butter, 257
Bars, Pecan Toffee, 254, *255*
Brownies, Lemon Ginger, 260
Cake, Biscuit, 243
Cookies, Almond-Cocoa Wedding, *255*, 256
Cookies, Oatmeal, *255*, 257
Mousse, Mint, 242
White Chocolate and Lime Tart with Strawberries, *6*, 238

Chorizo
Lasagna, Tex-Mex Chicken and, 179
Turnovers, Cheese, Jalapeño and, 16

Chutney
Dressing, Avocado-Mushroom Salad with, 78
Dressing, Crab and Shrimp Salad with Curry and, 92

Cilantro Rice, Saffron, 216
Cinnamon
Apple Pie, Grandma Clarice's, 230
Loaf, 50, *51*

Citrus Grilled Salmon, 154
Clam(s)
Bouillabaisse, Sally's, *8*, 157

Cocktails
Champagne, 32, *33*
Manhattan, Robert's Perfect, *33*, 35
Martini, Robert's Perfect, *33*, 34

Cookies
Almond-Cocoa Wedding, *255*, 256
Chocolate Oatmeal, *255*, 257
Ginger Spice, 258
Pecan Crispies, Bea's, 253

Coq au Vin, 114–115, *115*
Corn Salad, Prosciutto and, *10*, **210**
Couscous
with Dried Cranberries and Pecans, 220, 221
Ginger-Orange Chicken with Spicy, 108–109, *109*

Crab
Bouillabaisse, Sally's, *8*, 157
Salad with Curry-Chutney Dressing, Shrimp and, 92
Seafood Bundles with Creole Mustard Sauce, 158, *159*
Tetrazzini, Seafood, 172

Cranberries
Nantucket, 247
Relish, Golden Raisin and, 222

Cranberries, Dried
Couscous with Pecans and, 220, *221*
Mixed Greens with, 72

Cream Cheese
Chorizo, Cheese and Jalapeño Turnovers, 16
Green Chiles Stuffed with Goat Cheese, 182
Lemon Velvet, Frozen, 235
Onion Soufflé, Hot, 21
Smoked Salmon Mousse, 28, *28*
Taco Salad Dip, 31

Creole Mustard Sauce, Seafood Bundles with, 158, *159*
Crostini
Goat Cheese, Pesto and Tomato, 17

Cucumber(s)
Leek Vichyssoise, 56, *57*
Salad with Yogurt-Herb Dressing, Tomato and, 74, 75

Curry
Chicken, Dijon, 110
Dressing, Crab and Shrimp Salad with Chutney and, 92
Dressing, Spinach Salad with, 82
Sauce, Broccoli with Mayonnaise and, 206
Vegetable, 194, *195*

Custard
Pie, Blueberry Peach, 232, *233*
Sauce, Fresh Fruit with Brandy, 250, *251*

D
Desserts
Bars, Chocolate Peanut Butter, 257
Bars, Chocolate Pecan Toffee, 254, *255*
Bars, Pecan Shortbread, with Butter-Rum Glaze, 259
Brownies, Blonde, 261
Brownies, Lemon Ginger, 260
Cake, Chocolate Biscuit, 243
Cake, Sticky Ginger, 248
Cake with Lemon Frosting, Banana Raspberry, *228*, 246–247
Caramel Apple Slices, Sea Salt, 249
Cookies, Almond-Cocoa Wedding, *255*, 256

Cookies, Chocolate Oatmeal, *255*, 257
Cookies, Ginger Spice, 258
Cranberries, Nantucket, 247
Fresh Fruit with Brandy Custard Sauce, 250, *251*
Ice Cream, Peach, 252
Kuchen, Pear, 244, *245*
Lemon Velvet, Frozen, 235
Mousse, Chocolate Mint, 242
Pecan Crispies, Bea's, 253
Pie, Blueberry Peach Custard, 232, *233*
Pie, Frozen Strawberry, 234
Pie, Grandma Clarice's Cinnamon Apple, 230
Pie, Key Lime, with Ginger Whipped Cream, 231
Pots de Crème, Rum Pumpkin, 240, *241*
Tart, Rum Pumpkin, 239
Tart, White Chocolate and Lime with Strawberries, *6*, 238
Tarts, Individual Plum, 236, *237*

Dijon Mustard
Chicken, Curry, 110
Dressing, Arugula and Spinach Salad with Lemon and, 83
Green Beans with Caramelized Shallots, Lemon and, 208, *209*
Grilled Chicken Breasts, Rosemary and, 102, *103*
Sauce, Sautéed Pork with a Caper and, 143

Dips and Spreads
Hearts of Palm, 30
Mushroom Paté, 20
Onion Soufflé, Hot, 21
Pimiento Cheese, Zesty, *14*, 25
Smoked Salmon Mousse, 28, *28*
Taco Salad, 31

Dorothy's Potato Salad, 84–85, *129*
Dressing(s)
Arugula, Roasted Beet Salad with, 79
Avocado-Lime Yogurt, Layered Salmon Salad with, 90, *91*
Caesar, 87
Chutney, Avocado-Mushroom Salad with, 78
Curry, Spinach Salad with, 82
Curry-Chutney, Crab and Shrimp Salad with, 92
Lemon-Dijon, Arugula and Spinach Salad with, 83
Lemon-Tarragon, Tuna Salad Niçoise with, 94, *95*
Lime-Balsamic, Tomato and Peach Salad with, *70*, 73
Pesto, Tuna and Roasted Red Pepper Pasta Salad with, 96
Yogurt-Herb, Tomato and Cucumber Salad with, 74, *75*

E
Eggplant
Parmesan with Sausage, Mushroom and Olive Marinara Sauce, 137
Ratatouille, Slow Cooker Mediterranean Meatball, 136
Stuffed, 183
and Tomato Soup, Roasted, 63

Egg(s)
Benedict with Mustard-Dill Sauce, Smoked Salmon, 44, *45*
Frittata with Goat Cheese, Mushroom, Spinach and Onion, 47
Huevos Rancheros, 46
Salad and Smoked Salmon, Toasted Bagels with, 48
Soufflé, Cheese Grits, 213
Soufflé, Southwestern Chile-Cheese, 38
Soufflés, Individual Fontina Cheese and Broccoli, 188–189
Strata, Pesto, Sausage and Parmesan Cheese, 39
Tart, Peruvian Artichoke, 192–193

Elk
Tacos, Kidwell Family, 126, *127*

Enchiladas
Steak, with Roasted Tomatillo-Green Chile Salsa, 124–125

F
Feta Chicken, 105
Fig(s)
Tarts, Prosciutto, Goat Cheese and, 22, *23*

Fish and Seafood. *See also* **Smoked Fish**
Bouillabaisse, Sally's, *8*, 157
Crab and Shrimp Salad with Curry-Chutney Dressing, 92
Halibut with a Caper, Pine Nut and Tomato Sauce, Roasted, 149
Halibut with Celery Root Purée and Tomato Garnish, *146*, 148
Mahi Mahi with Herb Mayonnaise, 156
Salmon, Grilled Citrus, 154
Salmon Salad with Avocado-Lime Yogurt Dressing, Layered, 90, *91*
Salmon with Lemon-Lime Crumb Topping, 155
Scallops with Tomatoes and Pesto, 160
Sea Bass with a Pistachio Crust, 152, *153*
Seafood Bundles with Creole Mustard Sauce, 158, *159*
Seafood Tetrazzini, 172
Shrimp and Brown Rice Salad, Asian, 93
Shrimp and Rice Soup, Soy-Ginger, *54*, 68
Shrimp de Jonghe, Uncle Bill's, 164
Shrimp Jambalaya, Ham and, 165
Shrimp over Linguine, Thai Peanut, 170, *171*
Shrimp Tacos with Tomato Mango Salsa, Chipotle Lime, 162, *163*
Shrimp with Tomatillo-Avocado Sauce, Grilled, 161
Swordfish en Papillote, Lemon-Rosemary, 150, *151*
Tuna Niçoise Salad with Lemon-Tarragon Dressing, 94, *95*
Tuna Pasta Salad with Pesto Dressing, Roasted Red Pepper and, 96

Fondue
Tempura Vegetable, with a Soy-Ginger Dipping Sauce, 190, *191*

Fontina
Soufflés, Individual Broccoli and, 188–189

French Toast, Banana Caramel Baked, 42

Frittata
Mushroom, Spinach and Onion with Goat Cheese, 47

Frosting
Lemon, Banana Raspberry Cake with, *228*, 246–247

Frozen
Lemon Velvet, 235
Strawberry Pie, 234

Fruit with Brandy Custard Sauce, Fresh, 250, *251*

Fusilli, Sausage, Pepper, Mushroom and Onion, 178

G

Ginger
Brownies, Lemon, 260
Cake, Sticky, 248
Chicken with Spicy Couscous, Orange and, 108–109, *109*
Cookies, Spice, 258
Dipping Sauce, Tempura Vegetable Fondue with a Soy, 190, *191*
Soup, Carrot and, 60, *61*
Soy Shrimp and Rice Soup, *54*, 68
Whipped Cream, Key Lime Pie with, 231

Goat Cheese
Crostini, Pesto, Tomato and, 17
Frittata with Mushroom, Spinach, Onion and, 47
Green Chiles Stuffed with, 182
Tarts, Prosciutto, Fig and, 22, *23*

Golden Potatoes, 212

Grandma Clarice's Cinnamon Apple Pie, 230

Green Beans with Caramelized Shallots, Lemon-Dijon, 208, *209*

Green Chile(s)
Arroz con Pollo, 106, *107*
Canapés, 18, 19
Salsa, Steak Enchiladas with Roasted Tomatillo and, 124–125
Soufflé, Southwestern Chile-Cheese, 38
Stuffed with Goat Cheese, 182

Greens
Spinach, Broccoli, Mushroom and Cheese Pasta, *166*, 168
Spinach Risotto, Baked, 218
Spinach Salad, Roasted Butternut Squash and Mushroom, 80, *81*
Spinach Salad with Curry Dressing, 82
Spinach Salad with Lemon-Dijon Dressing, Arugula and, 83
Spinach Soup, Italian Sausage, Orzo and, 66, *67*
Vegetable Curry, 194, *195*

Grits
Soufflé, Cheese, 213

H

Halibut
with a Caper, Pine Nut and Tomato Sauce, Roasted, 149
with Celery Root Purée and Tomato Garnish, *146*, 148

Ham
Country, Split Pea Soup with, 64, *65*
Jambalaya, Shrimp and, 165
Prosciutto, Tomatoes Stuffed with Olives and, 202
Prosciutto and Corn Salad, 210
Prosciutto Wrapped Asparagus, *198*, 200

Hearts of Palm Dip, 30

Herb Mayonnaise, Mahi Mahi with, 156

Hill Family Meatloaf, 123

Hoisin Pork Tenderloin, Roasted, 138

Honey
Pork Tenderloin, Asian, 139
Pork Tenderloin, Balsamic and, 138

Huevos Rancheros, 46

I

Ice Cream
Peach, 252

Indonesian Brown Rice Salad, 86

Italian
Popovers, 227
Sausage, Spinach and Orzo Soup, 66, *67*

J

Jalapeño(s)
Turnovers, Chorizo, Cheese and, 16

Jambalaya, Ham and Shrimp, 165

K

Key Lime Pie with Ginger Whipped Cream, 231

Kidwell Family Tacos, 126, *127*

Kuchen, Pear, 244, *245*

L

Lamb with Lemon, Roasted, 134–135, *135*

Lasagna, Tex-Mex Chicken and Chorizo, 179

Layered Salmon Salad with Avocado-Lime Yogurt Dressing, 90, *91*

Leek(s)
Beef Stew with Caramelized Root Vegetables, 130–131
Cucumber Vichyssoise, 56, *57*

Lemon(s)
Brownies, Ginger, 260
Crumb Topping, Salmon with Lime and, 155
Dressing, Arugula and Spinach Salad with Dijon and, 83
Dressing, Tuna Niçoise Salad with Tarragon and, 94, *95*
Frosting, Banana Raspberry Cake with, *228*, 246–247
Green Beans with Caramelized Shallots, Dijon and, 208, *209*
Pork Chops, Glazed, 144
Roasted Lamb with, 134–135, *135*
Sauce, New Potatoes with Caper and, 211

Swordfish en Papillote, Rosemary and, 150, *151*
Velvet, Frozen, 235

Lime(s)
Crumb Topping, Salmon with Lemon and, 155
Dressing, Tomato and Peach Salad with Balsamic and, *70*, 73
Key Lime Pie with Ginger Whipped Cream, 231
Pork Tenderloin, Asian, 139
Shrimp Tacos with Tomato Mango Salsa, Chipotle, 162, *163*
Shrimp with Tomatillo-Avocado Sauce, Grilled, 161
Yogurt Dressing, Layered Salmon Salad with Avocado and, 90, *91*

Linguine, Thai Peanut Shrimp over, 170, *171*

M

Mahi Mahi with Herb Mayonnaise, 156

Mango(es)
Salad, Chicken, Blueberry and, 97
Salsa, Chipotle Lime Shrimp Tacos with Tomato and, 162, *163*

Manhattan, Robert's Perfect, *33*, 35

Marinara Sauce
Sausage, Mushroom and Olive, Eggplant Parmesan with, 137

Martini, Robert's Perfect, *33*, 34

Mayonnaise
Mahi Mahi with Herb, 156
Sauce, Broccoli with Curry and, 206

Meatball Ratatouille, Slow Cooker Mediterranean, 136

Meatloaf
Cajun, *120*, 122
Hill Family, 123

Mediterranean
Meatball Ratatouille, Slow Cooker, 136
Quinoa Stuffed Sweet Peppers, *180*, 186–187

Mexican Baked Chicken, 112, *113*

Mint
Mousse, Chocolate, 242
Pea Soup, Chilled, 58

Mixed Greens with Dried Cranberries, 72

Mousse
Chocolate Mint, 242
Smoked Salmon, 28, *28*

Muffins
Apple Butterscotch, *36*, 52
Raspberry Nut, Mini, *36*, 53

Mushroom(s)
Chicken Pot Pie, 116, *117*
Coq au Vin, 114–115, *115*
Eggplant, Stuffed, 183
Frittata with Goat Cheese, Spinach, Onion and, 47
Fusilli, Sausage, Pepper, Onion and, 178
Marinara Sauce, Eggplant Parmesan with Sausage, Olive and, 137
Pasta, Broccoli, Spinach, Cheese and, *166*, 168
Paté, 20
Portobellos, Sundried Tomatoes and Rice, 217

Ratatouille, Slow Cooker Mediterranean Meatball, 136
Salad, Roasted Butternut Squash and Spinach, 80, *81*
Salad with Chutney Dressing, Avocado and, 78
Sautéed in Bourbon, Grilled Pork Chops with, 142
Shiitake Bourbon Sauce, Wild Bill's Bison with, 132–133, *133*

Mussels
Bouillabaisse, Sally's, *8*, 157

Mustard, Creole
Sauce, Seafood Bundles with, 158, 159

Mustard, Dijon
Green Beans with Caramelized Shallots, Lemon and, 208, *209*
Sauce, Sautéed Pork with a Caper and, 143

N

Nama's Buttermilk Biscuits, 223

Nantucket Cranberries, 247

New Potatoes
with Lemon-Caper Sauce, 211
Salad, Grilled Steak, Tomato and Roasted, 88, *89*
Tuna Niçoise Salad with Lemon-Tarragon Dressing, 94, *95*

Noodle Soup, Chinese Chicken, 69

Nut(s). See also specific types of nuts
Muffins, Mini Raspberry, *36*, 53

O

Oatmeal Cookies, Chocolate, *255*, 257

Oklahoma BBQ Sauce, 128, *129*

Okra
Jambalaya, Ham and Shrimp, 165

Olive(s)
Arroz con Pollo, 106, *107*
Marinara Sauce, Eggplant Parmesan with Sausage, Mushroom and, 137
Sauce, Sautéed Chicken Breasts with Tomato, Caper and, 101
Tapenade, Tomato Shortbread with, 26, *27*
Tomatoes Stuffed with Prosciutto and, 202

Onion(s)
Breaded Chicken Breasts, Parmesan and, 111
Coq au Vin, 114–115, *115*
Frittata with Goat Cheese, Spinach, Mushroom and, 47
Fusilli, Sausage, Pepper, Mushroom and, 178
Soufflé, Hot, 21

Orange(s)
Chicken with Spicy Couscous, Ginger and, 108–109, *109*

Orzo
Soup, Italian Sausage, Spinach and, 66, *67*

P

Parmesan
Crusted Chicken with a Tomato Cream Sauce, 174–175, *175*
Eggplant, with Sausage, Mushroom and Olive Marinara Sauce, 137

Onion Breaded Chicken Breasts, 111
   Sauce, Cauliflower with, 207
   Strata, Pesto, Sausage and, 39
Parsley
   Argentine Chimichurri Sauce, Spicy
      Pork Chops with, 140, *141*
Parsnip(s)
   Beef Stew with Caramelized Root
      Vegetables, 130–131
Pasta
   Angel Hair with Chicken and
      Artichoke-Caper Sauce, 176, *177*
   Broccoli, Mushroom, Spinach and
      Cheese, *166*, 168
   Fusilli, Sausage, Pepper, Mushroom
      and Onion, 178
   Lasagna, Tex-Mex Chicken and
      Chorizo, 179
   Linguine, Thai Peanut Shrimp over,
      170, *171*
   Noodle Soup, Chinese Chicken, 69
   Orzo Soup, Italian Sausage, Spinach
      and, 66, *67*
   Parmesan-Crusted Chicken with a
      Tomato Cream Sauce, 174–175,
      175
   Ravioli with Roasted Red Pepper
      Sauce, 173
   Salad with Pesto Dressing, Tuna and
      Roasted Red Pepper, 96
   Shells, Zucchini Stuffed, 169
   Shrimp de Jonghe, Uncle Bill's, 164
   Tetrazzini, Seafood, 172
Paté
   Mushroom, 20
Peach(es)
   Ice Cream, 252
   Pie, Blueberry Custard, 232, *233*
   and Tomato Salad with Lime-
      Balsamic Dressing, *70*, 73
Peanut Butter Bars, Chocolate, 257
**Peanut Shrimp over Linguine, Thai,
   170, *171***
Pear Kuchen, 244, *245*
Pea(s)
   Arroz con Pollo, 106, *107*
   Soup, Chilled Minted, 58
   Split Pea Soup with Country Ham,
      64, *65*
Pecan(s)
   Bars, Chocolate Toffee, 254, *255*
   Couscous with Dried Cranberries
      and, 220, *221*
   Crispies, Bea's, 253
   Rolls, Mini Sticky, 49, *51*
   Shortbread Bars with Butter-Rum
      Glaze, 259
Peppers, Bell
   Eggplant, Stuffed, 183
   Fusilli, Sausage, Mushroom, Onion
      and, 178
   Mediterranean Quinoa Stuffed Sweet,
      180, 186–187
   Roasted Red Pepper Pasta Salad with
      Pesto Dressing, Tuna and, 96
   Roasted Red Pepper Sauce, Ravioli
      with, 173
   Roasted Red Pepper Stuffing, Rolled
      Turkey with, *12*, 118–119
Peruvian Artichoke Tart, 192–193

Pesto
   Chicken with Black Beans, *98*, 100
   Crostini, Goat Cheese, Tomato and,
      17
   Dressing, Tuna and Roasted Red
      Pepper Pasta Salad with, 96
   Scallops with Tomatoes and, 160
   Strata, Sausage, Parmesan Cheese
      and, 39
Phyllo Pastry
   Seafood Bundles with Creole Mustard
      Sauce, 158, *159*
Pie
   Blueberry Peach Custard, 232, *233*
   Cinnamon Apple, Grandma Clarice's,
      230
   Key Lime with Ginger Whipped
      Cream, 231
   Strawberry, Frozen, 234
Pilaf, Barley, 219
Pimiento Cheese Spread, Zesty, *14*, 25
Pine Nut(s)
   Sauce, Roasted Halibut with a Caper,
      Tomato and, 149
**Pistachio Nut Crust, Sea Bass with a,
   152, *153***
Plum Tarts, Individual, 236, *237*
Popovers, Italian, 227
Poppy Seed Puffs, *28*, 29
Pork
   Chops, Lemon Glazed, 144
   Chops with Argentine Chimichurri
      Sauce, Spicy, 140, *141*
   Chops with Mushrooms Sautéed in
      Bourbon, Grilled, 142
   Meatloaf, Cajun, *120*, 122
      with a Mustard-Caper Sauce,
      Sautéed, 143
   Sandwiches, Pulled, 144
   Stir-Fried, Asparagus and, 145
   Tenderloin, Asian, 139
   Tenderloin, Balsamic-Honey, 138
   Tenderloin, Roasted Hoisin, 138
**Portobello Mushrooms, Sundried
   Tomatoes and Rice, 217**
Potato(es)
   Beef Stew with Caramelized Root
      Vegetables, 130–131
   Golden, 212
   New Potatoes with Lemon-Caper
      Sauce, 211
   Salad, Dorothy's, 84–85, *129*
   Salad, Grilled Steak, Tomato and
      Roasted, 88, *89*
   Tuna Niçoise Salad with Lemon-
      Tarragon Dressing, 94, *95*
Pot Pie
   Chicken, 116, *117*
   Root Vegetable, Roasted, 184, *185*
**Pots de Crème, Rum Pumpkin, 240,
   *241***
Poultry. See Chicken; Turkey
Prosciutto
   Salad, Corn and, *10*, 210
   Tarts, Fig, Goat Cheese and, 22, *23*
   Tomatoes Stuffed with Olives and,
      202
   Wrapped Asparagus, *198*, 200
Puffs, Poppy Seed, *28*, 29
Pulled Pork Sandwiches, 144
Pumpkin Tart, Rum, 239

Q
Quick Bread(s)
   Cinnamon Loaf, 50, *51*
Quinoa
   Stuffed Sweet Peppers,
      Mediterranean, *180*, 186–187

R
Raisin(s)
   Relish, Cranberry and Golden, 222
Raspberry
   Cake with Lemon Frosting, Banana,
      228, 246–247
   Muffins, Mini Nut, *36*, 53
**Ratatouille, Slow Cooker
   Mediterranean Meatball, 136**
**Ravioli with Roasted Red Pepper
   Sauce, 173**
Relish
   Cranberry and Golden Raisin, 222
Rice
   Arroz con Pollo, 106, *107*
   Jambalaya, Ham and Shrimp, 165
   Portobello Mushroom and Sundried
      Tomato, 217
   Risotto, Baked Spinach, 218
   Risotto, Roasted Butternut Squash,
      196–197
   Saffron Cilantro, 216
   Salad, Asian Shrimp and Brown, 93
   Salad, Indonesian Brown, 86
   and Soy-Ginger Shrimp Soup, *54*, 68
Risotto
   Butternut Squash, Roasted, 196–197
   Spinach, Baked, 218
Roasted Red Pepper(s)
   Pasta Salad with Pesto Dressing, Tuna
      and, 96
   Sauce, Ravioli with, 173
   Stuffing, Rolled Turkey with, *12*,
      118–119
Robert's
   Manhattan, Perfect, *33*, 35
   Martini, Perfect, *33*, 34
Rolls, Anna Mae's Freezer, 226–227
Root Vegetable(s)
   Beef Stew with Caramelized,
      130–131
   Pot Pie, Roasted, 184, 185
Rosemary
   Grilled Chicken Breasts, Dijon and,
      102, *103*
   Swordfish en Papillote, Lemon and,
      150, *151*
Rum Pumpkin
   Pots de Crème, 240, *241*
   Tart, 239

S
Saffron Cilantro Rice, 216
Salad(s)
   Apple, Walnut and Stilton Cheese,
      76, *77*
   Arugula and Spinach with Lemon-
      Dijon Dressing, 83
   Asian Shrimp and Brown Rice, 93
   Avocado-Mushroom with Chutney
      Dressing, 78
   Beet with Arugula Dressing, Roasted,
      79
   Butternut Squash and Mushroom
      Spinach, Roasted, 80, *81*

Chicken, Blueberry and Mango, 97
Corn and Prosciutto, *10*, 210
Crab and Shrimp with Curry-
   Chutney Dressing, 92
Indonesian Brown Rice, 86
Mixed Greens with Dried
   Cranberries, 72
Pasta with Pesto Dressing, Tuna and
   Roasted Red Pepper, 96
Potato, Dorothy's, 84–85, *129*
Salmon with Avocado-Lime Yogurt
   Dressing, Layered, 90, *91*
Spinach with Curry Dressing, 82
Steak, Roasted Potatoes and Tomato,
   88, *89*
Tomato and Cucumber with Yogurt-
   Herb Dressing, 74, *75*
Tomato and Peach with Lime-
   Balsamic Dressing, *70*, 73
Tuna Niçoise with Lemon-Tarragon
   Dressing, 94, *95*
Sally's Bouillabaisse, 8, 157
Salmon
   Citrus, Grilled, 154
   with Lemon-Lime Crumb Topping,
      155
   Salad with Avocado-Lime Yogurt
      Dressing, Layered, 90, *91*
Salsa
   Chicken, Mexican Baked, 112, *113*
   Tomatillo-Green Chile, Steak
      Enchiladas with Roasted, 124–125
   Tomato Mango, Chipotle Lime
      Shrimp Tacos with, 162, *163*
Sandwiches
   BBQ Beef, 128, *129*
   Pulled Pork, 144
Sauce(s)
   Argentine Chimichurri, Spicy Pork
      Chops with, 140, *141*
   Artichoke-Caper, Angel Hair with
      Chicken and, 176, *177*
   BBQ, Oklahoma, 128, *129*
   Blueberry Balsamic, Cheese Blintz
      Soufflés with, 40, *41*
   Brandy Custard, Fresh Fruit with,
      250, *251*
   Caper, Pine Nut and Tomato, Roasted
      Halibut with a, 149
   Creole Mustard, Seafood Bundles
      with, 158, *159*
   Curry-Mayonnaise, Broccoli with,
      206
   Lemon-Caper, New Potatoes with,
      211
   Mustard-Dill, Smoked Salmon Eggs
      Benedict with, 44, *45*
   Parmesan, Cauliflower with, 207
   Roasted Red Pepper, Ravioli with,
      173
   Sausage, Mushroom and Olive
      Marinara, Eggplant Parmesan with,
      137
   Shiitake Bourbon, Wild Bill's Bison
      with, 132–133, *133*
   Soy-Ginger, Tempura Vegetable
      Fondue with, 190, *191*
   Tomatillo-Avocado, Grilled Shrimp
      with, 161

Tomato Cream, Parmesan-Crusted Chicken with a, 174–175, *175*

Tomato-Olive-Caper, Sautéed Chicken Breasts with, 101

Sausage(s)

Fusilli, Pepper, Mushroom, Onion and, 178

Lasagna, Tex-Mex Chicken and Chorizo, 179

Marinara Sauce, Eggplant Parmesan with Mushroom, Olive and, 137

Mediterranean Meatball Ratatouille, Slow Cooker, 136

Soup, Spinach, Orzo and Italian, 66, 67

Strata, Pesto, Parmesan Cheese and, 39

Scallops with Tomatoes and Pesto, 160

Sea Bass with a Pistachio Crust, 152, 153

Seafood. *See* **Fish and Seafood**

Shallot(s)

Caramelized, Lemon-Dijon Green Beans with, 208, *209*

Shiitake Bourbon Sauce, Wild Bill's Bison with, 132–133, *133*

Shortbread

Tomato, with Olive Tapenade, 26, *27*

Shrimp

de Jonghe, Uncle Bill's, 164

Jambalaya, Ham and, 165

Salad, Asian Brown Rice and, 93

Salad with Curry-Chutney Dressing, Crab and, 92

Seafood Bundles with Creole Mustard Sauce, 158, *159*

Soup, Rice and Soy-Ginger, 54, 68

Tacos with Tomato Mango Salsa, Chipotle Lime, 162, *163*

Thai Peanut, over Linguine, 170, *171*

with Tomatillo-Avocado Sauce, Grilled, 161

Slow Cooker Mediterranean Meatball Ratatouille, 136

Smoked Fish

Salmon and Egg Salad, Toasted Bagels with, 48

Salmon Eggs Benedict with Mustard-Dill Sauce, 44, *45*

Salmon Mousse, 28, *28*

Soufflé(s)

Cheese Blintz, with Blueberry Balsamic Sauce, 40, *41*

Cheese Grits, 213

Fontina Cheese and Broccoli, Individual, 188–189

Onion, Hot, 21

Southwestern Chile-Cheese, 38

Sweet Potato, Brandied, 214, *215*

Soup(s). *See also* **Stew(s)**

Black Bean, Puréed, 62

Butternut Squash, 59

Carrot-Ginger, 60, *61*

Chicken Noodle, Chinese, 69

Eggplant and Tomato, Roasted, 63

Italian Sausage, Spinach and Orzo, 66, *67*

Minted Pea, Chilled, 58

Shrimp and Rice, Soy-Ginger, 54, 68

Split Pea with Country Ham, 64, 65

Vichyssoise, Cucumber Leek, 56, *57*

Southwestern Chile-Cheese Soufflé, 38

Soy-Ginger

Dipping Sauce, Tempura Vegetable Fondue with, 190, *191*

Shrimp and Rice Soup, 54, 68

Spice Cookies, Ginger, 258

Spinach

Frittata with Goat Cheese, Mushroom, Onion and, 47

Pasta, Broccoli, Mushroom, Cheese and, *166*, 168

Risotto, Baked, 218

Salad, Roasted Butternut Squash and Mushroom, 80, *81*

Salad with Curry Dressing, 82

Salad with Lemon-Dijon Dressing, Arugula and, 83

Soup, Italian Sausage, Orzo and, 66, *67*

Vegetable Curry, 194, *195*

Split Pea Soup with Country Ham, 64, 65

Squash

Butternut Squash Risotto, Roasted, 196–197

Butternut Squash Salad, Mushroom Spinach and Roasted, 80, *81*

Butternut Squash Soup, 59

Ribbons, Zucchini and Yellow, 203

Vegetable Curry, 194, *195*

Zucchini Stuffed Shells, 169

Zucchini with Crumb Topping, Roasted, 204, *205*

Steak

Enchiladas with Roasted Tomatillo-Green Chile Salsa, 124–125

Salad, Roasted Potatoes, Tomato and, 88, *89*

Stew(s). *See also* **Soup(s)**

Beef with Caramelized Root Vegetables, 130–131

Bouillabaisse, Sally's, 8, 157

Sticky

Ginger Cake, 248

Pecan Rolls, Mini, 49, *51*

Stilton Cheese

Salad, Apple, Walnut and, 76, *77*

Stir-Fried Pork and Asparagus, 145

Strata, Pesto, Sausage and Parmesan Cheese, 39

Strawberries

Pie, Frozen, 234

White Chocolate and Lime Tart with, 6, 238

Stuffed Vegetables

Eggplant, 183

Green Chiles with Goat Cheese, 182

Peppers, Mediterranean Quinoa Sweet, *180*, 186–187

Tomatoes with Olives and Prosciutto, 202

Stuffing

Roasted Red Pepper, Rolled Turkey with, *12*, 118–119

Sweet Potato Soufflé, Brandied, 214, 215

Swordfish en Papillote, Lemon-Rosemary, 150, *151*

T

Taco(s)

Chipotle Lime Shrimp, Tomato Mango Salsa with, 162, *163*

Kidwell Family, 126, *127*

Salad Dip, 31

Tapenade

Olive, Tomato Shortbread with, 26, *27*

Tarragon

Dressing, Tuna Niçoise Salad with Lemon and, 94, *95*

Tart(s)

Artichoke, Peruvian, 192–193

Plum, Individual, 236, *237*

Prosciutto, Fig and Goat Cheese, 22, *23*

Rum Pumpkin, 239

White Chocolate and Lime with Strawberries, 6, 238

Tempura Vegetable Fondue with a Soy-Ginger Dipping Sauce, 190, *191*

Tetrazzini, Seafood, 172

Tex-Mex Chicken and Chorizo Lasagna, 179

Thai Peanut Shrimp over Linguine, 170, *171*

Toffee Bars, Chocolate Pecan, 254, *255*

Tomatillo(s)

Salsa, Steak Enchiladas with Roasted Green Chile and, 124–125

Sauce, Grilled Shrimp with Avocado and, 161

Tomato(es)

Arroz con Pollo, 106, *107*

Beef Stew with Caramelized Root Vegetables, 130–131

Bouillabaisse, Sally's, 8, 157

Crostini, Goat Cheese, Pesto and, 17

Garnish, Halibut with Celery Root Purée and, *146*, 148

Jambalaya, Ham and Shrimp, 165

Lasagna, Tex-Mex Chicken and Chorizo, 179

Mexican Baked Chicken, 112, *113*

Ratatouille, Slow Cooker Mediterranean Meatball, 136

Salad, Grilled Steak, Roasted Potatoes and, 88, *89*

Salad with Lime-Balsamic Dressing, Peach and, *70*, 73

Salad with Yogurt-Herb Dressing, Cucumber and, 74, *75*

Salsa, Chipotle Lime Shrimp Tacos with Mango and, 162, *163*

Sauce, Parmesan-Crusted Chicken with a Cream and, 174–175, *175*

Sauce, Roasted Halibut with a Caper, Pine Nut and, 149

Sauce, Sautéed Chicken Breasts with Olive, Caper and, 101

Scallops with Pesto and, 160

Shortbread with Olive Tapenade, 26, *27*

Soup, Roasted Eggplant and, 63

Stuffed with Olives and Prosciutto, 202

Tomato(es), Sundried

Rice, Portobello Mushrooms and, 217

Tuna

Niçoise Salad with Lemon-Tarragon Dressing, 94, *95*

Pasta Salad with Pesto Dressing, Roasted Red Pepper and, 96

Turkey

Rolled, with Roasted Red Pepper Stuffing, *12*, 118–119

Turnip(s)

Pot Pie, Roasted Root Vegetable, 184, *185*

Turnovers

Chorizo, Cheese and Jalapeño, 16

U

Uncle Bill's Shrimp de Jonghe, 164

V

Vegetable(s). *See also* **specific types of vegetables**

Chicken Pot Pie, 116, *117*

Chinese Chicken Noodle Soup, 69

Curry, 194, *195*

Root, Beef Stew with Caramelized, 130–131

Tempura Fondue with a Soy-Ginger Dipping Sauce, 190, *191*

Vichyssoise, Cucumber Leek, 56, *57*

W

Walnut(s)

Salad, Apple, Stilton Cheese and, 76, *77*

Wedding Cookies, Almond-Cocoa, 255, 256

White Chocolate Tart with Strawberries, Lime and, 6, 238

Wild Bill's Bison with Shiitake Bourbon Sauce, 132–133, *133*

Wine, Red

Coq au Vin, 114–115, *115*

Wine, White

Bouillabaisse, Sally's, 8, 157

Y

Yellow Squash Ribbons, Zucchini and, 203

Yogurt Dressing

Avocado-Lime, Layered Salmon Salad with, 90, 91

Herb, Tomato and Cucumber Salad with, 74, 75

Z

Zucchini

with Crumb Topping, Roasted, 204, *205*

Ratatouille, Slow Cooker Mediterranean Meatball, 136

Ribbons, Yellow Squash and, 203

Stuffed Shells, 169